If These WALLS *Could* TALK:

CALGARY FLAMES

D1016605

If These WALLS *Could* TALK:

CALGARY FLAMES

Stories from the
Calgary Flames Ice,
Locker Room, and Press Box

Peter Maher with George Johnson

TRIUMPH
BOOKS

Library of Congress Cataloging-in-Publication Data

Names: Maher, Peter, 1941– author. | Johnson, George, 1957– author.
Title: If these walls could talk : Calgary Flames : stories from the Calgary
- Flames ice, locker room, and press box / Peter Maher, with George Johnson.
Description: Chicago, Ilinois : Triumph Books LLC, [2018]
Identifiers: LCCN 2018025845 | ISBN 9781629373515
Subjects: LCSH: Calgary Flames (Hockey team)—Anecdotes. | Calgary
Flames—(Hockey team)—History. | Hockey—Alberta—History—
Miscellanea. | National Hockey League—History.
Classification: LCC GV848.C25 M34 2018 | DDC 796.962/6409712338—
dc23 LC record available at https://lccn.loc.gov/2018025845

This book is available in quantity at special discounts for your group or organization. For further information, contact:

Triumph Books LLC
814 North Franklin Street
Chicago, Illinois 60610
(312) 337–0747
www.triumphbooks.com

Printed in U.S.A.

ISBN: 978-1-62937-351-5

Design by Amy Carter

Page production by Patricia Frey

All photos courtesy of the author except where otherwise noted.

Frequently during my play-by-play days, hockey came first at the expense of family. I was able to enjoy my career thanks to their solid support. My wife, Nancy, has been a rock guiding the family allowing me to concentrate on work. My children, Jeff and Tricia, make me proud every day, along with their spouses, Amy and Russ, and grandkids Haylee, Sydney, and Kate. Love you all.

CONTENTS

Hero Worship: Danny Gallivan

Mentors and Tricks of the Trade

Building Trust

Captain Video

Billy Harris

The Ol' Redhead

A Lingering Disappointment

Turning Down *HNIC*

Don Armstrong

Five for Pat

Doing Double Duty

Eddie Whalen

"Yeah Baby!"

One Missed Flight

A Welcome Interview

Dissing Denis

Meeting Vin

The (Not So) Common Cold

Grapes

The Magic Elixir

Occupational Hazards

Broadcast Locations

FOREWORD

I'm pretty sure Peter Maher is the only person to see me play in every one of the 1,273 games that I suited up for the Calgary Flames. With that in mind I'm pleased to write the foreword for this book.

By the time I joined the organization for a couple of playoff games against Chicago in 1996, Peter had already been broadcasting the team's games for more than a decade and a half.

Veteran players on the team were very familiar with him, treating Peter as a trusted member of the group every day through games, practices, and travel. He was a walking encyclopedia about the franchise history, all the great players and all the great moments.

I soon came to know him well. He was always fair and considerate when asking for a one-on-one interview or a casual chat away from the rink.

I never heard a live broadcast of Peter's because I was always on the ice, but I heard a number of his highlighted calls from the radio after big games or big moments.

My family members listening in Edmonton followed our fortunes through Peter many, many times, be it on the radio or the Internet. My grandmother, who had lost some of her sight, would have Peter's call as her way of following games. In some ways, he was her eyes.

The night I scored my 500th career goal in Calgary, Peter was, as always, on the call, and following up with a "Yeah baby!" yell. Later when I heard it, I must admit I had goosebumps.

Peter also told me one of the greatest goals that he called was during the gold-medal game of the 2010 Olympics in Vancouver, when I assisted on Sidney Crosby's decisive strike against the U.S.

He'd also offer me encouragement at times when things weren't going so well, coming to me quietly after the morning skate on the day of a game to tell me, "On this date so many years ago, you had three goals," or to make mention of a past big night for the team.

Even after I'd left the Flames, Peter would occasionally leave a phone message or a text about that particular date having some historic significance, giving me a boost.

The day after I was traded to Pittsburgh and had a news conference at the Saddledome, I was trying hard to keep my composure and not get emotional but I must admit I came close to cracking near the end when Peter got up and thanked me on behalf of all the Calgary media and Flames fans.

I was very fortunate to play and live in Calgary for almost 16 years. I met a lot of great hockey fans, Flames fans, hockey personnel, and wonderful teammates. The one who I believe may have the most hands-on stories, game in and game out, over the past 30-plus years is my friend Peter Maher.

Jarome Iginla *spent 16 seasons as a member of the Calgary Flames and is the franchise's all-time leader in goals, points, and games played.*

INTRODUCTION

When I was 12 years old, my mother had already heard enough of me describing play-by-play of table hockey at home and during backyard games to last a lifetime.

As far back as I can remember, she would say, "You're going to be a broadcaster. I can just tell."

Turns out, she was right.

Then again, she was right about a lot of things.

As I reached my teens we lived close enough to Riverside Park in my hometown of Campbellton, New Brunswick, that she and my dad could hear me on the public address system, announcing softball games. And then on the morning reports about those games on CKNB radio.

In 1970, they heard my first radio play-by-play of a hockey game as the local senior team, the Tigers, played an exhibition game against the Nova Scotia Voyageurs of the American Hockey League.

They heard my broadcast of games for the next seven years on radio covering teams in Campbellton and those in nearby Dalhousie.

Mom helped with my grammar and pronunciation while Dad offered great support in all areas, wherever and whenever I needed him.

As I progressed, broadcasting senior, intermediate, and junior games in New Brunswick and started drawing a few compliments, I used to wish out loud what so many of us who fall in love with this game do: "If only I could broadcast just one National Hockey League game…"

In the end, I got to broadcast 3,162 of 'em.

And I say with some pride that I did it without missing one assignment, starting with the Toronto Maple Leafs and then moving on to the Calgary Flames.

My parents likely marveled at that durability, considering I was a skinny kid who had been quite ill with tuberculosis.

There were times, my mom admitted later, when she wondered if I'd even get to adulthood.

I've been so fortunate and blessed to have had such a wonderful, rewarding career, to be honoured by the Hockey Hall of Fame and to have a portrait plaque there for eternity in the building's Great Hall as a Foster Hewitt Memorial Award honouree.

Regrettably, Mom and Dad had passed away by the time that event took place, November 13, 2006, Dad missing by only seven months.

But they were such a big part of the journey, regardless.

My brothers, Allan and Noonan; sisters, Nancy and Wendy; wife, Nancy; son, Jeff; and daughter, Tricia; grandchildren, Haylee and Sydney; and a host of other relatives and friends were all on hand in Toronto to share in the moment. To be able to share something like that with them…there are no words.

I'd go on to broadcast hockey games for eight more years, including all the Canadian men's team games at the 2010 Winter Olympics in Vancouver.

Through it all, I felt I was the luckiest man in the world, with the world's greatest job.

It sure beat working for living.

I firmly believe that if I hadn't grown up in a relatively small, supportive community where the hockey teams were great in the early 1970s, I would never have been a big-league broadcaster.

There are so many people that helped me along the trail in numerous ways, I'll just say one giant "Thank you" to you all.

To aspiring broadcasters, I trust this provides some inspiration.

The key is working hard, getting some breaks, and making the most of it when the opportunity presents itself.

CHAPTER 1
THE BOOTH

Hero Worship: Danny Gallivan

As a kid back home in Campbellton, New Brunswick, I loved listening to Danny Gallivan.

Who didn't?

Sunday nights, I'd be by the radio without fail. I don't remember whether or not I had an interest in play-by-play before that, but listening to Danny Gallivan certainly acted as a spark.

I actually played the game until bantam level. That's when the forwards were allowed to start unloading slapshots and when I began to understand I wasn't a very good goalie.

It's also when I realized I could talk faster than I could move and things sort of went from there.

I actually got into broadcasting calling local softball games, doing the public address announcing for the Riverside Park Senior Softball League. Four teams. That's how it began, phoning in reports and going into the station. My last year of high school, the station manager asked me if I wanted to do the sports during the morning run, around 6:30 AM to 8:15 or 8:30. Then I'd go to school, come back to the station, and do the afternoon run.

A natural progression, I graduated to calling hockey games in the winter, in the old North Shore League.

That's when I began to really listen to the guys calling the games. Danny Gallivan was always my favorite. In those days, Foster Hewitt was the voice of the Leafs and I liked Foster. But Danny was the play-by-play guy I admired most.

Danny injected real excitement to his announcing. I know you get people from Toronto to this day who'll tell you Danny was partisan to the Canadiens, but I always felt he called a fair broadcast.

The fact he was from the Maritimes, like me, didn't hurt my enjoyment of his calls. I felt a connection there, for sure.

2

The winter of 1976, I sent him a tape of one of my hockey broadcasts. I'd met him previously though a friend of mine who was a policeman in Montreal, when I was there for an Expos game. I was sort of in awe and I didn't say much, but I did summon up enough courage to ask him if I could mail him my tape. He said sure and gave me the address. A while later I received a letter giving me some advice on my tape, which was great.

Then in June of 1977, he came to Campbellton for a hockey banquet as a guest speaker. The dinner was held in the basement of the St. Thomas Aquinas Church. I was in the audience like everybody else and in the course of Danny's speech, he said, "There's someone in this room who all of you know well who's not going to be here very much longer. He's too good a broadcaster."

Then he mentioned my name.

A shout-out from Danny Gallivan!

It was a big, big thrill, obviously.

As fate would have it, three months later I wound up going to Toronto to broadcast Maple Leafs games.

I'm happy Danny was on to something there.

Mentors and Tricks of the Trade

Through my formative years developing into a broadcaster, I was lucky enough to count any number of people generous enough to guide me. That started, naturally, back in my hometown, Campbellton, New Brunswick, and Dalhousie, 16 miles away.

Guys like Doug Young, the radio station manager who got me involved in the business to start with. Doug had done some hockey play-by-play himself, which made him a valuable resource. Bud Dow, who I listened to and talked to. Veteran broadcasters like Don Hume, host on our broadcasts.

3

I also did a lot of writing in those days for local newspapers, which put me in contact with old pros Eddie St. Pierre in Moncton and Bill Donovan in Saint John, both very helpful, as well as Al and John Anslow with the weekly *Campbellton Graphic*.

I learned a lot from Gerry "Red" Ouellette, a former 12-year professional who played in 34 games with Boston in the 1960s. He came to my hometown in 1971 to coach the senior-intermediate team, the Tigers, and taught me an awful lot about professionalism.

Listening to the greats of the era, Danny Gallivan, Foster Hewitt, and Bob Cole certainly helped whet my appetite and provided me with inspiration and instruction.

When I move to Toronto to begin my NHL career, I was pretty raw but helped along by people like Dave Ruskin, the general manager of CKO Radio Network, who hired me. He was someone who had a lot of history with the CBC on the news side and always had great tips. Ralph Mellanby, the long-time producer of *Hockey Night in Canada*, was part of the selection group that gave me a chance.

HNIC producer Jim Hough took me under his wing and helped get me acclimatized. I can't forget Brian MacFarlane and Dave Hodge on the TV side of things, John Iaboni and Frank Orr from the print media.

In my years in Toronto, guys such as John Shannon, Doug Beeforth, and Rick Briggs-Jude were basically runners on *HNIC* telecasts while attending Ryerson's broadcasting course. They would, of course, go on to become outstanding producers and directors at various levels. John, after being involved in production, is now an on-air commentator on Rogers Sportsnet.

As I was making my way and improving my broadcasts, I picked up tricks such as talking in the present tense when you're doing play-by-play. In other words, you don't say, "He shot the puck into the corner." You say, "He shoots the puck into the corner." Another valuable piece of advice was, when making a comment I wasn't 100 percent certain of, to say "I believe" rather than "I think."

They also were very helpful in drumming home that it's vital to follow the puck, to continually let the listening audience on radio know who has the puck and where it is on the ice, be it in the corner, in the neutral zone, at the blueline, etc.

Other important points:

- Keep the broadcast as conversational as possible, directed to the listener and not my colour commentator. I was also advised to concentrate solely on the game itself until I started feeling more at ease, and then to start working in some research into my broadcasts.

- Allow the fans do some of the work. If the Flames, say, scored at home in the Saddledome, identify the player, give the score itself, and then stop talking. Let the crowd noise in the building fill in for you for a few seconds. Give the radio listener the feeling they were there, in the rink, sharing the experience with the fans in the seats. I'd advise my colour commentators of this over the years, signaling by raising an arm in the air to briefly stay silent before talking about the goal.

- Not to "step on" the colour commentator or let him do the same to me. By that I mean don't talk at the same time. That's immensely irritating to an audience. I like to think over the years we did a pretty job of delivering a clean broadcast. When the play-by-play was on, I was on. When I stopped talking, either Doug Barkley, Mike Rogers, or Peter Loubardias—the three colour sidekicks over the course of my Flames career—would have a few seconds to jump in and comment. If they felt something was immediately pertinent during the play-by-play, all they had to do was give a little tap on the arm as a signal.

Building Trust

Gaining the trust of the people you were around was, and is, vitally important for a play-by-play broadcaster.

That's an aspect of this business I knew from the outset.

It was never my aim to create controversy. This book is all about sharing the experiences I had during my 36 years as a play-by-play guy in the NHL.

There were some controversial times, obviously, with players, coaches, management, and things I had to report on. But I never betrayed anyone's trust then and certainly won't now.

There was a chapter from my start as a broadcaster with the Toronto Maple Leafs when I described, from my vantage point, the 1979 firing and then un-firing of coach Roger Neilson by then Maple Leafs owner Harold Ballard. Roger, about 24 hours after he'd been fired, gave me some confidential information that he might be coming back as coach of the team and later confirmed that he was.

But he told me in strict confidence and I kept it that way.

Later on, when it was discovered that I'd had the information, I did get a little bit of flak from bosses. But later they came to understand that it was important for me to maintain the trust of people I was involved with on a day-to-day basis.

Players on teams change from year to year but my record with them was passed on through the generations and that certainly was helpful in allowing me to get closer to the players. There were times when players, coaches, managers, and team presidents confided in me knowing that the information wouldn't go any further.

It was important that I maintained the reputation of being trustworthy.

Part of my work involved providing two or three reports daily for about 30 or 40 seconds on the radio station, setting up games, talking about past games, etc. In those days, games were aired on stations that had music formats, so the reports were intended to bring everyone up to date with the team. If there is a big story, a development like a trade, if we get it first, great.

The arrival of sports radio changed things a lot.

I had my "Maher in the Mornings" segment at 8:00 AM, a hockey insider show at 5:00 PM Monday through Friday, and both of those programs were in popular time slots, so my goal was to pass on as much information as I could that would be new to listeners.

That required spending time in advance preparing for that audience and it meant closely following developments around the NHL and gaining insight through my sources, as well as scanning the Internet. Sometimes I'd receive information about a Flames trade from a member of management but was told not to reveal it unless approved to do so.

Often, they'd let me know in advance before a deal became public and sometimes another media source would get it first and that was frustrating, but it was very important for me not to betray the trust that had been bestowed upon me.

Captain Video

Roger Neilson was the first NHL coach I worked with doing a coach's show in my first years with the Maple Leafs in Toronto.

In fact, that initial season he almost led to what I thought might be a shortening of my broadcast career at the NHL level.

It was the 1978–79 season, late in the year, and the Leafs lost a game in Montreal. Afterward, as Harold Ballard, the owner, was leaving the Montreal Forum, he told members of the media that Roger had been fired and informed of the decision.

This was on a Thursday evening.

We flew back to Toronto with the team and Roger was on the flight. The next morning, I was contacted by David Ruskin, the manager of our radio station, CKO, which carried the broadcasts. He said, "In light of Roger no longer coaching the Maple Leafs, could you get in touch with him and ask him if he'd be interested in being colour commentator on our broadcasts for the remainder of the season?"

I had Roger's home number so I gave him a call about the offer. We didn't have a regular colour commentator at that time. Roger phoned back and said he'd be interested but he'd have to check with the old man, Ballard. He was still, after all, under contract with the Maple Leafs.

Early that Friday evening, Roger called and said he was definitely interested. Great. I told him David Ruskin would be in touch with him and he'd make the arrangements.

I got another call from Roger later on, probably around 10:00 PM, and said that he was still planning to be the colour commentator for the game the next night…but that there was a chance he'd actually be back as coach. He wanted me to keep quiet about the possibility.

The next afternoon, Roger gave me a call at home and told me that, indeed, he'd be behind the bench that night but that the Old Man wanted to make it a surprise for the people before the game and not to say anything.

I told him I'd keep the news quiet but that the radio station had been advertising him as being part of the broadcast. As a compromise, we agreed to meet wherever in the Gardens he was going to be hiding and record an interview to air on the pregame show.

We recorded the interview and just after the national anthem, I let the audience know that Roger—yes, Roger—was going to be behind the bench again as coach of the Maple Leafs. As soon as the words were out of my mouth, he appeared, just before the opening faceoff.

He told me later that Ballard had asked him to wear a paper bag over his head as he went behind the bench—adding to the surprise, I suppose—but he wouldn't agree to that. Thankfully.

So Roger returned as coach and finished the year before being let go. What was interesting is that on the Monday after his return game there was a Molson Cup luncheon, held at the Hot Stove Lounge in the Gardens to honour the winning player for the previous month, open to the public and press.

I was seated at the media table with some broadcasters and sportswriters. Stan Obodiac, the team's director of media, came to thank me for keeping the Roger Neilson coaching "comeback" a secret.

Seated close by, Scott Young, a columnist with the *Globe and Mail*, overheard. And got curious. I was very hesitant to respond but I did tell Scott that, yes, I'd been told in confidence by Roger that afternoon about his return.

The next day Scott wrote a column in the *Globe* reporting that I'd known about Roger coming back but didn't notify the public. He seemed to indicate that perhaps if I knew the story, I should have told it.

So then I got a phone call from my boss, Mr. Ruskin, and he was not happy that I had not told him. I told him that when somebody tells me something in confidence and not to tell anybody, I honour that confidence. I didn't feel it was the proper thing to do. He was still a little perturbed by that.

We were on the road for a game in New York and when I came back, Mr. Ruskin asked me to come see him at his office in downtown Toronto. As I went up to see him, I wondered if my future as the Leafs' play-by-play broadcaster might be over just as it was getting started.

Instead, he apologized for his reaction and told me I'd done the right thing.

A big relief.

Roger was a real innovative coach. He was way ahead of his time with his methods and tactics. He was the first guy to prioritize watching video, so they called him Captain Video. He'd record all the Leafs games and would stay long into the night dissecting games. He was a real student of the game, followed things very closely. He was very thorough. I remember one morning in Washington after a game the night before, the Leafs were at the hotel and at breakfast with Roger and some other people, Roger was bemoaning the fact that the video he'd received didn't have the third period. He was quite upset he wouldn't have the opportunity to look at that period and the chance to review of it.

So I said, if you'd like, I recorded the game last night on radio, I can let you have the broadcast of the third period. His response? "I'm sure there would be too much offence in that for my liking."

But that was Roger. Insightful, analytical.

Billy Harris

My first colour sidekick in Toronto was Billy Harris, a part of those storied Toronto teams of the 1960s, back when I was a kid and a Maple Leafs fan.

So naturally I considered working with Billy on CKO Radio and its network an honour.

After retiring as a player, Bill was coaching and lecturing at Laurentian University in Sudbury while helping us on the broadcasts of as many Maple Leaf games as he could.

Billy was a real student of hockey, very technical. That certainly helped me develop knowledge and enhance the on-air product. He could also speak in a language that made the game and its intricacies understandable for all our listeners.

Billy's wide net of hockey friends also aided me, a young play-by-play guy at a new job, in meeting many of the great names and influential people in the NHL and building relationships that in some cases lasted my entire career.

Nothing was more enjoyable than being out with him at dinner or for a few beers and listening to the tales of those Stanley Cup teams

My rookie season broadcasting Maple Leafs games from the Gardens on the old CKO-FM radio network.

I'd grown up idolizing, as well as all the legendary names—Dave Keon, Frank Mahovlich, Johnny Bower, Tim Horton, and the like. Sometimes I even met those guys, heroes of mine, at Maple Leaf Gardens.

After I'd moved on to Alberta, Billy would, too, joining the Edmonton Oilers as an assistant coach in the early 1980s, right at the time the Battle of Alberta was getting nasty.

Whenever I'd meet up with Billy at morning skates or elsewhere, we'd engage in some fun chats, talking over old times.

There weren't many civil conversations between Oilers and Flames people in those days, so bumping into Billy was always welcome.

When Edmonton visited the Dome, often an old teammate of his, Bert Olmstead, would be there to see Billy and that's how I got to know Bert, a five-time Stanley Cup winner who reached the Final an amazing 11 times in his 14 NHL seasons.

Certainly a thrill working with a guy like Billy Harris and certainly an educational time.

The Ol' Redhead

My second colour commentator in Toronto was one for the game's all-time greatest personalities and most engaging storytellers.

Red Storey was already a Hall of Famer in both hockey and football, and he'd trek in from Montreal to work Maple Leafs games with me whenever he could.

His style was totally different from the colour man of my opening year, Billy Harris.

Red was very humorous on the air, a highly sought-after public speaker.

He also wasn't shy about being critical of players and coaches, be it with the Maple Leafs or with another team if he didn't like what he was seeing.

In the way he approached things, he kind of pre-figured Don Cherry's on-air style.

You couldn't not like Red. It was utterly impossible.

He knew everybody in and around the game and would always make himself available to play Santa Claus for the Maple Leafs' Wednesday game during intermissions before Christmas, then he'd come back and be the colour commentator with me once the periods got going.

He was also very well connected with the Leafs owner at the time, Harold Ballard, and his noted sidekick King Clancy. That was helpful for me, getting to know those two powerful gentlemen better.

There were a couple of aspects about the game itself, evolutions I guess you'd call them, at the time that Red didn't much like.

For instance, he hated—absolutely loathed—players dumping the puck into the corner. Couldn't understand that tactic at all. He'd say, "You've got the puck, why are you giving it away to the opposition and then you have to fight to get it back again?"

This completely mystified Red.

Also, Red was reared in the game at a time when defencemen played defence. Period.

The arrival of Bobby Orr had changed all that, of course.

Borje Salming, who'd arrived over from Sweden, was an Orr-type defenceman for the Leafs, joining the rush and making all kinds of spectacular plays.

At one point, Salming was leading the Maple Leafs in scoring, racking up more points than either Darryl Sittler or Lanny McDonald.

Red's comment then was, predictably, "If you have a defenceman leading you in scoring, you don't have a very good team."

I'd remind him that the Boston Bruins—a pretty strong outfit at the time, winners of two Stanley Cups—had a guy named Orr who not only led his team but the entire NHL in scoring.

Didn't matter. Red still had a tough time with defencemen jumping into the offence.

Over dinner, he was an absolute wealth of stories, regaling us about his feuds with former NHL president Clarence Campbell as well as his days as a referee and player in the Canadian Football League.

Funny thing is, I never did get to hear him as an after-dinner speaker until I'd moved west to Calgary.

Red always had a twinkle in his eye that would jump out at you. He'd fly out each year for the Flames' charity golf tournament; he and Dick Irvin came for the first 15 at the Canyon Meadows Golf Club.

It became ritual that they would arrive two nights before the golf tournament and the day prior, Dick and Red would play my colour commentator of the time, Doug Barkley, and I would head on the course for 18 holes.

I think I got to know Red almost better then, despite the years working together.

Being around Red, with his style and his humour, was always like a jolt of fresh oxygen. He had that rare gift of making you feel better.

A Lingering Disappointment

Among the few regrets of a fantastic career is that I never had the opportunity to broadcast a game involving Bobby Orr.

I'd been lucky enough see him play live a few times as a fan, including the 1976 Canada Cup in Toronto. Such a game-changer, a revolutionary.

But to just once be able to say, "And here comes Orr up the ice..."

Imagine.

I thought I finally had that chance on November 8, 1978, while calling Maple Leafs games. The Leafs were in Chicago to take on the Blackhawks. Orr had played six times to open that season after being sidelined the entirety of the previous year with those recurring knee injuries that tragically cut short his brilliant career.

So I thought this would be my Bobby Orr Night. No such luck. During the morning skates at the old Chicago Stadium, the media got word of a news conference to be held at noon. That's when Bobby, only 30 years old, announced his retirement. My dream of calling a Bobby Orr game was gone. But at least I was there at the news conference.

You couldn't help but be struck by the emotion of the moment, even if, deep down, the number of knee injuries he'd sustained over the years shouldn't have made the decision a great surprise.

We lost so many great years, so much unparalleled entertainment.

Turning Down *HNIC*

Hockey Night in Canada is a television institution across Canada. The reason many of us fell in love with the game can be traced back to Saturdays on CBC TV.

Synonymous with cold winter nights and families huddled in front of their TV sets. The old theme music instantly makes you think hockey.

From the 1984–85 season through 1986–87, I had dual play-by-play commitments. My main job was broadcasting Flames games on Calgary radio, of course, but I also travelled when I could to Toronto to call mid-week Maple Leaf television games.

At the time *HNIC* produced those games mid-week as well as Saturday night and I was approached about moving back to Toronto permanently. I decided against it, but accepted a modified schedule—one Leafs mid-week game, which often meant broadcasting a Flames game on a Tuesday night, then taking the red-eye for a Wednesday game in Toronto and then hustling back to Calgary for a Thursday game.

I did that for three years as negotiations to return to Toronto continued. They were offering a mid-week Leafs game and the occasional Saturday *Hockey Night in Canada* game.

Unlike today, there were no doubleheaders, only a single game on Saturday.

At the end of that third year, Don Wallace, the executive producer for *HNIC*, sat down and made me another offer to move back east. After consideration, I told him no, mainly because at that stage of my career I didn't think the offer included enough games. Besides, I was happy in Calgary.

Don told me, "You know, if you take this position, you'd be the No. 2 broadcaster in our *Hockey Night in Canada* system to Bob Cole."

The Fan 960 crew during a 2006 game: (left to right) host Rob Kerr, colour commentator Mike Rogers, myself, and producer Tim Kallil. (© Calgary Flames)

That was a pretty good slotting but I still thanked him and declined. Years later, during the 2007–08 season, defenceman Anders Eriksson had joined the Flames. Anders just happened to be Don Wallace's son-in-law. So at one morning skate before Christmas, Don—no longer with *HNIC*—was there and we had a nice chat. I jokingly brought up my turning down his offer years before and that he'd promised I'd be the No. 2 man behind Bob Cole.

Turned out, I would've, all those seasons later, still been the second guy behind Bob, a job for which a lot of broadcasters wait a lifetime.

But I never regretted my decision to stay in radio and remain with the Flames.

Don Armstrong

There are so many people behind the scenes who contribute to producing a successful hockey broadcast. It's impossible to thank everyone because so much goes into what listeners watch and hear.

One guy who deserves every accolade possible is Don Armstrong, part of the Rawlco Communications group that purchased the rights to games after CHQR held them for the first decade of Flames hockey in Calgary.

Gord Rawlinson, the president/CEO of Rawlco and 66 CFR, along with Don, were huge hockey fans and made a very strong, winning bid after those 10 years at QR.

Don was one of those indispensable behind-the-scenes people. He went out and sold hockey, worked tirelessly to put a first-rate production crew together, and hired both myself and colour commentator Doug Barkley from Western Communications, owner of QR.

He was the one responsible for the sound and the feel of the pregame and postgame shows, as well as some intermissions, always with the listener in mind. Still, in my mind, the standard against whom all others can measure themselves against.

He brought in two analysts to go along with Doug, myself, and host Jock Wilson, on an alternate basis. They'd work the home games in the Hot Stove Lounge in the Saddledome—a name Don came up with that endures to this day—and at the station when the team was on the road. The pregame show lasted an hour and the postgame companion sometimes a lot longer than that.

Don was very, very strong in securing a great cross-section of hockey people to be involved, including ex-players Jim Peplinski, Perry Berezan, Mike Rogers (before Mike became the colour commentator following Doug Barkley's retirement), and Gerry Pinder, along with media types such as Eric Duhatschek, George Johnson, and Al Strachan. He also secured Ed Chynoweth, president of the Western and Canadian hockey leagues, to chip in, and Ed's lengthy list of contacts certainly helped in lining up guests for the programs. I remember the lockout season of 1994–95, we still broadcast a show every night on 66 CFR and Ed was instrumental in helping us with quality content.

One night he was able to land both NHL commissioner Gary Bettman and NHLPA executive Bob Goodenow to join us on the same night, if not at the same time, and offer some really interesting insights and perspectives on the work stoppage.

I remember comedian John Candy joining us on a couple of occasions, as well as golfer Craig Stadler, and others. Don worked tirelessly to secure guests.

If he knew you were in the building and someone the audience could relate to, Don would convince you to pay a visit to the Hot Stove Lounge.

When Theo Fleury scored his famous goal in overtime in Game 6 of the 1991 series against the Edmonton Oilers, the players flew back to Calgary on a charter immediately afterward and one of the first people to greet them at the airport was Don Armstrong. He'd driven over from the station with a commemorative cassette of my call of the goal to give to Theo.

He was so great, not only with the production, on-air people, and analysts, but he went out of his way for sponsors and everyone else involved in the broadcasts and around the Flames. A very caring guy for whom no detail was too small to address and no problem too large to solve.

When the rights were sold by Rawlco to the Rogers group, and the games moved on to 960, where they are today, Don's absence was certainly felt.

I often reflect on how unlucky those fellows—so instrumental in the standards we set—were in terms of team payoff.

Gord Rawlinson secured the rights for the broadcasts two years after the Flames hoisted the Cup in the spring of 1989 and sold them two years before the incredible run of 2004.

So, Gord and Don missed out on two of the highest points in franchise history. Which was, and is still, a shame.

Five for Pat

Twice over the course of my years in NHL broadcast booths I've had the opportunity to call a game in which an individual scored five goals.

For Flames fans, Joe Nieuwendyk's big night in 1989 pops immediately to mind, naturally.

But the first time can be traced back six years before that and involved a very unexpected source.

Right winger Pat Hughes did put up three 20-goal seasons for the Edmonton Oilers in the early-to-mid-1980s but I think it's safe to say he wasn't considered an offensive juggernaut.

But on February 3, 1984, he lit up the Flames a remarkable five times. Both of Calgary's goaltenders, Don Edwards and Reggie Lemelin, were victims of Hughes that night.

The Flames arrived at Edmonton's Northlands Coliseum on a nine-game win streak and with Wayne Gretzky, Jari Kurri, and Mark Messier all missing from the Oilers' lineup, the odds on increasing the run to 10 appeared awfully good.

No one, however, had considered the Pat Hughes Factor.

Hughes scored his first goal only 20 seconds into the game, added two more before the first intermission, and then had one each in the second and third periods.

The Oilers skated to a 9–5 victory.

Afterward, a media wag noted, "Five goals used to be a good *season* for Pat Hughes."

Doing Double Duty

The only year I combined hockey and football broadcasting duties during my career was 1985.

The radio broadcast rights for the Calgary Stampeders' Canadian Football League games had been purchased by CHQR, the station I was working for calling play-by-play of the Flames.

I was asked by Rod Gunn, the general manager of the station, to try the double for one season, rather than them having to go out and hire a football play-by-play man for something that may only turn out to be a short fling.

He said we should give it a go and make a joint decision moving forward and that the station would then make a call on whether or not they'd bid past the one season to retain the rights.

I was initially reluctant in combining the two, primarily because I'd never broadcast football before.

But after thinking it over, a one-season audition didn't seem like such a bad idea.

I was fortunate Mike Lashuk was hired on to do colour analysis, a former CFL player, assistant coach, and also a coach in the University of Calgary Dinos' program. Mike had a great way of describing the game and was able to assist me in learning some, if not close to all, of its intricacies.

Stan Schwartz, a former assistant coach with the Stampeders who'd gone on to become team president, was another great help.

The team did their bit by lending me reel-to-reel tapes of games from the past, so I could study them and do some practice play-by-play.

Have to admit I was very, very nervous the first few broadcasts. This was, after all, totally foreign to me. The two games—hockey and football—are completely different to call.

I decided quickly to basically focus on the offensive side of the ball and let Mike fill in during stoppages in play.

Owing to my football obligation, I missed out on Flames training camp, that year held in Moncton, New Brunswick, my home province. My hockey colour sidekick Doug Barkley travelled east and did reports for the station in my absence.

Through July, August, and the early part of September, I was able to focus primarily on the Stampeders with an eye half-cocked toward the upcoming NHL campaign.

When the Flames' regular season began, that's when things started becoming complicated.

There was one situation where I broadcast a Stampeder game on a Saturday night and had a Flames game to call on Sunday. Fortunately, they were both in Calgary, but the changing of focus that quickly really can hurt preparation.

The one time I found myself in a real bind, I had to call a Flames game against Boston one night, then rush out to the airport and hop

21

on the red-eye bound for Toronto and a Stampeders-Argonauts Sunday matinee, scheduled for 2:00 PM.

A pal, John Iaboni, a writer for the *Toronto Sun* at the time I broadcast Maple Leaf games, picked me up at the airport and then hustled me back after the hockey game to catch a flight to Winnipeg, where the Flames were playing that same night against the Jets, 7:00 PM start time. All quite chaotic.

Boarding the plane bound for Winnipeg, I immediately pulled out my notes on the Jets and Flames and began studying. Seated next to me, a man asked me what I was doing. So I detailed my hectic day for him. I'll never forget what he said to me: "Take it easy, young man. I'm just coming off heart surgery."

We had Bob Irving, a long-time local broadcaster, on standby in case my flight was delayed leaving Toronto and I couldn't get to Winnipeg Arena in time.

Logistically, it all worked out. Somehow. I reached the broadcast booth only minutes before the pregame show was ending.

After the game, it didn't take long for me to get to sleep at the team hotel that night, let me tell you.

A real exhausting situation. An eye-opening weekend and an indication that down the road, this double-duty might be too much for one person to commit to.

After the season(s) ended, I told Rod Gunn that I felt it best to stick to hockey. As the station didn't re-bid for the Stampeder rights, it became a moot point anyway.

But quite the experience.

Eddie Whalen

When I arrived in Calgary I'd never met Ed Whalen and only knew of him through a colour man in my early years, Peter Allison, a huge fan of Stampede Wrestling on TV.

He'd filled me in on all of Eddie's grappling catchphrases like, "It's a ring-a-ding-dong-dandy" and his signature sign-off, "In the meantime and in-between time…"

When I joined to call Flames games on radio, Ed's broadcast location was right next door to mine, at least in the early years on the road. In contrast, at the Saddledome the television broadcast booth was in the lower level, at centre ice, right above the lower-bowl seats. The radio booth was where it's always been—way up on top in the gondola, over-looking the crowd and the ice surface.

What always amazed me is that Eddie was often interrupted to sign autographs, and would accommodate, happily. I marvelled at how he could facilitate the fans and retain game focus, but he did.

When the Dome was remodelled in the mid-1990s the TV booth was also moved up to only a few steps from ours, so Ed and I were neighbours.

Eddie was a legend around these parts for his wrestling work. The reach Stampede Wrestling had on TV in those days was astounding.

To call him a busy guy would be a wild understatement. There was the wrestling and the hockey broadcasts, but he also wrote a column for the *Calgary Sun* and threw himself into charity work, most notably as host of the annual Children's Miracle Network telethon.

Listening to his stories about the wrestlers, joking at Flames practice, out for dinner on the road, or on a flight somewhere together, Eddie was always a fun guy to be around. And helpful, on a serious note, with advice and his scope of knowledge on so many things.

A gentleman who loved life and underscored the importance of giving back.

When he retired in 1999, one of the gifts presented to him by the Flames was travelling with the team on an eastern road trip. That's when I got to know his equally famous wife, Nomi, a city councillor and very well known for officiating at weddings.

She had great stories as well, and during that trip frequently played cards with coaches and players and did a lot of winning, as I remember.

The last time I saw Ed, early November of 2001, we bumped into each other at the Saddledome back door/media entrance. I was arriving to watch practice, Eddie was just leaving. We chatted for a few minutes and he told me how excited he was about his upcoming cruise, departing from Florida.

He got to enjoy that cruise but suffered a massive heart attack after returning to shore in Florida and passed away, with Nomi at his side.

That day, not only Calgary but the world lost an unforgettable personality and a great, great gentleman.

"Yeah Baby!"

The two-word catchphrase that would become my trademark can be traced back to April 28, 1986, the morning of Game 6 of the Smythe Division Final, Flames-Oilers, driving home after the skate in my car.

In those days, there were no all-sports radio stations, as music dominated the airwaves.

Against all odds, the Flames had the improbable opportunity to eliminate the back-to-back Stanley Cup champs that evening, send shockwaves crackling through the hockey world, and move on to the Stanley Cup semifinals.

I wish I could remember the name of the tune but on my drive the lyrics of this one song kept repeating "Yeah baby…"

For whatever reason, that registered in my mind.

I filed it away.

The Oilers beat the Flames 5–2 later that night so I kept the phrase in storage. Two nights later, though, Game 7, and seconds after the final horn signifying the series-clinching 3–2 victory, I yelled "Yeah baby!" for the first time and threw in a "The Flames have finally climbed the mountain!" for good measure.

That was the slogan Badger Bob Johnson had been preaching all season long in reference to beating Gretzky and his gang.

People loved it. So I kept the phrase handy but tried to save "Yeah baby!" for only significant occasions. In those free-wheeling, high-scoring days, hat tricks were common, but if a player scored, say, four goals—or in the case of Joe Nieuwendyk one memorable night, five—I'd clear my throat and let fly.

A milestone—say 50th of the season or a 500th career goal—also warranted a shout-out.

"Yeah baby!" really caught traction through the 2004 playoff run to the Final, though. Sports radio had become big by then, so when I'd unleash it, the sound bite was replayed over and over.

Martin Gelinas' OT goal to eliminate Detroit in Game 6 of the second-round series that spring took it to another level altogether.

Emotion got the best of me and I went into a heavy duty, overexuberant "Yeah baby!" three times in a row. I'd only done that once before, the night the Flames won the Cup in 1989.

Afterward, I went on our postgame show, the guys played the call for me again—my headset was on, my microphone was live—and I remember saying, "Oh, that was *awful*. Danny Gallivan would roll over in his grave."

Danny, of course, was my play-by-play idol growing up.

I just thought it was way, way overboard, considering it was only a second-round series. I didn't sleep very well that night and when I got to the Dome the next morning I went in to see coach Darryl Sutter and I apologized for going a bit over the top.

After I was through talking, he had that look on his face, the one everyone in Calgary remembers. Then he smiled and said, "I heard it this morning. I thought it was *outstanding.*"

ESPN played it over and over through the playoffs, which kind of surprised me.

For five straight weeks, Marty's goal and my call was the top-rated highlight from both the NHL and NBA playoff coverage.

That got me any number of phone calls and generated all kinds of excitement and attention.

Gelinas had quite a run that playoff year, as everyone in Calgary remembers, scoring three OT series winners.

So every time I've seen Marty in the ensuing years, I tell whoever he's with, "Marty actually put me in the Hall of Fame." And he gets kind of embarrassed.

Once I even mentioned that to his father but Marty was having none of it. "No, no, Dad," he protested. "He put himself into the Hall of Fame."

What's beyond dispute is that my calls of his goals that playoff year put some surprise focus on me as a broadcaster. Only two years later, I received the call that I was going to be honoured by the Hockey Hall of Fame. Coincidence?

So I have a great fondness for "Yeah baby!" A lot of others obviously do, too.

Anywhere I've gone, even now that I'm retired, fans ask about that phrase. It's become synonymous with me.

I still get a lot of people approaching me and asking me to yell it for them. I'm quick to point out I can do it, happy to, but it won't be with the same degree of enthusiasm that you'd hear when I was broadcasting a game, in the emotion of the moment.

One Missed Flight

Over the lengthy course of my career as an NHL broadcaster, I missed only one flight.

One of the perks of the job, of course, is that the team looks after all areas of transportation, ground and air, hotel reservations, etc.

My miscue happened in the early 1990s, in Ottawa soon after the Senators arrived on the NHL scene. I'd made arrangements to meet up postgame with my long-ago radio mentor from Campbellton, Doug Young. After leaving radio, Doug became a lawyer and later a politician and was a federal cabinet minister at the time of that visit into the nation's capital.

After the game we went back his house to eat, had a few beers and after-dinner drinks, talked and talked and talked. By the time I looked at my watch it was 4:30 AM.

Got back to the hotel and the next thing I remember—apparently a number of calls to my room had gone unanswered—there was a loud knocking on my door.

When I answered, there stood goalie Mike Vernon informing me the team bus was leaving for the airport in five minutes.

Well, I wasn't going to get packed and ready in five minutes so the bus left without me.

So did the flight.

The team had arranged to leave my boarding pass at the Air Canada counter. Fortunately, the next game was scheduled for Joe Louis Arena in Detroit the next night, a short hop 45 minutes away by air, so I caught another commercial flight later that afternoon to Windsor, Ontario, then took a taxi across the U.S.-Canada border to Detroit, rejoining the group at the team hotel.

I was none too pleased with myself and apologized to the coach of the Flames at the time, Dave King, for missing both the bus and the flight.

Dave actually had a pretty good chuckle over it.

And I suppose when you consider the thousands of flights I did take over three decades, missing one isn't *that* bad.

A Welcome Interview

To most fans I'm best known as a play-by-play broadcaster, and from time to time I'd also receive comments about the "Maher in the Mornings" segment I did on the radio and the insider show slotted in the afternoon for the commute home.

But over the course of my career I also conducted thousands of interviews on game days—pregame, postgame, intermission—and also on practice days. Sometimes as many as five in a day.

So I had lots of experience chatting with NHL players and coaches. Stars, role players, great coaches, scouts, agents.

You name it.

Occasionally I'm asked who was the best.

Well, if you're talking about someone who was long-winded and had a lot of things to say, Badger Bob Johnson always pops to mind from the five years he and I did the coach's show together.

But it might surprise you that in ranking interviewees, I put Wes Walz right at the top of my list.

Wes—for those who don't remember—was a utility forward who played parts of two seasons with the Flames from 1993 to 1995. In all, he'd log 92 games, picking up 56 points.

A Calgary kid who'd tell me he would listen to my broadcasts as a youngster, driving around with his father or at home at night, getting ready for bed, Wes put up big numbers in the Western Hockey League with Lethbridge before arriving in the NHL.

Drafted in the third round by Boston in 1989, he'd go on to play in the Bruins organization, as well as for the Flyers and Red Wings, but couldn't find the same scoring touch that had set junior hockey alight.

Wes took four years off and went to play in Switzerland and then had his NHL career resurrected in 2000 when the Minnesota Wild entered the NHL.

Doug Risebrough was hired as the first GM of the Wild and had managed the Flames at the time Wes was a part of the organization.

So he brought Walz back from Switzerland and Wes repaid Doug's faith with six solid seasons as a defensive centreman, finishing third in voting for the Selke Trophy one year.

I always thought that he'd make a first-rate coach and after retiring as a player; he served two years as an assistant with Tampa and then came back to Minnesota where he coached high school hockey and also served on Wild broadcasts.

I always found Wes' interviews enlightening. He was anything but shy about being critical of himself or his team when it was needed. Not in a derogatory manner, but very constructive.

Extremely, refreshingly, candid.

I remember one of the interviews I did with him when he was playing in Minny, he admitted of his younger self: "I was a dumb 20-year-old and I didn't figure things out until I was 30."

When he retired, I'd see him at Wild games from time to time when the Flames were playing at the Xcel Energy Center and I'd often ask him to come on the intermissions, if available.

During one of those, after he'd retired, I mentioned to him he was the best interviewee I ever met.

He was certainly flattered by that, but I meant it.

There were many other really good people I had the pleasure of interviewing through the course of my career. I had insightful subjects such as Robyn Regehr and stars who always made themselves available, like Jarome Iginla.

But many players, maybe out of self-preservation, felt the need to ⌃ employ a filter in their answers.

Wes didn't. And for that, he stands out.

Dissing Denis

Sometimes, things go wrong on broadcasts. It happens.

For the way he handled one of those situations, I've always felt indebted to Denis Potvin.

I'd always admired him during his Hall of Fame career with the NY Islanders, of course, and had interviewed him a few times during his playing career.

He always had good, thoughtful insights to share.

Soon after he'd retired, for some reason he was attending a game in Boston when the Flames were in town. I saw him prior to the start and asked if he'd be a guest during the first intermission. He agreed. Great.

Back in those days, our broadcasts were on 660 The Fan and Don Armstrong, in charge of the hockey production, had set up an outstanding feature—rotating analysts that would be part of the pre- and postgame discussion and also part of any live interviews we did during intermissions.

On this particular night, *Toronto Globe and Mail* hockey columnist Al Strachan and Mike Rogers, who'd later be my colour sidekick in the booth, were the analysts, set up in the studio back in Calgary.

Denis came to our broadcast location at the old Boston Garden just before the end of the first period, on cue, slipped on a headset, and I called for a commercial.

Well, while we were waiting for the commercial to conclude we picked up on our headsets the off-air audio going on back in the Hot Stove Lounge in Calgary.

Mistake.

Mike, of course, had played for the Rangers when they were bitter, bitter rivals of Potvin and the Islanders.

So as we settled in to wait for the interview to begin, there were some comments back in the studio being made about Denis that weren't, shall we say, particularly glowing. From both guys. Unbeknownst to them, Denis was listening.

I started to get uncomfortable. At one point, Denis turned to me and said, "Do they realize I can hear them?" To which I replied, "I hope not."

I thought he was going to get up and walk out. He certainly had enough reason. But I give him a whole lot of credit. He'd committed to doing the interview, so he stuck it out.

I ended up asking most of the questions and—thanks to Denis' professionalism—there were no ugly overtures when Mike and Al joined in.

Later on, of course, Denis would become a colour commentator himself, with the Florida Panthers and Ottawa Senators, and maybe then understood how things can get fouled up.

I'd see him from time to time and do interviews with him, but that unfortunate night in Boston never came into conversation. Denis Potvin, a real pro on and off the ice.

Meeting Vin

When Vin Scully retired after 67 years broadcasting baseball in the fall of 2016, I, like everyone else who loved his unique talent, felt I'd lost a friend.

I got hooked on his work when he was broadcasting network TV games. Always a treat to hear Vin call a minimum of nine innings.

I was lucky enough to have the opportunity to meet him twice, briefly. The first time at Dodger Stadium, the Dodgers were playing the Yankees in an interleague game. The operator for Vin on the radio side of things also worked our hockey games when the Flames played in Los Angeles. So he arranged for me to come down at meet Vin.

I got there a little later than I'd have liked. So basically it was just a "Hi, how are you?" kind of thing.

As a play-by-play guy myself, I know that when it's time to go on the air, that's where your total concentration has to be.

Years passed and I met Vin again, this time entirely by chance. The Flames were playing in Phoenix and the Dodgers were there for spring training. Turns out, they were staying in the same hotel.

As I was leaving my room to head out to the game I got on the elevator and there he was. We chatted, shook hands, and talked a little bit on the way down.

I do remember when we reached the lobby, he was besieged by Dodgers fans and autograph seekers.

What drew you in first was that voice. It captured your attention immediately. Absolutely perfect for baseball. The enunciation. The delivery.

It just fit.

He was so great at telling engaging stories, then quickly, eloquently, transitioning into the play-by-play.

A work of art to listen to, really.

The amount of research he did showed in his work. Tremendous balance in that he had interesting anecdotes, insights, and facts about players for both teams, not just the Dodgers.

That inspired me to do even more research because his preparation was so thorough, yet the delivery so effortless.

Broadcasting hockey is far different in style than baseball, naturally, but you can learn, pick up good habits, from great broadcasters in any arena.

He was able to raise his voice to accentuate important, exciting times in a game and not be too irritating on the ear. And that is sometimes not easy. He was tremendous at that.

The other amazing thing about Vin was not just his longevity but there was no dropoff in the quality of his work. Think of it, 67 years at the top of the game.

And he probably could've carried on longer if he'd wanted to.

Just a treasure. An absolute treasure. And an example for everyone in the business.

The (Not So) Common Cold

A bit of a cough. That unmistakable feeling of sluggishness.

The signs, for a broadcaster, are ominous.

Game 1 of the 2004 Western Conference Final was a matinee at the Shark Tank in San Jose.

I'd been fighting a cold, the unmistakable signs were there, and I have to admit to being quite concerned as game time approached.

I soldiered on, but as the game went on my voice was starting to crack, getting worse and worse.

Wouldn't you know it—overtime.

Compounding my raspy throat problems, the OT period went almost the complete 20 minutes.

Then, in the final 60 seconds, defenceman Steve Montador stepped up and scored, providing the Flames with a vital 4–3 victory and a valuable series lead.

It's funny how scratchy your throat can be but when a key moment of a game arrives, as Montador's goal certainly was, a rush of adrenalin hits you, and I was able to yell out the winning goal with customary vigour.

Got to admit, though, I was helped through the ordeal by my colour commentator, Mike Rogers. When I needed a break or my voice started to crack, he'd jump in and cover for me.

My gratitude to Steve didn't end with his OT snipe, though.

When the game ended and I'd completed my duties up in the broadcast booth, the next chore was racing down to the dressing room area and chatting with the star of the game.

In this case—naturally—Steve Montador.

By the time I got down there and had the opportunity to get Steve as my guest, my vocal chords stiffened up and I could barely get a word or two out.

I was hardly able to introduce Steve as our guest on the show and the fact that he'd scored the winning goal.

Steve, recognizing my difficulties, not only described in detail scoring the goal but continued to go on and talk about the ebb and flow of the game.

I believe he chatted for almost four minutes without any prompting.

I'll never, ever forget how he bailed me out on that occasion. (Unfortunately, Steve would pass away only a few years later and when that happened, it really hit home with me, along with so many others in the sport who'd known him).

After that game I went up to Dr. Jim Thorne, travelling with the team, and he gave me some medication and also had some advice.

He told me to go back to the hotel—it was a Sunday night—not to go anywhere that night or the next day, refrain from talking unless absolutely necessary, and get as much sleep as possible.

All that would help cure my situation.

Outside of the morning broadcast back to Calgary, I took his advice and didn't talk to a single soul.

Another thing he advised me to do was sit in the steam room in the hotel a few times during the course of the two days.

On Tuesday morning, for Game 2, my voice was much better but was still raspy.

As it turned out I was able to broadcast that day without any difficulty but there was a close call.

34

There were a few other near misses and I did struggle through some games due to a bad throat, a cold, flu, what have you. In my line of work, you're always worried about your voice, its strength. Hockey is a fast game to call and so fighting through a bad throat places a great a strain on your vocal chords.

One of the closest shaves I ever experienced was during my calling of the 2010 men's Winter Olympic hockey tournament in Vancouver, working with host Dan Dunleavy, interviewer Howard Berger, and colour analyst John Garrett. I started to develop a cold on the eve of the semifinals. Battling that bug and having to broadcast two games in one day certainly didn't do my voice any good. I got through the first game and half of the second before my voice started to crack.

I managed to finish the second semi, then went straight back to the hotel to rest. I spoke to Dr. Thorne, who was, luckily, working for the Canadian team, and he prescribed some medications to take and also the benefits of sleep.

By gold-medal Sunday, thankfully, the voice was working a lot better. That day, as all Canadians remember, Canada beat the U.S. in overtime on Sidney Crosby's goal, and I was able to unleash a "Yeah baby!" in celebration.

I couldn't have done it alone that day. Or any other day, for that matter.

During my career, I had the good fortune to not miss a broadcast, beginning in senior hockey and then moving along to the NHL level.

So I must stop and take time to thank family members for their support in my games-called record, as well as my three Flames colour men—Doug Barkley, Mike Rogers, and Peter Loubardias—who on nights that I did struggle helped fill in the gaps.

As well, I can't forget trainers Bearcat Murray, Terry Kane, and Morris Boyer with the Flames, as well as doctors such as Bill Blair, Kristin Yont, Terry Groves, and, of course, Jim Thorne. They all contributed to keeping me going and doing what I loved to do.

There were a lot of nights I didn't feel great, a couple in particular, but I persevered and did the best job that I possibly could every night I went on the air.

I take some small pride in that, and quite rightly, I think.

Grapes

The irrepressible Grapes, Don Cherry, is now one of the most recognizable faces on Canadian television via his Coach's Corner segments on *Hockey Night in Canada*.

Don, of course, has never been shy about giving his opinion and causing controversy.

What people might not know, or remember, is that he was a colour commentator for Flames games on *Hockey Night in Canada* for a while in the early 1980s, when his broadcasting career was just getting started.

He did get himself in a bit of trouble in those days, such as the night he questioned the intestinal fortitude of Flames defenceman Pekka Rautakallio, who was a pretty good offensive defenceman from Finland.

On or off camera, Don never shied away from saying what he thought and sometimes his comments looked like they might get him fired.

Then he'd sometimes go public, letting his fans know that his job was in jeopardy, and the support that he got was amazing, so much so that it convinced the higher-ups at CBC to keep re-signing him.

During his time as a Flames colour man, I asked Don if he'd be an intermission guest on our radio broadcast and, of course, he was great with his commentary.

In those days, the radio station provided gifts for our guests and on one occasion it was a hair dryer.

I gave the dryer to Don. I don't know what he did with it, but for years after that every time I'd see him he'd remind me of the hair dryer I gave him way back when.

Even at the 2004 Stanley Cup Final, over 20 years after the fact—the dryer surely must've short-circuited by then—he mentioned it once again.

I told him with my lack of hair, he certainly needed the gizmo more than I did.

The Magic Elixir

Vinegar.

It's gotten me through some rough nights in the press box when I wasn't feeling up to snuff.

A cold or sore throat is the avowed enemy of any play-by-play announcer.

In such situations, I found one or two sips of vinegar prior to each game and maybe again prior to the third period worked a charm.

You talk so fast and so loud doing play-by-play of a hockey game, there's quite a strain on the vocal chords.

Canadian pop star Anne Murray—one of my musical favourites, and a fellow Maritimer hailing from Springhill, Nova Scotia—actually suggested the vinegar trick to me during an interview when she was performing in Calgary.

Well, if vinegar was good enough for Anne Murray, it was certainly good enough for me.

This received a bit of attention over the years, and some people mistakenly believed I was chugging a whole bottle of the stuff.

I remember being in Dallas for a game during the 2005–06 season, having dinner at a pub with my colour sidekick, Mike Rogers, along with coach Darryl Sutter and a few members of the Flames coaching staff. Fish and chips was prominent on the menu, so in the middle of the table, there was a bottle of vinegar.

Televisions were showing NHL games from the night before. I had a bit of a cold at the time and mentioned that to ward off the effects, I used a couple sips of vinegar.

At that point, the guys at the table had yet to hear about that little trick. I remember Darryl leaving the table for a few minutes. When he returned, he had a full bottle of vinegar, wrangled from the cook in the kitchen, and presented it to me to use before the next night's broadcast and down the road.

A nice gesture.

What's interesting is that late in the 2016–17 season prior to a game at the Saddledome that featured Darryl's L.A. Kings, I was in the hallway near the visitors' dressing room when Darryl came out in the hall.

The first thing he asked me is if I was still sipping vinegar.

I told him I really had no need to since I'd retired, but I still had that bottle he'd given me more than a decade before.

Occupational Hazards

Broadcasts can be good or not so good.

Rarely are they dangerous.

But during a game at the Saddledome, mid-1990s, I unexpectedly smacked my head on a beam which was located just above my broadcasting position.

To this day, I have no idea how it happened. I'd leapt up so often over the years at crucial moments in games, out of excitement.

This time, though, I must've really launched myself.

Because...*Whack!*

Not having a luxurious thatch of hair, then or now, the blood really started to flow.

I was dazed, in a bit of shock, but there was nothing to do but continue on with the broadcast. I guess that's what's called "playing hurt."

Thank heaven, Don Armstrong, our executive producer of the broadcasts on 660 The Fan, hurriedly located some paper towels and applied them to my head. It was quite a mess, blood on my face, on the table, on my game notes. I remember my long-time sidekick Doug Barkley being a trifle amused by the whole thing but he did try to help out, too.

During the intermission after I'd had my little accident, Don and Al Coates, then the assistant GM, visited the Flames' dressing room and found an extra helmet from the training staff for me to wear, for "protection."

Never one to turn down a gift, I strapped the helmet on and worked the rest of the game.

Never did find out what happened to that helmet but luckily I've never had to use one again.

Another strange incident occurred late in a game against the Minnesota Wild that fans even to this day remain curious about.

The broadcast location at the Xcel Energy Center in St. Paul always concerned me, ever since my first visit. The problem is that the written media had been seated below us at such an angle that whenever the writers would flip up the top parts of their laptops, our view of the ice would be partially obscured. (Less than a year after opening the facility, the Wild broadcasters petitioned to be moved down and were accommodated, but the visiting radio location remained above the writers.)

Anyway, about a minute to go, tie game, faceoff to the glove side of Flames goaltender Miikka Kiprusoff. Wes Gilbertson, the beat writer for the *Calgary Sun,* was seated directly below me and flipped up the screen on his laptop. When he did that, it blocked my view of the faceoff dot and partially obscured the net.

An important faceoff. So I elected to stand up to get a clear view of proceedings.

Sure enough, the puck exited the zone and into the Minnesota end off the draw, where I had an unobstructed view, so I elected to sit back down and...

My chair, as it happened, was on wheels. It slid out from underneath me as I tried to sit back down and I tumbled spectacularly to the floor.

During a live broadcast.

I can only imagine what listeners back home were thinking.

Initially, my colour commentator Mike Rogers was quite concerned, wondering whether I'd had a heart attack or really hurt myself in the fall.

When he saw me struggling to get back up—I was carrying on with the broadcast, with as much dignity as I could muster—he started to laugh. I started to laugh. In the booth next to ours, assistant GM Craig Conroy had seen me disappear in the fall and he, too, wondered if something might not be very wrong, rushing over to provide any assistance possible.

Then he started to laugh as well.

The fortunate part of the whole incident is that if I'd happened to fall about a foot to the right, I'd have surely cracked my head on the desk behind us and none of us would've laughing.

While rushing to my aid, Craig had missed a controversial non-penalty call against the Flames and when he made his way to the dressing room area after the game, coach Bob Hartley asked him how he'd viewed the incident from up top.

"I'm sorry, I didn't see it," Craig confessed. "I'd gone to help Peter and see if he was okay."

So now everyone—coaches and players, too—knew about my fall.

And of course, being on sports radio, the audio of the fall was replayed countless times the day after that, the week after that, and, believe it or not, every once in a while years later.

Broadcast Locations

Over the course of my career, the best atmosphere for broadcasting had to be inside the old Chicago Stadium, located on the west side of the Windy City.

For those never able to see a game there live, believe me, it was as electrifying as its legend.

Nearly 20,000 fans, ready to party, and they were *loud*. The noise level they generated became almost a point of personal pride. Adding to the tumult was the fabled 3,663-pipe Barton organ.

An amazing, impossible-to-replicate environment. The Madhouse on Madison, indeed.

Our broadcast location there was another of those with an overhang and catwalk to reach. An incredibly long slog.

Players always complained about the walk up the stairs—10 or 12 steps—necessary to take to reach the ice surface from the dressing rooms. Well, for broadcasters, not in quite the same shape as pro athletes, believe me, it was a heckuva lot further.

To reach our location you had to go up 326 steps and then across a flat space and the catwalk to our booth.

How do I know? One night I counted them.

Best memory from the old Stadium was Game 4 of the 1989 semi-final, Al MacInnis scoring in overtime on a Flames power play after Hawks rookie defenceman Trent Yawney had closed his hand on the puck and tossed it toward centre ice.

That MacInnis goal prompted the now-famous kiss that Flames coach Terry Crisp planted on Al MacNeil's wife, Norma, after trying to scale the glass in impromptu celebration.

As a replacement, the United Center, located across the street from the now-demolished Chicago Stadium, comes as close as possible to replicating the unparalleled atmosphere of its predecessor.

In Los Angeles when I arrived to call Flames games, the Fabulous Forum was the home of the Kings.

It was, and is, located close to LAX, making it handy, but not exactly in the most glamorous part of the city.

Built without a traditional media press box, they ended up using a section of stands in the second level to house us. Our visiting broadcast location was in the last row reserved for media, right next to the Flames' management team.

The fans were right behind us. They'd use some colourful language from time to time so you had to keep talking over that so it wouldn't be heard on the broadcast back home. One particular evening, some unruly sorts took to throwing popcorn and beer at myself and Doug Barkley. Doug, a big, strong guy, took exception. Some verbal give-and-take and shoving ensued. Luckily his microphone was off and I just kept talking, as if nothing out of the ordinary was going on.

The next time we travelled to L.A., the visiting radio broadcast seats had been moved to the middle of the media area.

There were always Hollywood stars in the stands in those days and at the Forum Club after games, particularly after Wayne Gretzky arrived to join the Kings and made attending hockey the cool thing to do.

Our spot at the Forum's successor, the Staples Center, is much, much farther away from the ice. The most interesting thing about the setup there is the air-conditioning unit installed just above the visitors' broadcast booth. It was usually on full blast so I took to wearing a cap and a sweater-vest for games there.

The old Winnipeg Arena, famous for its portrait of Queen Elizabeth II, was an interesting place from which to call a game. The sight line was fantastic, fairly close to the ice. Trouble was, our booth was right next door to the one reserved for the Jets' general manager/management team.

And the general manager of the time happened to be John Bowie Ferguson.

That created some very interesting situations. Fergie was not, shall we say, shy about letting his feelings on officiating and opposing players be known.

So you'd have to be really guarded on those broadcasts because during any dead air you might pick up one of Fergie's four-letter verbal missiles. John also had an annoying habit of banging on the wall, and I often wondered if he was just frustrated or also very cognizant of the fact the visiting radio crew was on the other side.

Either way, I never found the nerve to ask him.

With Fergie, things were rarely quiet but they were always interesting.

New York's Madison Square, nicknamed the World's Most Famous Arena, had three different broadcast locations during my time in the business.

During the late 1970s to the late 1990s, our perch was located up behind the very last row of seats, at centre ice. Looking down, it was awfully difficult to pick out some of the Rangers tri-coloured numbers. Plus, there was the smoke—cigarette and, unmistakably, marijuana—to contend with.

Once again, we had to keep talking in order override a lot of the language emanating from the seats.

Later on, they moved us down to a location infinitely closer. Only three rows from the penalty box, in fact. Again, the proximity to fans made things difficult. Further compounding the issues, we were basically looking through two panes of glass. But we made it work.

The final remodelling was outstanding for media. Brand-new, an overhang with a catwalk, providing an outstanding view.

By far the best of the three incarnations of my time in MSG.

More Broadcast Locations

When the San Jose Sharks entered the league as an expansion team, they quickly gained a reputation for their teal-clad fans and the great atmosphere in the Shark Tank.

People tend to forget, though, that through their initial two seasons, the Sharks played at the old, atmospheric Cow Palace in San Francisco while the new arena in San Jose was being built.

The Cow Palace was an interesting setting. The media seats were right in the crowd, at centre ice. The way stands were built back in the early 1940s, they didn't rise up the way they do in new buildings, making the sightlines for hockey very difficult, especially if anybody stood up.

The building had been built essentially for rodeos along with agricultural shows, and all those decades used for that purpose had left a very, shall we say, distinct odour.

So you had to get used to that, too.

When the Sharks moved first into their own building, in the fall of 1993, in downtown San Jose, the broadcast location proved to be ideal, one of the league's best. An absolute dream to call a game from. We were located at centre ice, second level. Perfect. A little cramped, maybe, but the view more than made up for that.

I do remember saying to my colour commentator Doug Barkley on our first visit in there, "We'd better enjoy this. Because it's not going to last long as a broadcast location. We're taking up prime seating location. The Sharks are going to end up moving us elsewhere and selling these seats."

And sure enough—you really hate to be right sometimes—commerce eventually triumphed over our fantastic view of the ice and we were moved way, way up, going from arguably the best vantage point anywhere in the league to one of, if not the, worst.

I have a lot of history with calling games in Toronto, starting with my first NHL broadcasting job with the Maple Leafs, back in the Maple Leaf Gardens era.

The famed gondola that Foster Hewitt had made his legendary broadcasts from was gone by that time, done away with by cantankerous owner Harold Ballard. I know the *Hockey Night in Canada* people tried to locate the remains to maintain as an artifact, but to no avail.

So my early play-by-play career at the Maple Leaf Gardens was located in a suite area, back behind the general media location. Coming back as a member of the Flames' broadcast crew a few years later, we'd been moved near centre ice. The only issue there was a high overhang on the glass, and having to lean forward to see the entirety of the ice surface you literally had your nose up against the glass. But they needed that glass to stop things like pins or drinks and even people from falling over into the crowd below.

Broadcasting television games at MLG put you on the opposite side of the ice surface, at centre ice on an overhang. Good location.

The Leafs' move to the Air Canada Centre certainly dressed things up for us. We had our own booth, no crowding, no distractions. And, of course, all the media people and team personnel are located close by, making it easy to line up intermission guests.

Over the years, we had three different positions at the two rinks in Vancouver. The early years, of course, we spent at the Canucks' first home, Pacific Coliseum. There we were located on the opposite side of the press-box proper.

To get from one side to the other, over centre ice, you had to walk across a catwalk made of wood that actually had small holes in the planks. So you could literally see the ice surface below as you made your way across.

Even though I got more accustomed to the sensation as the years went along, the first time I remember holding on for dear life. One guest

I had lined up, Flames defenceman Charlie Bourgeois, flat-out refused to make trip after he saw that catwalk.

The move to GM Place, later rechristened Rogers Place, was certainly an upgrade, roomy and very functional, as new buildings tend to be.

I was lucky enough to do play-for-play for the 2010 Olympic hockey tournament for Rogers and one of the interesting aspects is that the IOC mandates media be seated in the lower bowl for hockey, taking away no end of prime seating locations.

An interesting experience, broadcasting from that unfamiliar, lower position.

The 2016–17 season was the final one of Joe Louis Arena in Detroit and I can say with certainty no broadcasters, at least, shed so much as a single tear.

The Joe's press area was a late addition to the facility, and that showed. Right behind the final row of seats, smack dab up against the fans, who could be somewhat derogatory when they realized you were on the visiting broadcast crew.

Very, very tight quarters, so you could be jostled, unintentionally, which could easily break your concentration, which is vital when doing play-by-play.

The working conditions were certainly far from ideal but I had a few memorable evenings calling games at Joe Louis. Back in the Flames' playoff run of 2004, Game 5, series tied 2–2, the heavily-favoured Red Wings had beaten the Flames fairly handily back at the Saddledome in the fourth game and the consensus was that Calgary's magical run was coming to an end.

But returning from a lengthy spell out due to injury, Dave Lowry's presence seemed to inspire the Flames, who they won the game 1–0, Craig Conroy scoring the only goal and Miikka Kiprusoff performing outstandingly in net.

The Flames would go home and wrap up the series at home 48 hours later.

Good-Guy Marty

Goaltenders are a notoriously quirky bunch.

Many have different pregame rituals. Declining game day interviews is a popular one.

Either they are sincerely superstitious or just use that line as an excuse to get out of talking.

I remember once trooping into the New Jersey Devils' room, sitting down to have a little chat with Sean Burke, the starting goaltender with the Devils. The tape recovered was turned off.

I'd gotten to know Sean through involvement with a number of charity golf tournaments in the nearby Red Deer area during the summer.

We chatted for about 10 minutes and then I asked him if could do a pregame interview with him and he said no, it was his policy not to do it on game day.

I told him I understood.

Another trip into the Meadowlands, Marty Brodeur was having an outstanding year and I'd interviewed him previously on game mornings. But on this particular occasion, there was no morning skate for the Flames, having played elsewhere the night before.

I got in touch with a member of the Devils' media relations department and made arrangements to meet someone outside the dressing room two hours or so before the start of the game.

I get to the dressing room and I'm standing in the hallway, waiting. No sign of the media relations guy. I was a little concerned because Lou Lamoriello, the Devils' GM, had a strict policy with regards to his players speaking to media too close to the start of the game.

I assumed the guy had forgotten.

A number of players came out, fixing their sticks and other things. I didn't feel comfortable asking one for an interview.

After a while, Brodeur came out in the hallway, didn't have his equipment on yet, and he asked me what I was doing there. So I explained.

He said, "Well, why don't you interview me?"

We ended up doing four or five minutes and I thanked him greatly. He certainly bailed me out.

That's the type of guy he was, an outstanding goaltender and away from the game always helpful to someone trying to get his job done.

Worth a Million

One of the great promotions during my time broadcasting Flames games had to be the Safeway Million Dollar Score and Win Contest.

The contest awarded a fan who had entered at a local Safeway outlet a prize every time a Flame scored a goal.

In each game there was also a chance to win a million dollars should a player be lucky enough to rack up five goals in that particular game.

Only once has a Flames player scored five in a game. That distinction is reserved for Joe Nieuwendyk, back on January 11, 1989, before the Score and Win contest had been initiated.

The closest we ever came to giving away the $1 million came in February 2003 at the old America West Arena in Phoenix, when Jarome Iginla had himself quite a night, scoring all four of Calgary's goals.

The Flames were leading 4–2 with a couple of minutes remaining in regulation time, and the Coyotes pulled their goaltender in favour of an extra attacker. And Jarome had a fantastic chance to register his fifth of the night, and win some lucky fan $1 million, in the final seconds, whipping a shot off a goal post from just inside the blueline. A shade more to the right and I would've had the chance to announce that, say, "John Smith has won $1 million!"

Or at least I thought so, anyway.

Unbeknownst to me, "John Smith" would not, in fact have won $1 million if Jarome's shot had found its target. What I hadn't noticed in the script that I scrupulously read before every game was that John Smith "could" win a million dollars.

I hadn't been informed that a stipulation to the contest was that the five goals had to be televised on the team's mid-week TV broadcast.

So in one way, I'm glad that Jarome's shot drifted a shade to the left. Saved a lot of confusion, and embarrassment.

Game Prep

I'm often asked how I prepared for games.

Really it was an ongoing thing during the season, the off-season, and then on game day.

At the beginning of my career, I'd collect notes from anywhere that I could and jot them down in a scribbler. I had a setup for each team and whenever I got information, whether it was trades or players switching teams, I'd enter them in that scribbler.

If I found interesting notes in newsprint or magazines or by word of mouth, I'd put those in there, too.

When computers started becoming more popular, I got in touch with a fellow named Murray Everett in Calgary who had some knowledge of them and he set me up with a program for notes and also to have a sheet ready on game nights. The whole idea was to compile interesting tidbits, on players and on teams, to pass along to the fans and enhance broadcasts.

On game days, from the minute I got up in the morning, my focus was on the game that night. Around 6:30 AM, sometimes earlier, I'd begin preparing for the morning show that I would do on radio.

[Handwritten notes top right:]
37 KYLE ROHMAN
78 CHRIS LEE
57 RYAN GALLOWAY
86 B. LAZAROWICH

[Handwritten notes top left:]
Friday at Minnesota, 5pm
ROAD 3-0-1 vs Caly fast
3-5-1 ... 3-4?

Vancouver Canucks		Notes
1 Roberto LUONGO	40W,2.57 & .913; PO 3.22,.895 in '9-10...47W,club rec 2nd Vezina & Hart '06-7...NYI-Fla at Calg Dft...6oshots vs Det'02...NYI4thOv'97...2 MemCup.	EXTRA TIME -- 3-2,lose 2 last 3...OT 1-1...OTG,Bourque...SO 2-1...In '9-10 were 5-6-4...OT 2-3...OTG Iginla & Phaneuf...Shootout 3-7 (Home 0-3)...6-4-3 in '08-9...3-5ot..SHOOTOUT 3-3 in '08-9.
35 Cory SCHNEIDER	1-way pact aft 35W, 2.51 & 919 '9-10 AHL; 0-1 Van...Top Goalie in '08-9,final...1st Rd '04 BostC...B-to-B NCAA finals...age24...From Marblehead,Mass	LATELY -- Pts last 5 last 7g (2-3-2)...Lose 11 last 15 (2 in ET).
2 Dan HAMHUIS	PA,Nash 6yr, 27M aft Philly & Pitt try sign,deals...24pt,78g '9-10...Age 27...Nash 1st Rd (#7) '01...From Smithers...	FIRST GAME BACK (OK Dec1) -- 2-1 in '10-11...In '9-10 - 2-2.
3 Kevin BIEKSA	Out 27g ankle '9-10...53pt,72g best '08-9...Last yr of 11M...42pt in 81g top scoring Def '06-7...4th Rd '01 Bowling Green...Age28.	LOST LEADS -- Now 11 times (3 in games at Det & 3 vs Colo)...REC 1-6...1G 8; 2G 8; 3G 1...In '9-10 - 39 times lose lead - 1G 29; 2G 5; 5G...OVL 15-18-5.
4 Keith BALLARD	From Fla, 1st Rd,Berner,Grabner ...Pho-Fla,Jokinen '08...Colo-Pho in Morris Trade...Buff 1stRd '02...Buff-Colo,Reinprecht...UMinn 3yr,2NCAA Titles.	1-GOAL GAMES -- 3-8, W at Philly aft lose prior 8,plus another 1-3...2-1 are 0-4; 1-0 have win; 5-4 are 1-2...'9-10 in 2-1 games (9-9-1)...OVERALL 18-16-9...43g either 2-1 or 3-2.
5 Christian EHRHOFF	AIR-Hoff...+36, #___ NHL '9-10 aft -12 SJ '08-9...44pt top Van D, 11G...3 Olys,age28k,1st 18 '02...Van-SJ,2 prosp...4th Rd '01 Germany.	HOME -- Win last 2...OVERALL 6-5...OVERALL 20-17-4 in '9-10 least wins since 18 in 00-01.
10 Jeff TAMBELLINI	FA,NYI aft 14pt,36g (groin inj)...Born Calg '84...15pt,65g '08-9...LA-NYI with DGrebheskov for MParrish & BSopel '06 DL...LA 3rd Rd '03 UMich.	ROAD -- Pts 3 last 5g (1-2-2)...OVERALL 4-7-2. In '9-10 - 20 - 15 - 6...Rec wins 22 in '87-88 & '88-89...21 twice.
13 Raffi TORRES	FA, 1yr,1M,Buff aft 19-17=36 in 74g '9-10...KneeSurg '07-8...27G '05-6,best...NYI 1stRd(#5)'00 Bramp...Tor,born MexCity,mom,Peru	AFTERNOON -- Now 1-1-1...In '9-10 were 3-4...All wins on road score...Iginla success.
14 Alexandre BURROWS	ShldrSurg at 35-32=65 in'9-10,with 5SHG,tie Hossa...52G last 114g to end '08-9...FA Nov9/05...Not draft jr Shawinagin...From Pte Claire,PQ...Age24	KIPPER SHUTOUTS -- 37 now with 12 of them in 1-0 games.
15 Tanner GLASS	4-3=7 with 115pim in 67g '9-10...9th Rd '03 from Regina...Born Regina...Tier BCJHL then 4yr Dartmouth...Age27.	MORRISON -- Had active conse game streak,3yr have hip,hernia & wrist...HAGMAN -- 91G last 4yr...BACKLUND - MVP Mac's '05...IGINLA - Top team pts 9yr row.
17 Ryan KESLER	75pt,top,Selke (#2) final,2nd str yr '9-10,12PPG of 25...US Nat Team Dev...Age26...Hip surg '06-7 aft 1.9M OSheet Philly...1stRd'03 Ohio St,ply 1yr	CONROY - Best yr 75pt '01-2...STAOIS - 1-2-3 Outdoor '03...TANGUAY - 2 shldr surg '08-9 (RH).
20 Ryan PARENT	From Nash,O'Brien...Philly-Nash Hamhuis aft 1-2=3 in 47g; 17g PO '09-10...'07 Philly-Nash,Forsberg deal...Nash 1st Rd '05...From PAlbert...Age23	IGINLA NOVEMBER -- Now 8-5=13...13-6=19 in 14g after 4-5=9 in 12g Oct.
21 Mason RAYMOND	#9 retire Camrose AJHL...25-28=53 in '9-10 add muscle to 186lb...Led UMinn-Duluth scoring '06-7...2ndRd'05 Camrose AJHL...From Cochrane.	IGINLA STALLED -- Since end Nov '09 has 24G in 80g.
22 Daniel SEDIN	Shooter...Not - since rook...#2 Team all-star LW,64pt,63g(T4th NHL)'9-10...36G,'06-7,best...1st Rd 2nd Ov '99...Inch smaller than Henrik	FIRST GOAL -- Monday first time 9g (3-3-2)...OVERALL 5-7-1...Overall team wins 70% of games.
23 Alexande EDLER	Brk Ankle last PO game '9-10 aft 42pt,76g...Pt increase last 3yr...3rd Rd '04 Sweden with in Tier 3 League, WHL Kelowna '05-6...Age24.	KOSTOPOULOS -- 30pim led Caro...Led 'Canes PIM, hits & blocked shots '9-10,only player 82g...166g in row...Age 31...Fav arena, Saddledome.
26 Mikhael SAMUELSSON	30G Reg & 15pt lead PO...FA aft 4yr Det...23G in '05-6,top...Age isk...SJ draft '98...NHL prior '05-6 49pt, 188g NYR,Pitt,Fla.	BABCHUK -- Chic 1st Rd '02 (#21) from Kiev,Ukraine...Age26...Omsk KHL '9-10 with 22pts & +17...'08-9 Caro 16-19=35 in 72g, best.
27 Manny MALHOTRA	FA, SJ 3yr aft 33pt,71g with +17,top faceoff '9-10 (62.5%)...CBJ-SJ aft rej 4yr Atla summer...#5 face-off NHL...NYR 1stRd'98(#7) Guelph...Age 30k.	KIPPER STARTS -- 13 Last 14. LAST 11 LOSSES -- 2 in Extra Time, 6 with 1 Goal and 1g 3-1 (with ENG) & 1-4 once.
29 Aaron ROME	0-4=4 in 49g '9-10...Part Ana Cup win but no ring but had day with Cup...FA, CBJ...Age 27...With 4 WHL teams...From Brandon.	SCHEDULE -- From Nov17 to Dec 10 and next 2 days between play 14 games in 24 days in all 4 NHL time zones.
32 Joel PERRAULT	FA, Pho 1G,2g & 36pt,47g AHL '9-10...Stl-Pho waivs '06-7...Ana 5th Rd '02 BComeau 3rd in League 116pt in '02-3...2yr Cincy,out 9mon conc...Age27k.	IGINLA 30 GOALS -- Seeks 10th straight to be only 9th player to it.
33 Henrik SEDIN	Passer..Win Ross & Hart 29-83=112 in '9-10 (30pt more prior top)...1st Rd 3rd '99...'99-00 Elite League co-MVP with Bro...Age30,10th Yr.	BIRTHDAY ODDITIES -- On Dec. 5 Jokinen 32 & Hagman 31...On Dec.28 Moss is 25 & Glencross 28.
36 Jannik HANSEN	Arbit 1yr,1way 850K aft 2way 550K '9-10 with 9G,47 (3 GWG),brk hand camp fite,GBrule...21pt, 55g '08-9...8th Rd '04 Portland...From Denmark...Age24	TANGUAY SHOOTS -- Composite stick now. Last time at Calgary wood...Iginla "His shot is harder now"...34 shots, 4 more than Jackman and 50 lines than Iginla.
41 Andrew ALBERTS	2pt,13g aft from Caro,3rd at DL;10pt,62g Canes...Bost '07-8,out 3mon conc...5th Rd '01...4yr BostonC...Age 28...Degree Communications	TANGUAY THRILLED -- "Mentally, I'm in a better frame of mind than the last few years. I know what I can bring to the table and can bring more. I'm having a blast. Its been fun"
0 Alain VIGNAULT	4th Yr,ext to '13-14...Top NHL Coach '06-7...Mtl Coach 3+ yr,once Adam final,replace MTremblay age36...Age47...Aft Mtl back QMJHL...Play 42g StL	*[handwritten:]* KIPPER Pulled 3 last 4 STARTS vs VAN - TWICE 1st PERIOD

After the program was completed, I'd begin focusing more on the notes to accumulate for that night.

Following that, I'd head down to the rink for the morning, gather interviews for the pregame show and chat with personnel from both teams, chart the lines and defence pairings.

When the opposition was warming up, I liked to sit closer to the ice and a do a mental play-by-play in my head. There was a time when players would be out there with regular practice jerseys on, including numbers on the back. That practice is long gone, leaving the small number on helmets for identification, so I'd make notes to identify players. Things such as how they would wear their helmet, their jersey, style of helmet, hair—anything that was helpful to identify players.

After that, I'd go back home or to the hotel to piece together final notes for the game in a few hours' time.

I travelled with a portable printer and would print out three separate pages of helpful hints; one including the lineup of the opposition, including information with tendencies of that team, streaks, power play numbers, etc., as well as up-to-date data on the Flames.

Once that was done, I'd begin concentrating on players on the opposing team. I'd memorize the numbers from top to bottom, then from high to low. When I was satisfied I had that down pat, I'd place the numbers in a bowl or a hat and draw them out and say the name of the player. It was a trick you learn over the course of time. After that, I'd have a little workout in the hotel gym if we were on the road, get physically ready and do my 15-minute Insider Show.

I liked to arrive at the game two hours ahead of time, head to the broadcast booth, and get settled there so that when pregame warmup arrived, I'd gotten all my papers lined up the way I liked them. During the warmup, I'd keep my eye trained on the team that the Flames were playing, doing a mental play-by-play in my head.

I liked to stay away from other sports on game days. Some years, there'd be a really important football game or the World Series on the television. Mostly, I'd ignore them, wanting to focus entirely on the Flames game for that particular night.

It's a habit I incorporated early in my career and maintained it.

When the game was finished, I'd go down to the dressing room; we always did a live interview with a player after the game and were involved in the coach's scrum. On home games, I'd also join the colour commentator, guests, and host for a one-hour postgame show.

That made for a pretty full day. And once you got the unwinding done, it was time to start preparing for the next one.

Game Openings

One of the aspects of a broadcast I most enjoyed doing, although it proved time consuming, was the pregame opening.

Normally, we'd air it seven minutes prior to each opening faceoff, and it was a feature that I began in the mid-1990s. Meaning I did well in excess of 1,000 of them over the course of my career.

It was kind of a takeoff of the TV openings *Hockey Night in Canada* enjoyed much success with, tying in the game with happenings around the league or matters outside the game while building excitement for the night's contest.

I usually always had mine scripted so that it would flow well, hoping it would be a good way to start the broadcast.

They'd run 60 to 80 seconds in length. I tried to tie them into holidays, significant dates like Friday the 13th, St. Patrick's Day; players going in search of a milestone that night; current goal or point streaks; or anniversaries of famous moments in franchise history.

A couple that stand out for me were one I did with Elton John playing the next night at the Saddledome, incorporating some of his hit

"Big Joel Otto," as coach Bob Johnson called him, in the 1980s preparing for a faceoff.
(Getty Images)

song titles into the narrative. The same for Rod Stewart, a favourite performer of mine, on another occasion.

Anything I found topical, quirky, or potentially of interest to the listener.

Once I talked about the Sutter family's gold-mining history, long before the boys became the most famous set of siblings in the NHL. Duane Sutter heard it while driving to the rink and brought the subject up later.

I like to think I took great care in selecting a topic that fit the particular game I was calling that night. So these openings added more workload to an already busy game day preparation.

But early on I decided they were important to the overall quality of the broadcast and eventually they became a sponsored segment of the pregame package.

What became gratifying was the positive feedback I received from fans. And, sometimes, players.

One that stands out came from former Flames centreman Joel Otto. After Joel retired as a player and moved back to Calgary, we got to talking one day and he said, "You know, there have been times I've been driving to games at the Saddledome and I find myself sitting in my car in the parking lot, waiting until your opening commentary had finished before going into the building."

Comments of that nature made the extra work so worthwhile.

After I'd finished, I'd hand it over to my colour commentator, be it Doug Barkley, Mike Rogers, or Peter Loubardias, to set up the keys to the upcoming game.

Then the national anthem, followed by my standard, "Tonight, live from the Scotiabank Saddledome…"

Mike Rogers

When my long-time game-calling sidekick and great ally Doug Barkley decided to retire, it left a huge hole in the broadcast booth.

Mike Rogers stepped in and filled in admirably.

Mike and I spent a dozen years together partnering on broadcasts, and I enjoyed them immensely.

He'd been an outstanding centreman, a local boy who played his junior hockey with the old Calgary Centennials before moving on to the pro ranks, four spent in the World Hockey Association and the final eight in the NHL.

Later on, I'd nominate Mike for both the Alberta Sports Hall of Fame and the Alberta Hockey Hall of Fame, noting the fact that he was one of only four players in NHL history to reach the 100-point plateau in each of his first three seasons—consecutive 105-point years with the Hartford Whalers and then 103 as a New York Ranger.

The other gentlemen? Why, only Gretzky, Lemieux, and Peter Stastny.

I had the opportunity to interview Mike the player and broadcast a few of his goals in the early 1980s when the Flames would be pitted against the Whalers or Rangers.

Mike spent his off-seasons in Calgary and following retirement came back home to stay, eventually settling in and working for companies in the oil patch.

He also held down a full-time job at the time he joined our broadcast team, but worked things out so that he was able to travel to away games, and also be on hand for home games and practices.

That juggling act couldn't have been easy.

Mike had actually cut his teeth in the broadcasting business on 66 CFR, after the station took over the rights for the 1991–92 season.

Starting out as an in-studio analyst on game nights, he applied for, and got, the colour commentating job when Doug retired.

Mike connections in the game were invaluable—he knew Gordie Howe well, for instance, after playing alongside Gordie in Hartford.

I must say, we had our share of laughs over those 12 years, both on air and off. Sometimes I wondered if maybe we didn't chuckle a bit too much. But that was an extension of the camaraderie we'd developed.

One night during a game in the Saddledome, I thanked those fans listening to our broadcast in the building on Walkmans for tuning in.

By that time, 2000, Walkmans were as out-of-fashion as 8–track tapes. Mike thought it was hilarious, chastising me during the game broadcast and then later on the postgame show: "Pete, *nobody* in the arena had a Walkman. In fact, nobody *anywhere* has a Walkman anymore."

I ended up getting the last laugh, though, receiving a couple of calls the very next day from different people supporting me, confirming that, yes, they did have Walkmans and still used them to listen to our broadcasts.

Mike was a very intelligent hockey guy. During his time in Hartford he operated on a line tagged with one of the great nicknames of all time— The Stash, Bash and Dash Line. The Stash was outstanding goal-scorer Blaine Stoughton; Dash was Mike, the speedy centreman; and Bash was Pat Boutette, a grinding type who worked tirelessly in the corners.

Mike certainly added greatly to our broadcasts with his insight. He did his homework.

He also took on the coach's show chores, the reasoning being that the colour commentator could glean more insight by talking to the man in charge every day.

We in the media understand that one of the curses of the business is waiting around for players, coaches, and management people to show up for interviews. But it sure frustrated Mike in the beginning.

One of his strengths was understanding that Flames fans were intelligent hockey observers and though he had a lot of positive things to say about the players and the team, he wasn't afraid to be honest, to call things as he saw them. He felt the listener deserved, and wanted, that degree of honesty.

Cassie Campbell

Cassie Campbell, or Cassie Campbell-Pascall as she was known after marrying current Flames assistant GM Brad Pascall, is someone I took notice of during her years with the Canadian women's national team.

Always impressed by the way she handled herself, the way she played the game and interacted with people. So after she retired as a player it came as no surprise to me that she'd get involved in broadcasting, ultimately moving up to work for *Hockey Night in Canada.*

I'll not forget the night she'd been assigned to work a Flames game in Toronto in, I believe, her first season on *HNIC* on Saturday nights. The teams had their morning skate and I recall running into her at Air Canada Centre and she'd just received word that Harry Neale, slated to be the colour commentator that evening, wouldn't be able to make it to the game. I'm not sure if a snowstorm where he lived, in Buffalo, or an illness was keeping Harry away.

Either way, Cassie, who had been slated to do interviews during intermissions, pre- and postgame, suddenly became the colour commentator, working with the great Bob Cole.

She was amazingly calm, getting the news that her assignment for that night had been much expanded. I asked her if she'd ever done colour before and she had, but not on an NHL game, *Hockey Night in Canada,* coast-to-coast.

That represents the big time.

The colour position involves more preparation and I wondered if she'd been put in a spot, so I arranged to get her the notes I'd compiled for that night's game.

I talked to her afterward and she seemed quite pleased at the way things had gone. And that pleased me, as well. Since then, of course, Cassie has gone onto a number of other projects for *HNIC* and Sportsnet.

Milestone Moments

Calling goals can sometimes prove problematic. The distance you're seated away from the ice, deflections, and screen shots can all conspire against you as a broadcaster.

But 99.9 percent of the time, you get 'em right.

Milestones, you *definitely* don't want to mess up. These are landmarks that can last a lifetime.

During my career, I had the good fortune of being behind the microphone for some of those moments, working on seven 500th career goals and five 1,000th career points.

There were more players achieving those plateaus against the Flames than for them, of course.

When it came to calling 500th goals, Flames players bookended my involvement—Lanny McDonald, on March 1, 1989, against NY Islanders goaltender Mark Fitzpatrick at the Saddledome, scoring at 10:34 of the first period, with Joel Otto and Jim Peplinski assisting, while my final Flames 500th call came on January 7, 2012, when Jarome Iginla counted against Minnesota's Niklas Backstrom, also at the Dome. Both, fittingly, were game-winners.

Jarome's arrived on a shot followed by a goalmouth scramble, so it was a bit tough to sort out but I managed to get it right.

Non-Flames who reached the milestone when I was in the booth working games: Bryan Trottier with the Islanders, Michel Goulet during his time in Chicago, Mark Messier in Manhattan as a NY Ranger, Patrick Verbeek while in Detroit, and Mats Sundin as a Toronto Maple Leaf.

Of the non-Flames, Sundin's goal stands out. It was October 14, 2006, in Toronto. It was his hat trick goal and came in overtime with the Leafs playing shorthanded.

So not a bad way to snag your 500th.

It also spoiled a big night for Flames defenceman Mark Giordano, scoring the first two goals of his NHL career in his hometown. After the game, I remember seeing the future captain surrounded by family members, proud of his accomplishment. Later on, my successor in the broadcast booth, Derek Wills, would call Giordano's 100th goal, who became only the fourth defenceman to reach that number while a Flame, joining Al MacInnis, Gary Suter, and Paul Reinhart.

Lanny and Jarome also represent my Flames' 1,000th-point calls. Lanny did it against Winnipeg goalie Bob Essensa on March 7, 1989, in a 9–5 triumph, assisted by Jiri Hrdina and Dana Murzyn. Iginla's milestone 1,000th point—another game-winner—was on April 1, 2011, versus the St. Louis Blues.

The first 1,000th point I had the opportunity to call had a personal attachment: Darryl Sittler did it with a goal on January 20, 1983, in Philadelphia. I called a number of Darryl's points while broadcasting Maple Leafs games earlier in my career.

Two other non-Flames notched their 1,000th career points in games I called: Dino Ciccarelli with Detroit in 1994 and L.A.'s Luc Robitaille four years later. Luc was my daughter Tricia's favourite non-Flame, so that provided a nice added touch. She got the chance to meet him soon afterward on the morning of a Kings visit to Calgary.

Exhausted in L.A.

On game days it was always my goal to be in a position mentally and physically to be at the top of my form, whatever time the puck would drop.

However, there were a couple of instances, both in Los Angeles, and neither of them having to do with Hollywood or late nights, that forced me through a game with less energy than I normally would have.

The first time was back in 1981, when the Los Angeles Dodgers and the Montreal Expos engaged in the National League Championship Series. The first game would be played in Los Angeles on October 13, as it happened the same day as a night game at the Forum where the Flames were facing off against the Kings. So Steve Simmons, then a writer for the *Calgary Sun*, and I decided we would go to the afternoon game at Dodger Stadium. Plenty of time, right?

The Dodgers wound up winning that game 5–1. When they scored three runs in the eighth, Steve and I headed back to our hotel, which was closer to the Forum. Being a broadcaster with few years of experience in the NHL, I didn't think that would be too much of an issue, but when I got to the game and started broadcasting, I found my energy level quite low after sitting out in the sun all day.

The moral of that story? Watch on the TV.

The other time that I had a similar type of situation was again in Los Angeles, on April 22, 1989, as the Flames and Kings were engaging in a second-round playoff series.

On tap that night, Game 3. As it turned out that same day my son, Jeff, was playing for the Calgary Buffaloes in the Air Canada Cup championship game in St. John's, Newfoundland, which was over on the other ocean.

I was disappointed not to physically be in the rink to cheer on Jeff's team but the Flames, after all, were in the playoffs and that was my job.

But on this particular day, the Buffaloes were playing against a team from Regina in the championship game for the Canadian midget title and the game was starting roughly around noon L.A. time.

The fine folks in television production for the Kings were able to set it up for me to watch via satellite—on CTV, with Bernie Pascall, Brad's father, doing the play-by-play—in their studio.

Jeff's game started roughly the same time the Flames were concluding their morning skate.

Where the television studio was set up in the Los Angeles Forum was just across the hall from the Flames' dressing room, so as the players were coming off the ice, a bunch of them would arrive and check in on how the game was going.

Flames general manager Cliff Fletcher came in and watched a full period, noticing how nervous I was. I remember him saying to me, "Now you know how we feel when we're watching our Flames games from our locations."

I told him would I'd rather be broadcasting this game as opposed to watching with a such vested interest.

I sat on the edge of my seat the entire game.

Speaking of the entire game, Scotty Bowman, who was colour commentator for that playoff series for the CBC *Hockey Night in Canada* telecast, came into the studio early on in the first period and watched with me until the final buzzer.

As the game progressed, he started making comments—the greatest coach in the game's history.

Certainly quite the companion for me during a nerve-wracking situation.

In the end, Jeff would score a go-ahead goal for the Buffaloes. It didn't turn out to be the game-winner, but nonetheless they went on to win by a score of 4–3.

After the game was over, I had a small celebration with Scotty as we exited the Forum, took a taxi back to the hotel, and started preparation for the game that night.

No real opportunity to rest.

By the time I got back to the Forum, I was completely exhausted, worn out by emotion.

The Flames would win their game 5–2 to grab a 3–0 series lead, a series they would claim in four straight.

Pronunciation

In broadcasting, you go out of your way to try and make sure you get the pronunciation right on names. That's your job.

There are various ways of getting them right.

Ideally, you'd like to go directly to the player or coach himself and ask him the correct pronunciation of his name.

Sometimes, you don't have that access. So then you depend on the visiting team's broadcaster or media relations person to give it to you.

Even then, there are no guarantees.

I well remember the first time the Russians sent a club team over to Calgary in 1985 to play an exhibition game against the Flames. The morning of that game I was down at the Saddledome for the morning skate, hooked up with the Russian interpreter, clicked my recording device on, and asked him to please go over the team lineup numerically.

After getting that done, I went home to memorize the numbers of the players and coordinate them with the proper pronunciation.

I got that to a point where I was very, very satisfied.

Then came the game. As the Russians skated onto the ice for the warmup and I was doing a pregame play-by-play in my head, I noticed that about half the players had changed their numbers!

Later, when I mentioned that to some people, they said the fans wouldn't know who the players are anyway, so it really didn't matter.

Nonetheless, you *try* and get them right...

Even going to the player is not always a guarantee of getting the proper pronunciation.

When they came over to North America, a lot of European players wanted to settle into their new environment and so were a little bit shy to give you the proper pronunciation. An example of that with the Flames was Finnish defenceman Toni Lydman. When he arrived, I remember approaching him and asking him how to pronounce his last name.

His reply: "Pronounce it any way you like."

I asked the question in a different way. "Is 'LIDman' the proper pronunciation?"

He said yes, so I went on and called him that for the entirety of his Flames career.

Later he would get traded to Buffalo and the broadcaster there started calling him "LOOdman." The very first time that the Flames and the Sabres played, I went over to Toni and asked, "So how do you pronounce your name, anyway? Now I'm hearing 'LOOdman.'"

He said the latter pronunciation was proper.

Those things happen.

Jeff Shantz was a guy that played four and a half years with the Chicago Blackhawks, a native of Duchess, Alberta, which is near Calgary.

Jeff, after his stint with the Blackhawks, was traded to the Flames back in October of 1998 along with Steve Dubinsky. I had pronounced Jeff's name the way it was spelled when he was with Chicago. The first game I broadcast with him as a Flame, the next day the radio station got a call insisting the proper pronunciation was "Shauntz."

I spoke with one of the Chicago broadcasters afterward and they hadn't realized that.

For years, we all called the current captain of the Flames, Mark Giordano, "Geeordano."

Then one night TSN's Gord Miller told us he had talked to a family member, I believe Mark's mother, and was told the proper pronunciation was "Jyoor-dahno."

So it's a tough job getting those names right, even, sometimes, when you go directly to the source.

The Hosts

The hosts on the broadcasts are always a key element of the shows.

In my time, there were six hosts on our broadcasts—Bart Dailley, John Henderson, Jock Wilson, Mitch Peacock, Rob Kerr, and Pat Steinberg.

These guys worked really, really hard coordinating pregame interviews, putting together the intermissions, chasing down people to come on for interviews, not to mention the postgame time, which in a lot of cases included a call-in show.

They performed in front of crowds in some instances: The Hot Stove Lounge had clients and friends come in, and for out-of-town games, they'd be working out of a sports bar that had large crowds.

So they were operating under a lot of pressure.

They also had to track down out-of-town scores, which got a little easier with the arrival of the Internet, but prior to that updating could be a bit tricky.

I certainly appreciated their assistance. These guys all had different on-air styles but did an excellent job controlling things. Also important on the broadcasts were the operators back at the radio station, people no one heard tell of, who had to sit there over the three hours of the game and be on the spot to get the commercials on the air, not knowing when they'd be called for.

While the team was on the road, arrangements would be made by the engineer of the radio station in Calgary to have someone be there with equipment to help get our broadcast on the air.

You also have to thank the radio station management, the sales people, and all the others who were very, very helpful in making sure we would have a broadcast and that they would go smoothly.

I could make a commentary about each and every one, but there is one individual who acted as a host for longer than anyone else: Rob Kerr.

Rob came from Edmonton and joined the broadcast crew for the 2003–04 season, bringing a call-in show with him after a few years' absence.

Rob was a tireless worker and still is, on the air with the afternoon show, then doing the pre- and postgame as well as the phone-in segment.

Some of those would go on until 3:00 or 4:00 in the morning. At the outset, Rob said he'd stay on the air until the final call came in; if there were no other callers, then he'd wait a little bit and finally sign off the show. So it made for some very long evenings.

During the 2003–04 run to the Stanley Cup Final, Rob even had Craig Conroy, still Jarome Iginla's centreman at the time, calling in to the show a few times.

One particular time in Detroit, I remember the team taking a bus out to the airport about two hours after the game had ended. The flight from Detroit to Calgary took off and it was approximately a four-hour flight.

I remember getting back to the airport in Calgary—it had been an afternoon game and it was well into the evening—and Rob was still on the air with the postgame talk show and Craig phoned in.

It was a great start to Rob's career at The Fan 960 with all of the playoff-drive excitement, but many years would follow where there things were pretty fallow. So Rob had to put up with the angry callers that had all sorts of suggestions. Rob handled that very well.

He was the one who initiated opening the door to the Hot Stove Lounge for pre-and postgames in the Saddledome. The door was adjacent to the visitors' dressing room. Over the early years, the door was mainly closed because in certain situations angry players from opposing teams would come into the Hot Stove Lounge while we were on air, leading to some embarrassing moments.

We also had a couple of fans sail in yelling and screaming while we were on the air. So we decided to keep the door closed.

But when Rob came in, he wanted the door open and in the end I told him that was okay, but he was going to have to police this. It definitely has worked out well.

Also during that time, during the games at the Saddledome, I would have Rob jump in and do the blow-by-blow on the fights as they developed and he called those with a tremendous amount of enthusiasm.

He travelled to Toronto when I was honoured at the Hockey Hall of Fame in 2006 and the day after that he got his first taste of NHL play-by-play action because they'd asked Harley Hotchkiss and I to drop the first puck to start the game that night. In those five minutes, Rob called a Flames goal and a fight.

Later he'd get involved in more play-by-play on television with the Flames' pay-per-view telecasts for a few years and then transition over to Sportsnet with their televised games.

Rob is still very well known as being the talking goaltender, always willing to take part in charitable events around town and be miked up and do the commentary as he tried to stop shots.

He continues to work very hard in the community of Calgary and area and still hosts in the afternoon.

All of us are indebted to the team's media relations people in helping to procure interviews. Over the years, the Flames have been great assistance in this area, starting with Al Coates, and his wife, Jane. Rick Skaggs, Mike Burke, Peter Hanlon, Sean O'Brien, Sean Kelso, and others have been wonderful resources as well.

CHAPTER 2
THE PEOPLE

The Epitome of Class

The night I was first introduced to Harley Hotchkiss happened to be the same night the Flames played their first NHL game in Calgary, at the old Corral.

Prior to puck-drop, a reception had been scheduled at the Rotary House, near the rink, involving the entire Flames ownership group—headed at the time by Nelson Skalbania—and various NHL dignitaries.

You knew, as soon as you shook Harley's hand, that he was genuine gentleman. Classy. Soft-spoken. Sincere. No airs whatsoever.

He made you feel like family.

So often around the team, Harley was one of the few owners to make the trek down to the dressing room after games, win, lose, or tie. Always there to lend an encouraging word.

When players would leave the organization via free agency or trade and return with their new employers, you'd see him waiting outside the visiting dressing room on their subsequent visits to Calgary, always happy to renew acquaintances.

That's the type of relationship he built with everyone on and around the team. Players. Coaches. Managers. Equipment staff. Trainers. You name it.

When the Calgary group bought out Skalbania, Harley became the point man for ownership and whatever issues might arise.

Every year, he and his wife, Becky, would make one trip with the team, a week, maybe 10 days, and there was always a memorable meal involving the coaching staff, training staff, media, and team personnel, usually 20 to 25 people.

He'd always pick up the tab, happily.

One particular time my brother and buddies from New Brunswick, "Peter's Posse," had travelled in for a game at the Colisée in Quebec City, renowned for its fabulous restaurants.

Harley, of course, invited them out, too. He insisted that everyone be included.

One of the great things about the year I was honoured at the Hockey Hall of Fame with the Foster Hewitt Memorial Award is that it coincided with Harley's induction as a builder.

With friend and long-time Flames owner Harley Hotchkiss moments before the ceremonial opening faceoff, November 14, 2006. The night after we'd both been honoured at the Hockey Hall of Fame. (© Calgary Flames)

I'll never forget a wonderful Sunday evening in Toronto, the annual party night for the Hockey Hall of Fame festivities. The Flames rented out the Great Hall, the room that houses all the plaques and trophies.

To share my big moment with Harley, a man I'd gotten to know so well—along with Becky and his son, Jeff—over a 26-year span was so special.

On Monday at the luncheon when I received my HHOF jacket, Harley attended to support me. That night he was enshrined for everything he'd done not only for the Flames, but the NHL as its long-time chairman of the Board of Governors.

No one deserved it more.

Harley wasn't merely an owner. He was a huge fan of hockey and, of course, his beloved Flames.

He worked tirelessly, as did a number of other Flames owners, when the team went on that run of missing the playoffs for seven consecutive years, from the late 1990s to the mid-2000s. Crowds were down, the Canadian dollar was taking a hammering (while salaries were being paid in U.S. funds). There were rumbles that other cities were interested in purchasing the franchise and rumours that some of the ownership group might be ready to pursue such a sale.

Harley was among the group steadfast about staying, saying that was the mandate when the franchise was purchased back in 1980. I remember him commenting at the time that he hoped one day the NHL would have a salary cap to help all teams in the competitive aspect of the game.

That came true in 2005.

As chairman of the Board of Governors, Harley was among the most respected voices in the game.

We never spoke directly about the subject, but the work stoppages must've been very, very difficult on him. Business was business but this man loved the game so much. He was a major player in limiting the 2004–05 stoppage to only one season.

After so many memorable dinners with him and Becky over the years, I remember one night when the Flames were on the road in Philadelphia, just before the Thanksgiving holiday in the U.S. No Harley. It seemed so strange.

By that point, though, his illness was well known and he wasn't travelling with the team anymore.

A week or so after we returned from that road trip, I received a call from Harley's secretary inviting me to lunch with him and Becky, along with Doug Barkley and Al Coates.

That was really the last time I had a chance to chat with Harley. Just a great hour and a half, talking hockey. He knew the cancer had taken hold of him but remained the consummate host, the down-to-earth, concerned friend, asking questions about our family and mutual acquaintances.

We did see him again at the outdoor game, the Heritage Classic, in February of 2011, and the Flames alumni there for their game against the Canadiens alumni—so many retired players he'd forged such lasting relationships with over the years—held a reception for him to swap old stories.

That was the last time Harley was around the old gang.

He passed away too soon, a few months later, on June 22, at age 83. As befits a great man, a community-minded person, a voice of reason, and a friend to so many, a huge outpouring attended the memorial service.

We all continue to miss him.

Dave Hindmarch

Watching players being injured is another tough part of the job.

One particular injury that stands out, because it ended a player's career but also because it brought about a safety innovation in the NHL, happened to Dave Hindmarch.

Dave was a member of the Flames for 98 games, drafted when the team was still based in Atlanta, No. 14 overall. He attended the University of Alberta and played for its team before moving on to play for Canada in the 1980 Olympics at Lake Placid, New York, and then turning pro. He got to play one game with the team in the 1980–81 season and made it count, scoring his first NHL goal.

The next year, he came up from the minors for a nine-game stint, scoring three times before becoming a Flames regular in 1982–83.

Originally hailing from Vancouver, Dave's career would end in that city on December 16, 1983, at the old Pacific Coliseum.

That night, he was playing on a line with a couple of veterans, Doug Risebrough and Lanny McDonald, when he was tripped up by Vancouver Canucks defenceman Rick Lanz.

Dave slid hard into the goal post, which did not give, and he suffered serious damage to cartilage in both knees. Doctors looking at the knees later said it appeared more as if he'd been in a car accident than in a collision with hockey goal posts.

As it turned out, Dave spent a few months in a wheelchair and underwent major knee surgery and subsequent rehabilitation for a year and a half before being advised by medical experts not to continue his hockey career.

With today's modern medicine, they might've been able to repair the knees to a point where he could've played again. That wasn't the case back in 1983.

But his injury did help bring about the introduction of Marsh Pegs, which still are in use in all rinks where hockey is played. These are the pegs put into the ice for nets to go on top of, but are moveable and safely break away when hit by any degree of velocity by an oncoming player.

That innovation has saved countless players major injuries in the years since. Dave wasn't that lucky, of course, but if there's any consolation it's that his injury brought about meaningful change that allowed other players to enjoy lengthy NHL careers.

"Reg-gie! Reg-gie! Reg-gie!"

He arrived in Calgary as Rejean Lemelin, a goaltender hailing from Quebec City who was a long shot to be the Flames' No. 1 when the franchise relocated from Atlanta in 1980.

He quickly became a fan favourite and the chant of "Reg-gie! Reg-gie! Reg-gie!" would reverberate around the Saddledome for years.

Part of a three-goaltender group that also included the veteran Dan Bouchard and up-and-coming Pat Riggin, Reggie would serve some time in the minors before coming up and establishing himself.

And, of course, with a French Canadian name, there was the movie *Slap Shot* that had the French Canadian goaltender Denis Lemieux as one of the star attractions.

Reggie was drafted by Philadelphia as a seventh-round pick in 1974 and never did play for the Flyers, just one of their minor-league affiliates.

Ultimately, he'd sign on as a free agent with the Atlanta Flames and play 21 games over a couple of years at the Omni before the franchise was sold and shifted north.

He then became part of a two-man goaltending duo during the 1980–81 season, about midseason, after Bouchard was shuffled off to Quebec City.

So it was Riggin and Lemelin.

Reggie took over as the mainstay in 1983 and held that spot until late in the 1985–86 season, when Mike Vernon supplanted him prior to the start of the playoffs.

Mike, of course, would go on a lengthy run as the Flames' top guy. Reggie stayed one more year as the Flames' backup before moving on.

While in Calgary, though, he certainly made his mark. Second in the voting for the Vezina Trophy in 1983–84, a year in which he put together a 19-game unbeaten string as the Flames goalie, a record that still stands. He won the Molson Cup—presented at the end of each season to the Flame player that amassed the most points in the three-star selections at the end of each game—in back-to-back years.

What I remember most about the off-ice part of Reggie's spell in Calgary was when he would speak at the segment luncheons once a month. This was an extremely funny guy. He unloaded some great one-liners and of course he still had that French Canadian accent that went over really well with the fans.

While with the Flames, he played in the Canada Cup tournament in 1984 in a tandem alongside Grant Fuhr that collaborated on a gold medal.

Reggie would move to Boston in 1987 and then teamed up with Andy Moog to post the best goals-against average in the NHL and win the Jennings Trophy in 1990 with the Bruins.

He eventually retired and became the goaltending coach with the Flyers for a dozen years or so. We'd see him quite a bit when the Flames and Philadelphia would meet, and we'd reminisce.

When Reggie was in Calgary, we both lived in the same part of the city in the southwest and frequently would drive to and from the airport together. So I got to learn an awful lot about Reggie and the game.

A really interesting guy to chat with, and also a very good on-air interview.

He really enjoyed some tremendous success in the old Stampede Corral. In his three years of goaltending in that venue, he lost only nine of the 51 starts.

Reggie's big problem—and it was a big problem with a number of goalies of the era—was the difficulty in beating the Edmonton Oilers. Some of those games against Edmonton were high-scoring affairs and eventually Reggie got slapped with the nickname "Reggie 'Let-'Em-In,'" mostly coming from fans in Edmonton.

A bit unfair. I mean, he wasn't the only goaltender who had trouble beating the Oilers in those days.

Taken in its totality, he had a great career with the Flames and will always be remembered for that "Reg-gie! Reg-gie! Reg-gie!"chant.

Al Coates

Al Coates spent two decades in the Flames organization, working his way up the corporate ladder from public relations all the way to general manager.

Quite the rise.

Al's NHL career began in the Motor City with the Detroit Red Wings, where he served as trainer and then in the media relations department.

When the Flames arrived from Atlanta in the spring of 1980, he was hired by then general manager Cliff Fletcher to be the team's media relations/public relations director.

After a short time, Al graduated into the managerial side of things, serving as assistant GM before he was elevated to the top job in November of 1995, becoming the third man to hold the position, following Cliff Fletcher and Doug Risebrough.

Al inherited the job at an extremely difficult moment. Due to a sinking Canadian dollar, escalating salaries, and the departure of many top players, the team's power days were at an end.

Nevertheless, Al—very personable, very well connected—worked like a demon trying to maintain the standards set when the financial playing field had been level.

Two trades, under duress, that he made rank among the best in franchise history. The Joe Nieuwendyk deal, Christmas 1994, was probably the best holiday-dateline swap ever, if not the best of any time made by a Flames general manager.

Nieuwendyk, team captain, had left the team prior to the regular season due to a contract dispute with Al's predecessor, Doug Risebrough. So Al inherited a major problem: How to get back fair compensation for a great player who was very publicly sitting out.

But at Christmas, he was able to swing a deal with the Dallas Stars to acquire a bright young prospect named Jarome Iginla, and the versatile Corey Millen. The whole point in making the deal, of course, was Iginla, then playing junior for the Kamloops Blazers of the Western Hockey League.

Iginla would, as everyone knows now, turn out to be one of the greatest players in franchise annals, if not *the* greatest.

The other shrewd trade arrived when he was forced into dealing the immensely popular Theo Fleury, set to become an unrestricted free agent at the conclusion of the 1998–99 season. Contract discussions weren't, to be blunt, proceeding smoothly.

Although Coates dearly wanted to keep Fleury, the financial landscape of the time simply wouldn't allow it, so his aim was to get back the best assets possible.

As in the Nieuwendyk deal, he went for youth, bringing promising young defenceman Robyn Regehr over from the Colorado Avalanche, along with utility forward Rene Corbet and defenceman Wade Belak.

The key, once again, was the junior-age player from the Kamloops organization, and once again Coates and his staff had thoroughly done their homework, scouting players the Avs listed as being available in a deal to bring Fleury to Denver.

Ultimately, he chose Regehr, who would go on to play the second-most regular season games as a Flame (826), trailing only Iginla's 1,219 total.

So, in terms of service, Al Coates' deals brought the players ranked first and second in Flames longevity, the foundation—along with Darryl Sutter acquisition Miikka Kiprusoff—for the unexpected push to the Stanley Cup Final in 2004.

Mighty impressive, given the circumstances.

Unfortunately, Al didn't reach his goal as GM—to win the Stanley Cup. Although he did own a Cup ring from the 1989 title team, when he served as assistant manager.

He'd win another championship as a part of the management crew with the Anaheim Ducks in 2007, also working in the NY Rangers and Toronto Maple Leafs organizations, as well as with Hockey Canada.

He and his wife, Jane, very much people-persons, are back in Calgary now and the community's all the better for that.

Cliff

Cliff Fletcher's impact, his influence, on the franchise is incalculable. His fingerprints on the formative years, the foundation, of the Flames are there for all to see.

Before Cliff came to Calgary as president and general manager, a position he held in Atlanta prior to the relocation, I became acquainted with him a little bit, when I was broadcasting Maple Leafs games.

I obviously got to know him a whole lot better during his years as GM in Calgary from 1980 through 1991.

Ask anyone of that era. This was someone who operated with consummate class. A very caring person. One of the tells that really stands out to me is that oftentimes when you'd meet him, the first thing out of Cliff's mouth was, "Is everything okay?"

He had a genuine interest in the well-being of people around him, whether they be players, members of management, his office staff.

Or, yes, even the media.

He wanted to make sure everyone was taken care of.

You always got the feeling that if you had a problem, Cliff would try and fix it. I heard stories of players and people employed by the Flames who had issues, things that needed sorting through, and very quietly Cliff would go about as best he could to get things worked out.

Taking over in Calgary, he realized this was going to be whole different situation than Atlanta, which, to be honest, wasn't much of a hockey market.

What held him in good stead for that unique challenge was that he'd worked for many years in the Montreal Canadiens organization— one of, if not the, classiest in hockey—and also later in St. Louis.

From day one, he worked on assembling an on- and off-ice team that would be highly competitive in the NHL with, of course, the ultimate goal to lift the Stanley Cup.

Another thing that stands out—Cliff was a very superstitious guy about many things. For instance, for some reason, he shied away from doing any radio or television interviews in the second-period intermission.

Why the *second* period, specifically? Beats me.

Of course, I wasn't aware of that quirk early on, and one particular game the Flames played on the road, I asked if he'd come on for a live second-period chat.

He mentioned that no, he didn't like doing them at that time.

He didn't go into any details as to why not, only apologized when he saw my confusion.

Soon after that, though, he returned and said, yes, he'd agree to it. But it was obviously breaking protocol.

As it played out, the Flames went on to win that game, but during his tenure in Calgary I never asked again for Cliff to join me during a second period. Years later, when he was working for the Leafs, I ran into him prior to the game in the press box at a game in Phoenix and he told me he'd gotten past that particular superstition. Why? I didn't ask and he didn't offer any explanation.

In the late 1980s, as our contract as Flames rights-holders was expiring, Cliff was considering making the broadcast crew a part of the organization. In other words, hiring them to work for the team as opposed to the stations employing the broadcasters.

He had me come to his office one day and asked my thoughts on the idea, wondered if I'd have any problem with it in terms of giving a fair, impartial broadcast.

I was very appreciative that he'd take the trouble to ask and told him that I, personally, would not have difficulty with it as long as I wouldn't be asked to change my style.

In that sort of situation, because the team is paying you, they want you to be more "on board," so to speak.

I expressed that concern and his immediate response was, "No, the way you broadcast games right now is outstanding. It's very, very fair."

Nice of him to say, because you do want to find that correct balance.

The conversation brought me back to the time I was starting out in the business in New Brunswick. Listening to my idol Danny Gallivan call Montreal Canadiens games on *Hockey Night in Canada* is when I learned the value of calling a fair game.

Cliff's take on the matter also fit in with what Harold Ballard told me when I met him in Toronto the morning of my first game. I asked him if he had any advice. In typically blunt fashion, Ballard said, "Remember there are two teams on the ice."

On the business side of things, Cliff certainly wasn't shy about making trades and pulled off some dandies to improve the team and ultimately to win a Stanley Cup.

He didn't get the moniker Trader Cliff by chance.

Bringing in Alberta-born icon Lanny McDonald, then with the struggling Colorado Rockies, was his first big, bold trade.

Later on, Cliff gambled by dealing Kent Nilsson when the Magic Man was the leading scorer in Flames history to acquire a draft pick that would become Joe Nieuwendyk.

Later, he'd acquire sniper Joey Mullen from St. Louis, and also add Doug Gilmour and Mark Hunter from the Blues.

Cliff always seemed to be able to strike when the iron was hot.

One deal that a lot of people still feel he got fleeced on came during the 1987–88 season when he dealt rookie Brett Hull to St. Louis, getting back rock-solid defenceman Rob Ramage and goaltender Rick Wamsley in return.

At that time, Brett, the kid with the famous last name, had scored 26 goals in the 42 games that he had played with the Flames. A pretty significant contribution.

But in analyzing his personnel, Cliff's thinking was that he had enough goal-scoring wingers, allowing him to make the swap.

I remember when he completed that deal, chatting with him off the record, and he admitted, "You know, Brett Hull is probably going to go on and score 50 goals in the NHL."

I don't think he could ever have dreamed that Hull would go on to score 70 and 80, but his whole idea was that he was trading a surplus for needed depth. The Cup was his aim.

That 1987–88 season didn't bring about a Stanley Cup, but Cliff's work in adding key pieces did deliver that elusive championship the next year and I thought those two players, Ramage and Wamsley, while they weren't major factors, made very solid contributions.

In the case of Ramage, he found himself thrust into some heavy-duty action after Gary Suter was injured in the opening round and couldn't play.

Ramage stepped in and played solidly.

Wamsley, meanwhile, made a perfect backup, a quality person, supportive teammate. His biggest contributions came during the regular season, spelling off No. 1 goalie Mike Vernon.

Vernon didn't have to work 70 to 75 games that year and that made him quite fresh to backstop the team in the Stanley Cup playoffs.

Cliff was always the brains of the operation.

Al MacNeil

Ironic how things happen in life.

I first met Al MacNeil, the first coach of the Calgary Flames and also the last coach of the Atlanta Flames, in the early 1970s when he held the twin titles of general manager and coach of the Nova Scotia Voyageurs.

At that time I was play-by-play broadcasting in New Brunswick and the Voyageurs would come to Memorial Gardens in Campbelltown, my hometown, for exhibition games. I was part of arranging those dates, so that's when I got to know Al.

The night that I did my audition for the job in Toronto in September of 1977, when the Montreal Canadiens and Toronto Maple Leafs were playing, there was Al, and I met up with him beforehand outside the Habs' dressing room.

I told him what I was doing and asked him for advice should the audition go well.

I'll never forget him saying to me: "You have nothing to lose, kid. Take it!"

So I did. Al, I owe you.

A couple of years later I'd see him again in Atlanta when he was coaching the Flames and as fate would have it, we would hook up again in Calgary when he was coaching and I was doing play-by-play for the team.

Sometimes I think Al's just been following me around.

In 1971, of course, he was behind the bench for the Canadiens when they won the Stanley Cup, after gaining the distinction of the being the first Maritimer ever to be a head coach in the NHL.

He'd go on to win three American League titles with the Voyageurs.

As a player, I'd heard he was a very rugged defencemen in the 524 games he logged in the super-competitive, rough-and-tumble six-team league.

He would also play in that first expansion, when they moved up to 12 teams and gained a reputation as a very hard-nosed type of guy. After retiring from active duty following the 1969–70 season, he moved into the coaching ranks.

Cliff Fletcher had initially hired Al to coach the Flames in what would turn out to be the team's final year in Atlanta. He then made the move to Calgary.

Jarome Iginla presenting long-serving Flames coach and executive Al MacNeil with a plaque after Al was inducted into the American Hockey League Hall of Fame. (AP Images)

When Cliff decided on a coaching change for the Flames' third season here, 1982–83, and made the bold hire of Badger Bob Johnson from the University of Wisconsin, I can remember him telling me, "We have to keep Al." He convinced him to stay on in a management position. Al has stayed loyal to the organization ever since.

He was always helping out in various areas, different capacities, but the one that became his highest-profile occurred on December 10, 2002. That was the day the Flames let Greg Gilbert go as coach.

In a momentary bind, midseason, needing some time to hire the right replacement (which would turn out to be Darryl Sutter), Al stepped into the breach, two decades after his last coaching assignment.

When Al was behind the bench, he was kind of like a favourite grandfather coming in to look after the kids for a weekend or so.

The stint was only supposed to last three or four games but it wound up being 11.

And the Flames actually compiled a decent record with four wins, five losses, and two ties before Darryl took over.

Afterward, Al continued on with the organization, travelling with the team, attending home games, passing on his insights to coaches and tips to players.

If they had concerns, they'd feel free to talk to Al, knowing that he'd be as helpful as possible, and if the conversation was confidential, it would stay between them.

I loved listening to the entertaining conversations he would engage in at the rink with stars of yesterday such as Mr. Goalie, Glenn Hall, and Bert Olmstead, a five-time Stanley Cup winner from nearby High River, Alberta, both contemporaries of his.

For over a half century, Al's been involved in the game as a player, coach, and in management, four times a Stanley Cup winner, including with the Flames in 1989 as assistant general manager.

One of hockey's class acts.

The Other Al (MacInnis)

When Al MacInnis shot the puck, I was happy to be up in the broadcast booth, a long ways from the ice surface.

Al certainly had a rocket of a drive from the blueline. He attended his first Flames training camp in 1981 after being the team's first draft pick, 15th overall, three months earlier.

Introducing myself to him for the first time I knew we had a little bit of a bond, something in common: We were both Maritimers. Al was from Port Hood, Nova Scotia, born in nearby Inverness, and me being from New Brunswick.

I remember he'd played in a bantam tournament in my hometown with a team from Port Hawkesbury and already was beginning to gain a bit of a reputation.

Later, when we'd gotten to know each other better, he'd refer to me as "the pride and joy of Campbellton, New Brunswick" and I'd refer to him as "the pride and joy of Port Hood." Both small towns.

Few Maritimers reached the NHL, let alone played for the Flames, but when Al joined the organization Al MacNeil from Sydney, Nova Scotia, was the team's head coach (Big Al had been slapped with the nickname Chopper long before, so it stood to reason that Little Al would inherit it).

Later, Charlie Bourgeois from Moncton would join the team in 1981–82 as part of the defensive corps, adding to the Maritimer flavour.

Naturally, I pulled for these guys.

When Al first arrived in Calgary, he was already noted for that big shot but other aspects of his game needed work, such as skating and conditioning.

What people today maybe overlook—familiar with only the finished product—is how diligently he worked to shore up the areas and turn himself into an All-Star.

After Al's first taste of a pro camp he realized how much stronger he needed to be to turn himself into an NHL player. Returning to his junior team, the Kitchener Rangers of the Ontario Hockey League, he set about doing precisely that.

Over the course of his stellar Kitchener career, he'd play on two OHL champions and a Memorial Cup winner in 1982. He also had brief stints with the Flames, suiting up for his first NHL game on December 30, 1981. I well remember that day. The old Corral was the site and the Flames doubled up on Boston 4–2.

He'd receive one more in-game look before heading back to Kitchener.

The next season, Al logged 14 games for the Flames and 51 for the Rangers. Despite the lengthy audition in Calgary, with that blistering shot of his, he still managed to score 38 goals, tying the single-season OHL record for defencemen set by a guy you may have heard of—Bobby Orr.

His first game of that campaign for the Flames was in Toronto, at Maple Leaf Gardens on October 23, 1982. With Kitchener being nearby, GM Cliff Fletcher called Al up for just the one start, and he'd register his first point, an assist on a goal by Denis Cyr.

Over the course of his Hall of Fame career, he'd go on to collect 1,273 more points.

That keepsake first NHL goal arrived about a month later, on November 20 in Hartford, a 4–4 tie against the Whalers. Later on, he wouldn't have such fond memories of the Connecticut capital, dislocating his hip at the Civic Center during the 1992–93 season after colliding with the end boards racing the Whalers' Patrick Poulin for a loose puck.

Al found himself hospitalized after the incident and there was some concern about whether or not he'd be able to continue his career. He'd end up missing three months.

He anchored a tremendous power play in those days. He told me in an interview, "We should always score on a 5-on-3." During that era, they almost always did.

Indisputably, Al's finest year in red and white was 1990–91, when he piled up 103 points in 78 games, one of only four defencemen in history to reach or surpass the century mark in points for a season.

That same year, his mother became seriously ill and he'd miss the final two games to return to Nova Scotia and thankfully got to see her before she passed away.

Over his 11 seasons as a Flame, he'd establish all sorts of records for defencemen before becoming embroiled in a contract dispute that led

Al MacInnis, the Flames' all-time top-scoring defenceman, preparing for a Flames rush before unleashing his howitzer slapshot. (Getty Images)

the St. Louis Blues to sign him to an offer sheet of $3.5 million U.S. per season—$1 million more than he was being offered by the Flames.

Finally, almost inevitably, Al was traded to the Blues for another gifted offensive defenceman, Phil Housley, and a pair of second-round draft picks.

He left for Missouri as the franchise's all-time leader in points (822), assists (603), games played (803), playoff assists (77), and postseason points (102), and, of course, as a Conn Smythe Trophy recipient.

With the Blues, he continued to be a standout on defence, finally winning a richly deserved Norris Trophy—a personal honour that eluded him in Calgary—in 1999.

Retired since 2005, after more than 1,400 games and 23 seasons of excellence, the "pride and joy of Port Hood" was named one of the NHL's Top 100 players during its centenary celebrations.

Not so much since I myself retired, but I still get to see him from time to time, when he visits Calgary for games as vice-president of hockey operations for the Blues. Always a pleasure.

Just a couple of Maritime boys.

Lanny

My career and Lanny McDonald's seem somehow entwined.

One of the first interviews I conducted as an NHL broadcaster featured Lanny, when we were both in Toronto.

The first NHL goal I ever called was scored by Lanny, as a Maple Leaf.

Then I was fortunate enough to be in the broadcast booth for the final goal of his Hall of Fame career, that Cup-clinching evening for the Flames at the wonderful old Montreal Forum.

Our friendship has never wavered.

I well remember that morning down at the Corral, receiving the word that Lanny had been traded to the Flames from the struggling Colorado Rockies.

He'd actually played against Calgary the night before and left that very morning with the Rockies, heading east for a game in Winnipeg against the Jets. Arriving in the Manitoba capital, he was immediately told to catch the next flight back to Calgary.

And so began a love-affair relationship between a city, a franchise, and a very, very special player and person.

Who can forget the great year of 1982–83 when Lanny scored 66 goals? It still stands as a Flames record.

Many of those goals arrived via that great shot he had. Quite a few of the others came on the wraparound move he became renowned for.

The night that he collected his 50th goal was one that caused us no end of concern, though. A Friday night in Buffalo, and Lanny needed only one to hit the magical number.

There was no television coverage of that game against the Sabres and when Doug Barkley and I got up to our broadcast location in the old Aud, we were told by our producer that he was having trouble making a connection with the station back in Calgary.

So the game started out with myself on the a regular telephone land line doing the broadcast. I'd do play-by-play and then hand the phone over to Doug when the play was whistled dead.

It was pretty primitive stuff.

Anyway, we eventually lost that connection and I was really worried Lanny would score this monumental 50th and we'd be off the air.

As it turned out, the broadcast line was restored about five minutes or so before Lanny delivered.

On the bus from Buffalo to Toronto afterward, I recall Guy Chouinard, Lanny's centreman, popping open a bottle of champagne to toast a great accomplishment.

So many indelible moments for me and Flames fans everywhere involve No. 9.

Lanny scored the first Calgary goal after the team moved across the street from the Corral to the shiny new Saddledome. Then there was his overtime snipe in 1984 that sent a spectacular series against the Oilers the maximum seven games. Another OT playoff goal, this time in 1986 at Winnipeg, swept the Jets aside in a best-of-five series.

Bringing Lanny into the Flames' fold was obviously one of the smartest moves made by a very smart man, GM Cliff Fletcher.

So respected, Lanny helped nurture a group of young players— Nieuwendyk, Roberts, MacInnis, Suter—to a point where together they would rise to the pinnacle of the game.

That keepsake 1988–89 season had its share of ups and downs for Lanny. He was in and out of the Flames' lineup, both because of injury and as a healthy scratch. After scoring only four times in the first 39 games he went on an absolute tear late, notching seven in seven to reach the 500-goal and 1,000-point milestones.

No. 500 was the last regular season goal of his career, against Mark Fitzpatrick of the NY Islanders at the Dome. You wondered whether the cheering would ever stop.

The moment that sticks in everyone's mind, of course, is his game-changing goal in Game 6 of the Stanley Cup Final at the Forum, an iconic image in franchise history.

It'd be the only goal he'd score that postseason. A lot of people remain convinced it stood as the Cup-winner, when in reality it staked the Flames to a slender 2–1 lead in the second period.

Lanny was actually in the penalty box just prior to breaking down the ice with Joe Nieuwendyk and Hakan Loob, and chatting with him later he was really concerned whether he'd be getting any more ice time that night given the fact he'd taken the minor.

Normally, when broadcasting on radio, I pretty much stuck with the pass going from player to player, as opposed to television, where you can throw in how so-and-so is open. On this particular play, though, Nieuwendyk got the puck heading into the Canadiens' zone and I did say on the broadcast, "McDonald is open on the right side."

The words weren't even out of my mouth before Lanny sailed in and stuck the puck past Patrick Roy.

Until that point in the game I thought the Flames were playing rather tentatively but that goal—and the emotional resonance of the man who had scored it—seemed to take the edge off the team and Calgary went on to win 4–2.

One of the unforgettable aspects of that game, to me, was the Canadiens fans, who'd never seen their team lose a Stanley Cup Final on home ice, staying around for the presentation.

The Flames received a huge ovation when they received the Cup and I believe to this day that a major reason for that reception was Lanny's great popularity and how everyone—regardless of rooting interest—were overjoyed in his finally lifting the Stanley Cup.

Not long afterward he announced his retirement out at his home in Springbank.

As a champion, at last. The perfect way to go.

During his time in Calgary, I was once invited to his hometown of Hanna to speak alongside Lanny and help raise funds for a community program.

I had the opportunity then to meet his parents, as well as other members of his family. It was interesting seeing how much reverence and respect there was and, I'm sure, still is, for a favourite son.

So many memories of the man.

I'll never forget the day in Montreal at the 1992 draft, when the Hockey Hall of Fame selectors announced he'd been voted in, only three years after his career came to an end.

I had a chance to celebrate with him a little in the Flames' suite. Wonderful times.

Then 14 years later, when I was fortunate enough to be inducted, in 2006, Lanny was there. Of course.

And the day I announced my retirement in 2014, he got wind of the announcement in advance and cut short a trip to Phoenix to be there for me at a morning news conference at the Saddledome.

He also made it to the Dome on the night I was honoured in 2014 by the Flames.

Typical of him.

I'll always have such great respect for Lanny, be thankful for how so much of my career was tied into his, and for the great friendship we forged through the years.

Joel Otto

Sometimes, people simply get things wrong.

When nobody had yet heard of Joel Otto, during his early days in the minors with the Moncton Golden Flames of the AHL, a friend of mine in New Brunswick who watched quite a few of their games came down with this pronouncement: "Joel Otto will never be an NHL player."

Goes to show.

The big guy from Bemidji would go on to play 943 NHL games, 730 wearing the Flaming C, which slots him in at fifth on the franchise's career list.

He'd also log 87 playoff games, trailing only Jim Peplinski and Al MacInnis among Flames.

I suppose my friend can be cut some slack, though. He made his call on Joel during the big fellow's first pro season after playing Division II college hockey at Bemidji and subsequently being signed to a free-agent contract by Flames GM Cliff Fletcher.

In those days, Cliff was miles ahead of his peers in terms of unearthing quality free agents, especially those out of the U.S. college ranks. And Joel Otto was one of his most important.

Joel had the size, of course, at 6-foot-4 and 220 pounds, a virtual giant in that era. And by the end of that first taste of pro hockey, in Moncton, my friend had changed his tune.

The guy who would never make it up top scored 27 goals and 63 points in the 56 games he played in 1984–85 and, in fact, was a full-time Calgary Flame the very next season.

Joel's role was to shut down one of the very best centremen of the era, Mark Messier, the Raging Bull located only three hours north in Edmonton.

Through dedication, hard work off the ice, and help from coaches like Badger Bob Johnson, Joel Otto ultimately became a solid two-way centre who made a quiet but significant impact in the Flames' Cup runs of 1986 and '89.

Checking and his work inside the faceoff circle is what he was noted for, but he could chip in offensively, too.

Never forget, Joel scored one of the most important goals in franchise history. It came at 19:12 of overtime in Game 7 against the Vancouver Canucks and might've saved the President's Trophy–winning Flames from a shockingly early exit in the year they won their only Stanley Cup.

A pass from Jim Peplinski glanced off Joel's skate and into the net behind goalie Kirk McLean after the Canucks had generated the better scoring chances through that OT period. The sense of relief in Calgary was palpable.

From there, the Flames just got better and better, going a collective 12–3.

Overall in that 1989 playoff run, the guy known for a brand of muscular defensive hockey also collected 19 points in 22 games, two goals and six points in the six-game Final series against Montreal, assisting on or scoring the winning goals in three of Calgary's four victories.

Hardly the numbers of a one-way player.

An oddity in Joel's career, he notched only two hat tricks but both came on a November 3, seven years apart. The first in 1986 against the L.A. Kings, the second in 1993 versus the Hartford Whalers.

He'd go on to play the final three seasons of his NHL career for the Philadelphia Flyers, signing a free-agent deal there in the summer of 1995.

Upon retirement, he and his family returned to his long-time professional home, where Joel works as an assistant coach for the Western Hockey League's Calgary Hitmen and remains a valuable part of the Flames' Alumni.

Jim Peplinski

Jim Peplinski could be considered the consummate team guy.

On those wild Battle of Alberta nights through the 1980s, he'd stand up for his teammates, often dropping the gloves against bigger foes and more reputable fighters.

Wherever trouble broke out, Pep would sail in to be there for the cause.

His leadership skills reached far beyond the ice, though, even during his early years with the team.

He was forever organizing social events for his teammates, knitting people together, a prankster not above stealing one shoe from a certain radio play-by-play announcer during a commercial flight, forcing said announcer to walk around Chicago's O'Hare Airport for a while, one-shoed, one-socked, as we were readying to change flights.

Eventually he tied the shoe to a fishing line and placed it out in the corridor where the gates were located. The idea was that I'd chase

93

the shoe and he'd keep pulling it further and further away. Just as I was leaning down to pick up the shoe, a guy inadvertently stepped on the line, giving me the shoe and Pep a broken line and no satisfaction. This was someone who kept everyone loose but took the game and his role on the team extremely seriously.

Pep holds the distinction of being the only player of the core group of that 1989 Cup-winning team to spend his entire NHL career as a Flame (Soviet Sergei Priakin, acting as an advance man for the release of the legendary Red Army star Sergei Makarov in the fall of 1989, spent all 46 of his NHL career games spread over three seasons as a Flame, but I don't really think you can count him).

The other superb players of that era—Vernon, MacInnis, Suter, Mullen, Nieuwendyk, and the rest—had either spent time before or would spend time later as part of other organizations.

Peplinski joined the Flames for their first year in Calgary, which is only fitting, coming straight out of junior and the Toronto Marlies. He fit right in, scoring 13 goals and 38 points that season. The second year turned out to be his best production-wise, 30 goals and 67 points in 74 games, finishing fourth on the team in scoring.

He also became the first Calgary Flame to score four goals in one game, at the old Stampede Corral against the Winnipeg Jets on November 17, 1981, and it turned out to be the only hat track of his NHL career.

The outburst very nearly doubled his season output, Pep having scored five goals in the opening 19 starts. That year he also tied a club record set by Kent Nilsson, counting four game-tying goals in an era when ties were part of the NHL landscape.

During both of the Flames' trips to the Stanley Cup Final during his career, he was a key factor. In 1986, he collected five goals and 14 points in 22 games while amassing 107 minutes in penalties. By 1989, he'd graduated to co-captain, reflecting his importance in the dressing room.

Jim Peplinski, the first Flame to register a four-goal game and scorer of the 1986 game-winner that ended the longest losing streak in team history. (Getty Images)

When Lanny McDonald scored his milestone 500th on March 21, 1989, Pep had the primary assist on the goal.

Jim was a very durable winger, missing only 24 games during his entire NHL career, playing in every game of a season four times.

He was also handy in the airline/hotel loyalty card department, the first Flames player to apply and get me involved.

Following that cameo-keepsake Stanley Cup year, his role on the team diminishing, he suited up for only half a dozen games before announcing his retirement, at 29 years old.

During the 1987–88 season, while still a part of the Flames, he was loaned to the Canadian National Team for the XV Olympic Winter Games being held in Calgary in February.

After calling it quits after those six games in 1989, he launched a comeback in the 1994–95 season, playing another half-dozen before retiring a second time and for good.

At the time of his retirement, he ranked as the all-time games-played leader in franchise history at 705, since passed by others.

After exiting, Pep dabbled in broadcasting, later getting involved in management with the Flames and acting as alumni president for the team for 18 years.

He remains part of the organization as vice president of business development and has been highly successful in other business ventures, which is no surprise to anyone who knows him.

Badger Bob

Everyone who found themselves around the Flames between 1983 and 1987 has favourite Bob Johnson stories.

Cartloads of them.

He's been gone over a quarter-century now, but Badger was one of those people you simply cannot forget.

Full of such life, such energy, such optimism.

Bob, of course, came straight to the Flames from the University of Wisconsin, where he'd already become a legend, a superstar, while coaching the NCAA powerhouse Badgers.

He arrived in Calgary with the reputation of being a teacher and very much an innovator. It's become kind of a cliché now, but we all remember Bob behind the bench, notebook in hand, jotting things down, looking for an edge.

Bob's business was making players better.

Ask Joel Otto. Or Colin Patterson. Neil Sheehy. Jamie Macoun. All undrafted players out of the U.S. college ranks. No one was quite sure whether any of them would make it at the top level.

Well, they all turned out to be long-term NHLers, solid pros, major parts of that '89 Stanley Cup team, and to a man they credit Bob Johnson's influence.

He was quite the innovator, always trying new things. When the team would receive a bench penalty for, say, too many men on the ice, Bob would send one of his top-scoring players over to serve the two-minute minor.

At the time, this was novel.

His thinking, of course, was that in those days, top players didn't usually kill penalties and—here's where his innovation came into play—he wanted someone in the box who, when the penalty was over, could perhaps be sprung for an excellent scoring opportunity—usually a breakaway—and would know what to do if one presented itself.

This was so different from the thinking of the time that at first the guys being ordered into the box—for instance, Joey Mullen or Lanny McDonald—felt they were being punished in some way and weren't very happy.

But after a few goals resulted from the strategy they caught on.

For Badger Bob Johnson, every day was "a great day for hockey." (Getty Images)

Bob's signature line, of course, was, "It's a great day for hockey." And for him, it was. He loved the game. Absolutely loved it.

It would be difficult to name a more positive person anywhere, in any business.

During the 1985–86 season the Flames suffered through 11 losses in a row, which remains a (dubious) franchise record. That streak tested the limits of even Badger Bob's optimism.

I'm not sure how he was around the players during that spell, but he was always—or almost always—upbeat around us, the media. I do remember after one lopsided loss during that streak he actually seemed a bit pessimistic, a bit deflated.

You just weren't used to seeing him that way. Nothing, you felt, could get Bob Johnson down.

Typically, after a minute or two of hesitancy, though, the old Bob resurfaced, and he perked up, saying something like, "Well, we had a great shift in the third period. A *great* shift. That's something we can build off."

With positively like that, it shouldn't be that surprising they'd reach the Stanley Cup Final a few months later.

But that was Bob. He was always comparing success, winning hockey games, to climbing mountains and shooting low scores on famous golf courses.

One of his quirks: He used to make a lot of his personnel decisions while sweating away in the sauna.

During those years there was a monthly Molson Cup luncheon for the players who'd been one of the postgame three-star selections most frequently. Bob was often the victim of pranks during those events.

He'd be seated at the head-table, which naturally had a tablecloth covering it. Often during the luncheon, while Bob was eating or engaged in conversation—once he got talking, nothing could distract him—a player would crawl underneath the table, pour ketchup on Bob's shoes, and return to his seat. Someone would then yell, "Shoe check!" And sure enough, there'd be Bob, with ketchup all over his dress shoes.

I've never been around anyone so superstitious. On game days, we'd always pre-record a coach's show to run that night. Any time the Flames were on a winning streak, Bob would insist on going back to the same location we'd recorded the previous show. When the streak came to an end, we'd move on to another spot.

During one streak, we did the show with Bob sitting on the Zamboni, me standing beside it asking questions. That carried over into a road trip and Bob was insistent that he climb up on top of the Zamboni. Unfortunately, one of the arena attendants at the rink caught us and wouldn't let him make the trek.

Bob wasn't very happy about that.

Other times, we'd be on the bench or have to sit in the row and the seat number corresponding to the number of wins the team was going for evening. One night in Buffalo at the old Aud we were up in Row 30 and he seemed kind of torn, because everything is easier when the team's winning, naturally, but if this streak kept going much longer we might end up on the roof somewhere.

On one run, the penalty box was our lucky area. During a game in Vancouver at the Pacific Coliseum when that was in vogue we got to the box about two hours before game time—there'd been no morning skate—but it was locked.

So we had to climb up on the ledge of the boards and over the glass to get in the box. We did, but I was looking around to make sure no one was watching because they'd have thought we were both crazy. Anyway, an hour or so later heading up to the broadcast booth, Jim Robson, the Canucks' veteran play-by-play broadcaster, strolled up to me and asked, "What on earth were you and Johnson doing climbing over the glass?"

I started to answer, but then shook my head and said, "Jim, you really don't want to know."

(For the record, the boiler room in the Saddledome was the location that produced the most wins.)

The highlight of Badger's time in Calgary had to be the 1986 Campbell Conference semi-final against Edmonton. The Flames had finished 39 points behind the Oilers that year and no one gave them a chance against Gretzky, Kurri, Coffey, Fuhr, Anderson, and the rest. Just a powerhouse of a team.

The Oilers were coming off consecutive Stanley Cups and looked pretty close to invincible.

But Bob Johnson played all kinds of little games to push and prod his underdog team to remarkable heights over those two weeks. He had a lot of fun with Oilers boss Glen Sather. The two coaches came from vastly different hockey backgrounds and had vastly different personalities.

Bob was always pushing buttons, doing things to annoy Slats. He brought in a left-handed goaltender from the University of Calgary for practices because Grant Fuhr was one of the few left-handed goalies at the time. He made a big show of telling the media, of course.

Another day he took his players to the upper reaches of the Saddledome and had them sit down and watch the assistant coaches down on the ice below demonstrating how the Oilers would attack.

Of course, all these little tricks would get back to Sather, an old-school hockey guy.

As Flames fans undoubtedly remember, Bob and his team pulled one of the great upsets that year, beating the Oilers in seven games.

Whenever you'd see him after he left the organization to head up U.S. Hockey, he was always so proud of that victory. He'd set the bar high since he arrived in Calgary, and the Oilers were always the target.

Not only his team's, but every outfit in the league.

In that series, though, they'd climbed that mountain he was always talking about.

Do You Believe in Magic?

In my mind, Kent Nilsson is the single most talented individual ever to don the Flaming C.

Best player? Perhaps not. But those are, after all, two entirely different things.

He'd been dubbed, of course, Magic Man. With justification.

I'm unsure of whether he truly felt he could do more on the ice or actually didn't care. Set a challenge in front of him and he didn't really seem to want to take it on.

I remember one night during the Flames' second season at the old Stampede Corral. Kent and Wayne Gretzky were tied for the NHL scoring lead at the time and the Oilers were in town. A marquee matchup between two great teams and the two great talents.

I interviewed Kent the morning before the game and mentioned the showdown with Wayne and how he could perhaps use it as a springboard to winning a scoring title.

I'll never forget his response: "Oh, no, no, no. Wayne Gretzky is a great player. Much better than I am."

Interestingly, Gretzky—pre-Mario days—would call Kent the most talented player he'd seen. I don't know if I'd go *that* far, but he'd certainly have ranked right up there.

The first year the team arrived from Atlanta he was absolutely astonishing, establishing a record for points by a Flame (131) that may never be surpassed. Somewhat surprisingly, he wouldn't reach the 50-goal plateau but did creep to within one.

In those days, Nilsson had the hockey-fan citizenry of the city divided into two camps—supporters and detractors. You either loved him or hated him. Among those who loved him was Russ Parker, Mr. Baseball in Calgary for more than 30 years. Transfixed by his talent,

Russ wouldn't hear a negative word against Kent. And a lot of fans felt the same way.

His critics mostly felt he never reached his true potential, that there was always more to give on too many nights.

When he was "on," he could lift fans—pro-Kent or con—out of their seats. That everyone agreed on.

I remember my brother and a bunch of his pals arrived to catch one particular game in Montreal. Kent had put up a lot of points, so they were excited to watch him play live for the first time.

Afterward, we were having a couple of beers, and one of the guys, speaking for most of them, said, "You know, I expected a whole lot more from Nilsson. He was kind of floating around out there."

And I felt compelled to point out, 'Well, guys, he did have four assists…"

But that was the Kent Effect.

The Flames always felt they could push him to greater heights. Coach Bob Johnson at one point referred to him as a "novelty player" and tried to come up with new ideas to interest Kent and prod him to shine on a more consistent basis.

I remember one time Bob suggested to Kent that he sharpen his own skates and Kent actually did for a few games, after learning the basics from equipment manager Bobby Stewart.

He went on a tremendous scoring run at that time, too, but eventually the novelty wore thin and he was back to being…well, Kent.

As maddening as he could be on the ice, though, this was such a fun-loving guy it was difficult to dislike him off it.

Ultimately, Flames GM Cliff Fletcher dealt Kent away at the 1985 draft to the Minnesota North Stars in a deal for two second-round picks. Those selections turned out to be Joe Nieuwendyk and Stephane Matteau.

Stephane had a decent run as a Flame and Joe, of course, would go on to great things.

There were rumours at the time of the deal that an agreement had been put in place between Cliff and Minnesota GM Lou Nanne, a friend, that Kent would never be traded to Edmonton, the Flames' most bitter rival.

Turned out, he eventually was dealt to the Oilers, and was a part of a Stanley Cup winner in 1987, leaving many people in Calgary wondering why that couldn't have happened once or twice during his days as a Flame.

One and Done

Darryl Olsen had the distinction of being the only Calgary Flame to lead the team in preseason scoring and then start the season in the minors.

Olson was a local Calgary kid, a defenceman whom the Flames selected 185th in the 1985 NHL draft.

During his minor hockey career, Tier II junior, and then at Northern Michigan University, he gained a reputation of being a smooth-skating, slick point-producer from the back end.

After turning pro, he toiled in the American Hockey League, the IHL, and later on would play in Europe.

At the 1991 Flames training camp, Olsen excelled, racking up a team-high 10 points—a goal and nine helpers—over his seven-game preseason audition.

When it came time to start the regular season, though, he was shipped off to Salt Lake City, the Flames' IHL farm team in the International Hockey League.

Not surprising, as the Flames' defence at the time boasted Al MacInnis, Gary Suter, Jamie Macoun, and Ric Nattress—who would all be key components on the 1989 Stanley Cup–winning team—as well as Frank Musil, Neil Sheehy, Jim Kyte, and Trent Yawney.

Darryl would be called just once, on December 14, after injuries to Suter and MacInnis, and play his only NHL game—at the Saddledome, against the Detroit Red Wings.

His stat line read: No points, three shots on goal, and a minus-2.

Two nights later, MacInnis was back in harness and Darryl Olsen was back in Utah. Never to make another NHL start.

Swedish Delight

Among the most unusual calls of my career, this would have to rank right up there:

"Looby-dooby-do!"

Not a word of a lie.

That one-time-only call marked the afternoon right winger Hakan Loob became the first Swedish-born player in NHL history to score 50 goals in a season, his fifth in the league.

April 3, 1988.

He is, by the way, *still* the only Swedish-born player to score 50 goals in a season.

The milestone arrived on the final day of the 1987–88 regular season, at the Saddledome, with 3:05 left in a 4–1 win over the Minnesota North Stars.

The Flames had already clinched the President's Trophy. Loob's goal just finished the regular season off in style.

Hakan mentions my call of his historic goal whenever we've met up over the years.

A ninth-round draft pick the summer the team arrived from Atlanta, he turned into quite a find. Another little guy—5-foot-9, 175 pounds—with lots of competitive fire married to a considerable talent. Very personable, meshed well with his teammates, the media, and fans. All business on the ice but a keen sense of fun off it.

In the beginning, having countryman Kent Nilsson nearby helped with language and customs and something as apparently easy as just finding your way around town.

Given Loob's demeanour and talent, though, the adjustment period was short.

His career in the NHL lasted only six seasons. He decided to go back to Sweden after the Stanley Cup win in 1989, although still in his prime, so it was a bit of a shock to the Flames to lose his services. But he made the decision strictly for family reasons, so his kids would be brought up in their homeland, and you had to admire him for that.

A few summers later, when he was visiting with Calgary pal Jim Peplinski, I met up with him and he mentioned that he kind of regretted leaving when he did.

No surprise that following his playing career Hakan would become involved in hockey management. For years he was manager and president of hockey operations with Farjestad of the Swedish Elite League, his former team before joining making the jump to North America.

He stepped down from that role in the summer of 2017 but joined the Flames as head European scout in 2018.

The neat thing about Hakan is that even after he'd left the Flames, he'd still listen to their games via the Internet, ignoring the eight-hour time difference between North America and Sweden, and occasionally even call into the postgame radio show to talk about his time in Calgary.

He's always remained as close as possible to his NHL home.

Doug Risebrough

Just prior to the opening of the 1982–83 season, on September 11 to be precise, general manager Cliff Fletcher swung a culture-changing deal in acquiring Doug Risebrough from the Montreal Canadiens.

A hard-nosed centre, Risebrough understood the dynamics of winning, having seen it up close as part of four Stanley Cup winners with the powerful Montreal Canadiens in the 1970s.

Cliff instinctively understood Risebrough's value in nurturing the younger players being assimilated into the organization. On the ice, in addition to experience, he brought a fiery, indomitable attitude, a great competitive hunger, and a reputation as an expert agitator.

No opponent was too big or too tough for Doug to tackle.

I'll never forget the night he found himself involved in a fight against Edmonton enforcer Marty McSorley, hauling McSorley's discarded jersey into the penalty box before shredding it with his skates.

That act of defiance got him in hot water with Oilers boss Glen Sather, who, probably tongue-firmly-in-cheek, later sent Risebrough a bill for the cost of the jersey that he'd ruined.

But that was Doug. Never one to back down.

He played way above the 5-feet-11 and 183 pounds he was listed at, but to his credit he didn't miss many games. I made the comment on air one time that they must just stick him in an ice freezer between games, then take him out and get him ready as best they could for the next one.

Doug was a co-captain for five years in Calgary, one of the spark-plugs of the trip to the Stanley Cup Final against his old employers, the Canadiens, in the spring of 1986.

After retiring as a player, he transitioned into a job as an assistant coach with the team and was in that capacity when the Flames gained revenge on the Habs for the earlier Cup disappointment, in 1989. When Terry Cup was relieved of his head coaching duties following a six-game, first-round exit to the L.A. Kings the very next season, Fletcher asked Doug to step into the breach.

Which he did, guiding the Flames to a 46-win season, ended prematurely in the opening round of playoffs by the Edmonton Oilers in seven games.

The ever-willing company guy, Doug also said yes a year after that to assume double-duty in the wake of Cliff Fletcher's exit to become general manager of the Toronto Maple Leafs. A tough act of follow, for sure.

Doug himself would later admit that he lacked savvy in the managerial end of the job. Owing to accelerating salaries around the NHL, these were turbulent waters even for an experienced GM to try to navigate.

At that time, remember, the Flames still had many star players starting to command sizeable salaries.

I've always thought Doug managed the way he played, which I suppose in retrospect shouldn't be surprising—he'd get into battles over salaries with guys he'd played with previously or coached. The hard bargaining sessions turned off some of those players.

But everything Doug did was designed to win. That never changed through his many incarnations in the organization.

We had a lot of chats, he and I, in hotel lobbies, on planes, or in airports. Before a game in Vancouver, mid-1980s, I was fighting a bad cold. As Doug and I waited for the bus to take us from the Hotel Vancouver to Pacific Coliseum, he remarked on the rasp in my voice. I remember him saying, "You have to broadcast the game tonight with that voice?"

I kinda nodded to him, yes.

What was really amazing to me was that particular night, the closer we got to game time, the stronger my voice became. I guess Doug's admiration at my giving it a go gave me a shot of adrenalin.

Doug was always inquisitive, keen to learn.

He's often cited for that 10-player trade that saw Doug Gilmour leave Calgary and head east to Toronto and become a superstar. That certainly didn't work out in the Flames' favour and Doug later acknowledged that his inexperience in the role of GM played a part.

The night before the deal was consummated, I talked on the phone to Doug and in confidence we discussed various potential swaps involving Gilmour.

The Toronto option never came up.

After leaving Calgary, Doug would sign on with the expansion Minnesota Wild as their GM and now works for Glen Sather, president of the NY Rangers.

Don't believe he ever did pay Slats the cost of that McSorley jersey, either. But Sather did joke about the long-ago incident in July of 2017, with Doug in attendance, when Slats was being inducted into the Alberta Hockey Hall of Fame.

Good-Time Charlie

Over the years in this job, you come in contact with any number of famous players, household names.

Charlie Bourgeois certainly can't be counted among those faces, those names.

All the same, he was one of the funniest, most personable guys you could ever hope to meet. Great, great sense of humour.

Just a big-hearted person.

Long before I'd met him, I'd been aware of the tragic death of Charlie's father, a policeman in Moncton, New Brunswick When Charlie was 15, his dad and another officer were kidnapped and killed in a crime that shocked the nation.

Later, I'd heard of Charlie's exploits with the Moncton Blue Eagles university team, and went out to watch him play the year the national championships were held in Calgary.

After he signed on with the Flames and was heading west for training camp, the sports editor of the *Moncton Times*, Eddie St. Pierre, told Charlie to look me up.

Being fellow New Brunswickers, we naturally hit it off and I was very pleased when he made the team. That year, 1981–82, the defence included Paul Reinhart, Kari Eloranta, Steve Konroyd, and Phil Russell.

I've called a number of significant goals by great players over the years, but one of the highlights for me was Charlie's first, scored in the cradle of the game, Montreal.

Fitting, too, because it's the second-closest NHL city to Moncton.

His mother was there that night, along with his brothers. Getting together with them and celebrating the great occasion was a wonderful time for us all.

After four and a half seasons in the Flames' organization, Charlie was part of the trade that brought future 50-goal sniper Joey Mullen to Calgary from St. Louis in early February of 1986.

The year the Flames won the Stanley Cup in Montreal, Charlie was playing in the Hartford Whalers' system, for Binghamton. But with the chance for his old team to lift the trophy they all dream of, he made the trek from Moncton for Game 6 to see a few ex-teammates and hopefully see them accomplish the ultimate.

He didn't go in the dressing room afterward, feeling a little awkward, maybe, but knowing Charlie, he would've been thrilled for the organization.

Now heavily involved in coaching at hockey schools in Moncton, he was able to purchase the ice rental times for all buildings in the city outside of the Moncton Coliseum.

Mike Vernon

The emergence of Mike Vernon as the No. 1 goaltender for the Flames late in the 1985–86 season is really an interesting story.

Back then, I recall chatting with friends in New Brunswick while he was playing there in the American Hockey League. They both had the same opinion: No way this guy was NHL calibre.

Well, it wasn't until 1986, really, that the hometown kid became entrenched as the hometown team's go-to guy. That year, he began in the minors, in Moncton, with Reggie Lemelin and Marc D'Amour installed as the 1-2 punch on the big club.

Mike did get called up to play just before New Year's Eve in an exhibition game against the touring Moscow Dynamo team at the Saddledome. He made quite an impression, too, producing 34 saves in a 4–3 Flames victory, but ended up heading back to Moncton in short order.

Then on January 10, Mike was summoned again to play a game against Vancouver at the Dome, that coming after the Flames had lost 11 straight, a dubious club record. Mike arrived, played, and ended up winning, making 32 saves in the 5–4 triumph.

He'd play the next game as well, as the Flames started a road trip in Philadelphia, losing that game 3–0. Five days later he was—you guessed it—back in Moncton.

But D'Amour had begun experiencing all kinds of trouble with nagging injuries and, more worrisome, dehydration. It didn't seem to matter how much water he'd be given. In a couple of games he wasn't even able to finish the 60 minutes, dropping to the ice on one knee to alert the trainers that he was having difficulty.

As Marc left the Flames and moved on to other teams, the problems persisted, which was very unfortunate, as no one ever really saw what kind of goaltender he might've been at the NHL level.

Maybe in the minds of Cliff Fletcher and the Flames' management team, Mike had already been pegged as the heir apparent and they wanted to keep him sharp playing in the minors. But D'Amour's physical issues certainly sped up Mike's ascension to the big club.

It really wasn't until the middle of March that he began to take hold of the Flames' goaltending position, starting six of the last 10 games of the regular season, winning five and tying one.

With the playoffs set to begin, he'd gotten on a pretty solid roll. So coach Bob Johnson rolled the dice, started him in the opening-round

Cup winner Mike Vernon diving to make another outstanding save. He has the longest shutout streak in team history (164:40). (Getty Images)

series against the Winnipeg Jets. He won the first three games of that series and then the opening game against Edmonton in the second round.

He continued winning as the Flames marched on to the Stanley Cup Final.

Three or four years after Mike Vernon had retired as an active player, the late Ed Chynoweth and I engaged in drafting a nomination for him to the Hockey Hall of Fame. By then he'd won a second Cup and a Conn Smythe Trophy in Detroit.

Ed was on the selection committee and submitted Mike's nomination. It was before the board three years but didn't gain much traction.

I still believe he's deserving. I feel very strongly about that.

He put up Hall-comparable numbers and excelled through two eras.

He might have collected another Conn Smythe, when the Flames won in 1989, if it weren't for Al MacInnis narrowly nudging him out on that occasion.

Talking once to Terry Crisp, the coach of that '89 title team, he told me he hadn't watched the replay of that Game 6 for maybe 25 years.

His comment then was, "Wow! I didn't realize how great Mike Vernon had played in that deciding game."

After playing in Calgary and Detroit, Mike moved on to San Jose, Florida, and then came back to the Flames to conclude his career in a second tour of duty.

One of the first things Craig Button did after being named general manager of the team was secure Mike's services from the Panthers.

Mike's year with Calgary didn't go as well as he would have liked. In fact, I'd hazard a guess that he probably wasn't all that thrilled about coming back to finish his career in his hometown. I think he would have preferred to go to a team that was more of a contender as opposed to a struggling, rebuilding one.

He ended up being the backup goaltender.

And there was a controversy late in that season while the team was on the road—I believe it was a Friday night game in Boston. The Flames lost the game and the next morning had a practice scheduled.

But by the time I got to the rink I'd learned that Mike had been sent to the minors.

No doubt a tremendous blow, after the career he'd had.

I called him and he was very down. I wanted to get an interview with him to send back to the radio station before he left. I found him waiting for me back at the hotel, even holding up his transportation to the airport to talk to me about going back to the AHL—a league he hadn't played in for 14 years.

One of the things he asked me when the interview was over was, "What's your brother's phone number?"

He knew my brother Noonan and felt that if he was going to New Brunswick to play, at least there would be somebody he knew there. Unfortunately, Noonan lived six hours away.

Mike took the flight to Saint John and the Flames packed up and flew to Raleigh, North Carolina. I stayed in contact with Mike, who was supposed to be the starter for the Saint John Flames that Sunday. Mike Rogers and I went out to dinner that night. When I got back to the hotel, the first thing I did was go online and see how Mike had fared—only to find out that not only had he not played, but he wasn't the backup either.

A lot was going on behind the scenes.

Flames president Ken King had intervened, along with Lanny McDonald.

They got in touch with Mike and had him fly to Miami where the Flames were headed after playing the Hurricanes. Mike went there, King and McDonald arrived, trying to patch things up.

They tried to keep everything quiet.

They got into the hotel before the team and had him hide in a room by himself, making sure no one travelling with the Flames knew he was there. The next morning I happened to be up early preparing for my radio show, went down to the coffee shop and happened to see Mike. We had a brief chat. He didn't want me to say anything publicly and we learned later in the day that Mike was back with the team and would be dressing for the next game.

It's unfortunate it ended that way.

You talk to NHL players present and past who played in their hometowns and get wildly mixed reviews. Some liked it. Some didn't, feeling there was more undue pressure and distractions.

Mike Vernon, of course, also played his junior hockey with the Wranglers in Calgary. I would have to think overall Mike enjoyed playing near family and friends.

The challenges and pressures inherent with the situation, he more than met.

However, his Calgary stay wasn't without its issues.

He was particularly sensitive about how his parents were sometimes treated at the rink. Everybody knew them, knew where they sat, and at times they were victims of catcalls and verbal abuse.

I remember Mike telling me, "I don't mind them yelling at me and swearing at me, but they should leave my parents alone."

It reached a point where his mother had stopped going to the games.

I know his dad didn't appreciate the fact that his son, who'd given so much to his hometown team, should be ridiculed in that way.

So it was a difficult time for the organization.

By the mid-1990s, the Flames had lost a number of their top players due to skyrocketing salaries and it was difficult for a Canadian organization with a weak dollar to match the contract demands from American clubs.

Trevor Kidd, another Flames goaltender, was emerging as the No. 1 guy for the team so Mike knew that he'd be traded and ultimately was, to the Red Wings.

Mike had some interesting times. A little guy who wanted to prove that he was a bona fide NHL goaltender. He did that.

Hopefully one day he'll be enshrined in the Hockey Hall of Fame.

Until then, he can savour being only the second Flame—after Lanny McDonald—to have his number retired by the organization.

A richly deserved honour.

Joey Mullen

To anyone who watched him play during his stay in Calgary, scoring goals in the greasy areas or after getting up off the seat of his pants, it's no great surprise that Joey Mullen won the Lady Byng Trophy as the league's most gentlemanly player twice as a member of the Flames.

On his way to scoring 190 goals and 388 points in the 345 regular season games he played during four seasons and change wearing the Flaming C, Joey absorbed more punishment than most did over the course of a career and rarely retaliated.

For every slash or cross check designed to stop him or slow him or intimidate him, he'd just turn the other cheek and get even via the scoreboard.

The two years he claimed the Byng as a Flame, he scored a collective 98 goals and 197 points, while incurring only 30 minutes in penalties.

A truly amazing player.

Cliff Fletcher made the trade with St. Louis to acquire Mullen in 1985, and it proved to be another smooth move by the Flames' general manager.

Fletcher knew the scoring talent that Mullen would bring. He was another little guy who had a tremendous hockey IQ. That he could take that punishment and not slash or hit back at an opponent was a marvel to me.

Always a gentleman.

As much as I was in awe of his play on the ice, my best memories of him came off the ice. He was never a great interview, being a shy guy, and the first to admit it.

In the 1980s and 1990s, the Flames presented the Molson Cup to the player who had the most three-star selections over the course of a season.

A luncheon would be held each month and about 700 fans would come to honour the segment winner.

Those recipients were required to come up and say a few words. I was assigned the task of hosting those luncheons and Joey, naturally, was a frequent honouree during his stay in Calgary.

The first time he made an appearance at the luncheon, he came up and said two words in his very distinct New York accent: "Thank you."

That got lots of laughs from the people in the ballroom.

The second time he doubled his word count to four: "Thank you very much."

More laughs.

When he was traded by the Flames during the 1990 off-season, I remember him being totally perplexed.

"Why did Cliff trade me?" he kept asking.

I had no idea, considering he'd scored 36 goals in the previous campaign with the Flames. Not great by Mullen standards, but still pretty healthy.

However, I assured him he'd likely score lots in Pittsburgh and he did, helping the Penguins to two Stanley Cup titles.

Later, at the end of his career, when he was about to be inducted into the Hockey Hall of Fame, Joey was honoured in Pittsburgh on a night the Flames were in town, at the old Igloo, during the pregame ceremony.

Remembering those Molson Cup luncheons, I warned everyone that Joey's speech would be short.

Well, he spoke for 10 minutes!

I was absolutely shocked.

He thanked everybody, also had some interesting anecdotes, then came up to our broadcast area during the intermission as a guest.

The first thing I said to him was, "Joey, that was an amazing speech you gave. You thanked everybody but me!" He laughed and then gave the best interview I ever had with him.

When I was honoured by the Hockey Hall of Fame with the Foster Hewitt Memorial Award in 2006, a number of players called to congratulate me.

Joey Mullen was among them.

Five-Goal Joe

Among magical, dominant nights in franchise annals, January 11, 1989, certainly ranks right up there.

That evening, Joe Nieuwendyk lit up the Winnipeg Jets for five goals—one off the modern-day record shared by Red Berenson of the

St. Louis Blues and Toronto's Darryl Sittler—to the delight of the crowd at the Olympic Saddledome.

Nieuwendyk scored 'em every way possible, two even-strength, a pair on the power play, and one shorthanded.

In those days, shorthanded goals were nothing out of the ordinary for Joe, given his tremendous puck sense, great hands, and ability to read developing situations on the ice.

After scoring once in the first, he hit for four in the middle stanza in a span of 12 minutes and five seconds to become only the ninth player in league history to net that many in one period.

Naturally, the talk in the press box during that second intermission centred on Joe's chances to tie, or maybe even eclipse, the record.

As I remember, he had a number of good looks to etch his name in the NHL record book but couldn't quite find the range.

The Flames cruised to an 8–3 victory. Twelve of their 36 shots came off the stick of No. 25.

Jets goaltender Daniel Berthiaume, for you trivia lovers out there, was the victim on all five of Nieuwendyk's tallies, which ran his goal total on the season to 31 (he'd finish with 51 for a second straight year).

Joe had already set a franchise record that season, scoring 20 goals in the first 28 games—no Flame had ever done that. And he'd be a part of another slice of history, assisting on Lanny McDonald's 500th career goal. Knowing how much Joe respected Lanny, that must've been quite the thrill.

But that night against the Jets showed him at the peak of his predatory form.

In those days, we didn't have the Safeway Score and Win Contest, a radio station/TV promotion whereby a Safeway shopper would win $1 million if a Flames player scored five or more times in a game.

A shame, because the second-year sniper from Cornell could've made someone an awful lot of money.

And all these years later, no Flame has equalled, must less bettered, Joe's lethal display.

Gary Roberts

Selected 12th overall with the Flames' first draft pick in 1984, Gary Roberts arrived at his first training camp believing he was in pretty good shape.

After being put through the circuit, he realized otherwise.

To his credit, he returned to his junior club, the Ottawa 67s, determined to improve his fitness.

Gary's near-fanatical level of conditioning and interest in nutrition today is well known around hockey circles—the company he formed has become a haven for NHL players looking to stay in top shape during the summer months—but back then he was a teenager with a lot to learn.

Arguably the best left winger over the team's first three decades in Calgary, he'd develop to a level where he'd score 53 goals during a phenomenal 1991–92 season, still the second-highest single-season aggregate in franchise history, trailing only Lanny McDonald's 66.

Gary quite likely could've put together back-to-back 50-goal campaigns, too.

The year following his breakout offensive season, 1992–93, he went on a tear to tie a club record for goals in consecutive games (eight), accomplished previously by only Kent Nilsson.

During his goal-scoring binge, Gary notched his 30th of the season in the third game of that run, then scored twice and added two assists in the highest-scoring game the Flames have ever been involved in, a 13–1 obliteration of the San Jose Sharks.

The goals just kept coming.

The closest Gary came to having the streak ended was the night he had to wait until overtime to extend it to seven, in a victory over Hartford.

He then tied the Magic Man's record at 19:54 of the first period with the Flames up against the Philadelphia Flyers, the game played at a neutral site, in Cincinnati.

The goal was his 37th of the season. Well on his way to 50, right?

Unfortunately, Gary suffered what was described initially as a charley horse later during that very game.

Being a neutral-site affair, the medical staffs on hand weren't quite the same as if the game was being held at a normal NHL arena and he was given the green light to fly on a charter that night to Toronto for the second end of back-to-backs, against the Maple Leafs.

During that flight, the swelling of the leg, exacerbated by the altitude, increased to such a point that Gary couldn't hide his distress. A lot of yelling on that flight. And Gary, remember, was a tough guy.

Once up in the air, of course, there was no going down, at least not until we reached Toronto.

After landing, Gary was whisked to a hospital where he underwent surgery, keeping him out until the final game of the regular season, against the San Jose Sharks at the Dome. He scored a goal that night, too, but the streak, of course, had officially stopped because of the injury.

No carryover. And no second 50-goal season.

Gary returned for the 1993–94 campaign and continued his scoring exploits, leading the Flames with 41 goals, before suffering a serious neck injury, damaging nerves, that ruled him out for the final two weeks.

Unfortunately, the problems with his neck were only beginning.

The next season, lockout-shortened, he appeared in only eight games due to degeneration of the nerves.

The injury was considered career-threatening and required two surgeries, in March and October of 1995. As I said, this was one tough cuss,

Gary Roberts, the greatest left winger in club history. His 53 goals in 1991–92 rank as second-most in a single season. (AP Images)

and he returned to action but the risk was deemed too great and Gary announced his retirement, an emotional day, on June 17, 1996.

At 30 years old. It seemed so wrong, so unfair.

The NHL dream remained strong inside him, though, and through diligent rehab he ultimately made an amazing return to the game, moving on first with the Carolina Hurricanes, then a number of other teams.

A testament to his indomitable will, persistence, and willingness to keep searching for avenues to regain the strength in his neck, Gary would go on to play 11 seasons following that first "retirement."

An individual so many of us have a such a great amount of admiration for.

Crispy

Run through the list of coaches who handled the Flames over their three decades in Calgary, and Terry Crisp owns the best record.

Two President's Trophies, one runner-up finish, an astounding .669 winning percentage (240–144–52) through three regular seasons at the helm, and, of course, the 1989 Stanley Cup championship.

Immensely impressive.

When he was brought in to the coach the Flames prior to the opening of the 1986–87 season, general manager Cliff Fletcher chose someone vastly different than the last man to hold the job, Bob Johnson.

Bob was a teacher, a motivator, who adopted a hugely positive approach.

Crispy was more from the old school, someone who pushed the players, a disciple of his boss through two Stanley Cup runs in Philadelphia, Freddie "The Fog" Shero.

On the bench, in the dressing room, here was a hard-driving guy, striving to get the most out of his players in concert with his assistant coaches: Tom Watt, goaltending coach Glenn Hall, Doug Risebrough through the first two years of Crispy's reign, and then Paul Baxter.

Crispy was very loud and animated. Talking to fans who owned season tickets near the bench, they often commented on being able to hear him several rows back, barking instructions, yelling encouragement and criticism when required, questioning the referees' calls, and occasionally engaging in banter with opposition players and coaches.

All designed, of course, to win. And clearly Crispy was a winner.

As I mentioned, he'd been a part of those Broad Street Bullies title-winning teams in 1974 and 1975, anchored by captain Bobby Clarke and goaltender Bernie Parent. As a player he was a checking centreman and superb penalty killer—an important job on those wild Flyers teams of Dave Schultz, Don Saleski, Moose Dupont, et al.

After Crispy retired, he worked as an assistant coach alongside Shero for two years and I'm sure picked up a lot of technique there. He then moved on to great success in the Ontario Hockey League in charge of the Sault Ste. Marie Greyhounds for three years before Cliff Fletcher chose him to head up the Flames' top farm club in Moncton, the Golden Flames.

He prepped in Moncton for a couple of seasons before Bob Johnson moved on to become president of USA Hockey in the summer of 1986, opening up the job on the big club.

Being a Maritimer, familiar with Moncton, the arena there, and the owners of the Golden Flames, Crispy and I had much in common when he arrived in Calgary to begin his NHL head-coaching career.

A real family guy, he and his wife, Sheila, are great parents to their kids: sons, Jeff and Tony, and daughter, Caley. In fact, my son, Jeff, and Crispy's son Jeff became pals playing on the same minor hockey teams. Jeff Crisp would go on to be an NHL scout and owns a Stanley Cup ring himself, from his time with the Anaheim Ducks. He currently works for the Buffalo Sabres.

Away from the game, Crispy had a very different persona than the one those fans with tickets near the bench became accustomed to. Just an open, gregarious, fun-loving guy.

Looking back, people point out the fact that he had many, many superb players on those Flames teams. Agreed, but anyone involved in hockey will tell you it takes a quality coach to properly handle talented players given some of their idiosyncrasies, and Crispy was certainly able to pull the best out of the ones at his disposal.

He also went through tough times, of course. Lanny McDonald was in the twilight of his Hall of Fame career during that Stanley Cup–winning season. Lanny had been an outstanding winger, of course, and remained so popular in Calgary, and before that, during his seasons in both Toronto and Colorado.

So those were difficult, uneasy times when Crispy felt he had to take Lanny out of the lineup. A tough call with such a star player.

Terry also made the decision to insert Lanny back into the lineup for Game 6 in Montreal, one game away from the Cup, and feeling No. 9's presence would provide the team with an emotional lift in a tough place to play, let alone win, the fabled old Montreal Forum.

Of course, Lanny responded by scoring that goal everyone remembers, off the setup from Joe Nieuwendyk, giving the Flames a 2–1 lead.

I'll never forget a few months earlier, January 13, 1989, celebrating my 1,000th NHL broadcast, in Buffalo. My buddies from New Brunswick would stage a party every time I'd hit a milestone game, so one had been arranged for No. 1,000.

The Flames lost that night to the Sabres, 3–2, but at the hotel afterward my bathtub was full of Moosehead beer that the boys had brought along.

As the night went along, coaches and management came and left, which meant the players started to filter in and the party went on until the wee small hours.

A couple of times we received calls about the noise in the suite and the hotel staff finally phoned Crispy, who came up to investigate.

When he arrived, that sent the remaining players scurrying but Crispy stayed on for another hour, hour and a half, having a couple beers and swapping stories with my New Brunswick pals.

Given the team at the time, the mandate in Calgary was Stanley Cup or bust. So when the Flames were eliminated in L.A. in six games the year after the great success, Crispy paid the price with his job.

He went on to work with Dave King and the Canadian National Team and then became head coach of the Tampa Bay Lightning for four years and change.

A career switch arrived when he joined the new boys on the block, the Nashville Predators, as a colour commentator.

Such a personable person and amusing storyteller, he was perfect in that role, selling hockey to a new market as sidekick to play-by-play man Pete Weber.

When Crispy did retire from the broadcast booth following the 2013–14 season—the same year, coincidentally, that I did—he stayed on as an ambassador for the Predators.

It was wonderful to see him whenever he'd visit with the Preds, flying into town for alumni golf tournaments, to visit his kids who'd remained in Calgary, or for the 25th anniversary of the Cup-winning team in 2014.

Always a joy to get together with Crispy and reminisce.

Barks

Doug Barkley and I are synonymous with one another. A radio tag team, if you will.

For the first 21 years I called Flames game, Doug was the guy in the booth beside me, certainly a great, great boost to any broadcast and to me personally, in learning the ins and outs of the game and getting to know the people who inhabit it.

Unfortunately, Doug didn't enjoy the playing career he deserved, a very serious eye injury cutting it short in only his sixth NHL season.

Playing for the Red Wings against Chicago on January 30, 1966, Doug was clipped in the eye by the stick of the Blackhawks' Doug Mohns. In an attempt to lift the stick, Mohns missed, accidentally striking Doug's right eye.

Doug never played another game.

With today's modern technology, he likely would have been able to repair the damage and continue his career.

Unfortunately, those technologies didn't exist in the 1960s.

A break in the action with my friend and broadcast partner of 21 seasons, Doug Barkley, in the booth at the Saddledome. (© Calgary Flames)

He'd already made an impact in a short time with the Wings, finishing second in voting for rookie of the year, just behind Kent Douglas of the Toronto Maple Leafs the season prior.

Anyone who saw Doug play and were students of the game felt he would have had an outstanding career in the NHL with his hard-nosed style, skill level, and hockey IQ.

Following the forced retirement, he'd go on to do some coaching, a couple of times with the Red Wings. He was also in charge of Red Wings farm teams and also was involved with a team they set up over in London, England, the start of the NHL's involvement in international hockey. Doug certainly had some great stories from that season, touring Europe with the London Lions.

Everyone in hockey knew Doug and after he joined our broadcast team he was instrumental in lining up pregame and intermission guests, including his former roommate with the Wings, Gordie Howe.

Doug also had the distinction of the being Gordie's last coach wearing the Winged Wheel. Which was apropos.

Doug was a guy who, on the road, was always quick-witted, whether we were in a taxi, on the team bus, at meals, or in arenas for morning skates.

He dished out some great one-liners over the course of our professional time together. He'd also serve as a sort of protector for me, like Dave Semenko for Wayne Gretzky.

I'm just a little guy. Doug is anything but.

One night, he also got the chance to do some play-by-play. It was a game in Edmonton and was one of those situations where the play went on without a whistle, maybe five minutes.

When you're calling a game in that situation sometimes you can get a knot in your voice and have to stop momentarily.

That's what happened to me.

Suddenly, I couldn't talk.

I had to stop, catch my breath, and take a quick drink of water. While I did that, Doug jumped in and did the play-by-play for a few seconds.

When I jumped back in, at the first stoppage of play, I teased him. "Gee, you did a great job on the play-by-play," I said.

Doug fired back: "Well, it was real easy. Gretzky and Kurri had the puck the whole time."

Colin and the Cup

These days, members of the Stanley Cup–winning organization—coaches, management, players—are eager to snap up the opportunity to physically take the Cup for one day to a special place, be it their hometown, or to a charity they're particularly involved with. Wherever.

Totally their call.

That one-day rule wasn't the case back when the Flames got their hands on it.

The winning team would receive the Cup the night it was won, and keep it for only a short period of time.

But Calgary can, in a sense, be credited with initiating the one-day-for-each tradition in the summer of 1989. And it can be traced back to left winger Colin Patterson.

Colin was living in a Toronto suburb in the off-seasons back then and happened to know someone who worked at the Hall of Fame and had access to the Cup.

So he arranged for the gentleman to bring it to his house one Saturday afternoon and invited a bunch of family and friends to help celebrate.

In 1994–95, when the New Jersey Devils won the title, the ritual of everyone having spent his own day with the Cup began in earnest.

Colin was one of those players GM Cliff Fletcher unearthed from the U.S. college system, at that time a largely untapped talent pool.

A solid, solid two-way winger noted more for his checking abilities, Colin was a finalist for the Selke Trophy as the best league's top defensive forward back in the 1988–89 season. He finished plus-44 that year, a pretty phenomenal stat for a guy often sent out to muzzle the opposition's top-scoring wingers.

His career stats for the Flames—88 goals, 187 points in 416 games—didn't begin to illustrate his value on the ice.

But he could chip in offensively at the most timely of moments. Often lost in recollections of the title-clinching night of May 25, 1989, at the Montreal Forum is that Colin was the guy responsible for the all-important first goal, scoring at 18:51 of the first period to give the Flames a lead.

Scroll back three years to 1986, and he also notched a vital goal in a run to the Final, scoring the game-winning goal against the St. Louis Blues in Game 7 of the Campbell Conference Final.

Early on, Badger Bob Johnson put three forwards together and memorably christened it The Dice Line, owing to the numbers each of its members wore—centre Carey Wilson, No. 33; left winger Patterson, No. 11; and right winger Rich Kromm, No. 22.

During his eight seasons wearing red and white, before moving on to the Buffalo Sabres, Colin never managed to register a hat trick but did pitch in with nine two-goal games and was an integral part in one of the big comebacks in franchise history. On January 26, 1987, the Flames fell behind 5–0 after 40 minutes at the old Maple Leafs Gardens before roaring back to erase the hefty lead, scoring five times to send the game to overtime.

And in OT, Colin was the man to end it after a minute and a half, leaving the Leafs and their Gardens faithful stunned.

These days, when I introduce him at Flames alumni events, I often refer to him as "Hall of Famer." The reason is that when I myself was being inducted, I played tourist, moseying around the Hall, and found a mural of Colin on the wall in the space devoted to international hockey.

Well, actually the photo was primarily of Sergei Priakin, the first Soviet player to make the jump to the NHL, with the Flames during their Stanley Cup year.

But I spotted Colin there, too, in the background of the image. So ever since I've jokingly referred to him as a Hall of Famer.

Turned out, as I found out wandering the concourse one day at the Leafs' practice rink in Etobicoke, Ontario, he's actually been enshrined in the Etobicoke Hall of Fame, a list of his accomplishments up on the wall alongside his citation.

So he's a legitimate Hall of Fame player. Not to mention a Hall of Fame person.

Gary Suter

Some people you just seem to hit it off with.

In the late 1980s and early part of the 1990s, I got to know a number of players on the Flames quite well. One of those who became a friend was Gary Suter.

The night Gary won the Calder Trophy as rookie of the year, I remember attending a celebration with his family in Montreal, where the NHL awards were being staged.

The recognition was richly deserved.

I also remember George Pelawa, a huge teenage winger out of Bemidji whom the Flames selected with their first pick in the draft, being there, too. Tragically, Pelawa would die in a car accident that summer.

Suter's arrival from the University of Wisconsin, Badger Bob Johnson's alma mater, heralded a change in provincial fortune for the Flames against their bitter rivals from the north.

The tables tipped, in my mind, in a late-season 10–3 shellacking the Flames administered on the Oilers. The comprehensiveness of that scoreline instilled Badger's boys with belief.

Suter, by the way, tied a franchise record with six assists that night.

Away from hockey, Gary was probably the only player who was as bad a golfer as I was. Naturally, that made us golf pals.

Gary and I wouldn't break 100 while the other guys, the better guys, were in the 70s and 80s. We were a little bit out of our class but we certainly had a lot of fun. Left winger Colin Patterson dubbed Suter and me "The Legends of Golf."

We were at the Bearspaw course one day, with Perry Berezan and Al MacInnis, and as we got to the 18th and final hole we found ourselves tied.

There was water in front of the 18th green and both of us had a lot of difficulty getting the ball over the water and onto the green. Finally, after putting a number of balls in the water, we elected to throw our balls over the water hazard.

Another time, at Pinebrook Golf and Country Club, we had a similar situation.

That fall, Suter, involved in the Canada Cup tournament for the USA, had engaged with Wayne Gretzky, injuring No. 99, and Gary wound up being suspended by the league.

Wouldn't you know it, the day his suspension was announced—unbeknownst to him at the time—we were out on the course. Making our way up the 18th green, we noticed all kinds of cameras and media people standing around the green. Again.

We weren't sure what it was all about. There were no cell phones at that time to alert as to what had transpired.

So Patterson said, "Those TV cameras must all be here to see Suter and Maher coming down the final hole to see which was going to win the Legends match."

But no, they'd hustled to the course to get Gary's comment on the suspension he'd been slapped with that day.

Another time we hit the links together was during the Stanley Cup playoffs in 1989, the year the Flames laid claim to the Cup.

Gary had suffered a broken jaw in the first round against Vancouver, so between Games 3 and 4 of the second round, in Los Angeles, he and I went out and had a golf match near the airport.

I had a pretty good game going, and had an eight-stroke lead with just two holes to go. However, I quickly watched that lead evaporate and Gary would win our challenge match.

I don't know if I blew the match because I was distracted by all the planes flying overhead or because Suter, because of his broken jaw, didn't talk very much over the first 16 holes.

But he was certainly talking later, telling his teammates that he'd overcome that eight-stroke deficit to beat me.

Name That D-Man

Trivia question: Name the first Flames defenceman to register a hat trick.

If you answered Al MacInnis, Paul Reinhart, or Gary Suter...you're wrong.

Big Dana Murzyn holds that distinction.

Noted more for being a solid, defensive blueliner during his seasons as a Flame, including the 1989 Cup-lifting campaign, the Calgary-born former fifth-overall pick of the Hartford Whalers hit for three goals on February 22, 1990, at the Saddledome.

All of them were even strength in a 12–2 shellacking of the Toronto Maple Leafs. The first goal came at the expense of starter Jeff Reese, giving the Flames a 5–0 lead. The next two beat backup Alan Bester.

In the closing stages of that game, I recall, players on the bench were pleading with coach Terry Crisp to throw Murzyn out on the ice to shoot for the hat trick.

Terry obliged and Dana held up his end of the bargain, scoring with only 2:47 remaining.

While Murzyn was the first Flames defenceman to hit for three goals in a game during the regular season, Reinhart actually twice had hat tricks during his Calgary stint, both on the road and both in the playoffs. The first time was April 14, 1983, in a 6–3 loss at Edmonton, then a year later, on April 4, he potted one in each of the three periods as the Flames rolled over the Canucks 5–1 in Vancouver. He also scored a regular season hat trick on November 24, 1986.

Most of his career Paul did play defence, but on that night, against Edmonton, centremen Mike Bullard, Perry Berezan, and Doug Risebrough, as well as right winger Lanny McDonald, were all absent due to injury.

So Reinhart was shifted up to the centre position and scored the first three goals of a 6–5 victory.

I remember my colour commentator Doug Barkley, a defenceman during his playing days, was amazed that Paul, an awfully skilled guy, could move up and play forward so seamlessly.

But, technically, the hat trick came as a centre.

Over the course of career as an NHLer, Dana logged 838 games and scored only 52 goals. His hat trick season, he wound up with seven.

This was a guy who, while playing junior for his hometown Calgary Wranglers, was actually noted for goals, netting 32 in the 1984–85 campaign.

To date, Dana and MacInnis, against Hartford in 1992, are the only Flames blueliners to post a hat trick.

An interesting note: The game following Murzyn's three goals, 48 hours later against Edmonton up north, the Flames torched the Oilers

10–4. Dana didn't manage a point that night, but Sergei Makarov—a more logical choice as offensive star of any evening—indulged himself with a franchise-record seven.

Makarov the Magnificent

General manager Cliff Fletcher was able to convince the Russian hockey people to have Sergei Makarov come over to play with the Flames starting with the 1989–90 NHL season.

The prior year, Sergei Priakin had preceded him, becoming the first Russian to receive permission from the hockey authorities there to make the jump to the NHL.

But Priakin was not a star, certainly not up to the standard of Sergei Makarov.

Makarov began his NHL odyssey at 31 years old, after a distinguished career with the Soviet national team, gold medals at the Olympics and world championships on his résumé.

One of the most prolific scorers in the history of Russian hockey while operating on the world-renowned KLM Line alongside Igor Larionov and Vladimir Krutov, Makarov made a pretty big impact in the NHL, too, winning the rookie of the year award in the 1989–90 season in which he had his best point campaign, picking up a total of 86.

The Makarov night I remember most was February 25, 1990, when he established a Flames record that still stands for most points in a single game, with seven.

After Sergei joined the Flames and anybody wanted to interview him, all he would say was, "No speak English."

He probably could speak better English than he was letting on, but certainly he wasn't comfortable with it. His teammates told me that on the ice and in the dressing room he was okay to communicate with.

He'd certainly picked up on it pretty well by the time he was inducted into the Hall of Fame in 2016. Sergei's speech went on for a full 10 minutes and a lot of it was delivered in English.

The big night I mentioned earlier came in a 10–4 victory in the Saddledome over the Edmonton Oilers, only three nights after the Flames had walloped Toronto 12–2.

Against the Oilers, Sergei was simply unstoppable, tallying two goals and five assists. He had a goal in the first, two assists in the second, then came on even stronger in the third period, notching his 20th goal of the season and adding three assists.

That night, and much of the season, he played on a line with Joe Nieuwendyk and Gary Roberts. The night Sergei ran wild, Nieuwendyk counted goal No. 36 of the season and Roberts his 30th.

Almost lost in Makarov's brilliance was defenceman Gary Suter and his five assists.

Dave King

Bob Johnson, Terry Crisp, and Darryl Sutter all won Game 7s during their tenures as head coach of the Flames.

Ultimately, following each of those occasions, they'd guide the team on to that season's Stanley Cup Final.

In the case of Dave King, though, if he could've found a way to win a Game 7, his stay at the Dome would've been far, far longer.

The final two years of his three seasons in charge ended in heart-breaking Game 7 losses. Both in double overtime.

Suffering that fate in back-to-back tries hardly seemed fair but that's the way things played out.

Stellar regular seasons—point totals of 97, 97, and 55 (in a work-stoppage-shortened 48-game schedule. A second-place finish in the Smythe Division, followed by two straight Pacific Division titles.

Dave's first year in charge, the Flames were eliminated in Game 6 of the opening-round series, at Los Angeles.

The next two postseasons proved to be wildly dramatic. And excruciatingly painful.

The unsettling images are seared into the memory banks of Flames fans of the time.

In 1994, Vancouver's Pavel Bure used that Russian Rocket liftoff to leave defenders in his wake at the blueline and score on Mike Vernon at 2:20 of double OT.

A year later, same circumstance, San Jose's Ray Whitney did the dirty work, at 1:54 of the second overtime, beating Trevor Kidd.

Following the bitter loss to the Sharks, the organization decided it needed a different voice at the top coaching position and Dave was let go.

I'd known him a bit before he became coach of the Flames, of course, as one of the most respected hockey minds in the international game and his years spent in charge of the Canadian national team program, based in Calgary, and Olympic competitions.

But his three years in charge of the Flames certainly gave me a full perspective of the man. Especially interviewing him virtually every day for the coach's show.

Dave was always very, very insightful about the game, not a big talker but he answered hockey-technical questions in layman's terms, which helped give the audience a better understanding of his coaching style and what he was aiming to achieve.

I told him more than once if coaching didn't work out for him, he'd make a heckuva broadcaster, given the way he could communicate the game to people.

Dave, however, was a career teacher, and that was his passion, his love.

Following the stint in Calgary he was hired to take charge of the Columbus Blue Jackets and stayed in Ohio for two and a half seasons.

To this day he remains involved in coaching, back in the international arena, and signed on with Hockey Canada as an assistant coach for the country's entry at 2018 Winter Olympic Games in PyeongChang, South Korea.

Theo

Theoren Fleury was different, unique.

Through the course of a career that averaged more than a point-per-game, a Stanley Cup ring in 1989, and an Olympic gold medal at the 2002 Winter Games at Salt Lake City, many people refer to him as being a great little player.

I refer to him as a great player. Period.

When you consider all that he overcame to have the NHL career that he had, after all of the personal difficulties arising from the Graham James scandal and so forth, you really have to admire all that this young man accomplished.

I'll never forget his draft day in 1987, which was being held in Detroit, in Cobo Hall just down the street from Joe Louis Arena. He was really only an afterthought, selected in the eighth round, 166th overall, from the Moose Jaw Warriors.

Listed as a centreman, he'd become a star after being shifted over to right wing.

By the time the Flames selected him, I had all of my broadcast equipment packed up and was just waiting for the draft to end, sending in periodic reports to the radio station about who the Flames were selecting in the later rounds.

Then Ian McKenzie, one of the Flames' scouts who travelled extensively across western Canada covering the WHL, came up to me and said, "You should call the guy that we just drafted, Theoren Fleury."

I told Ian that we didn't usually make phone calls or do interviews with eighth-round picks.

But Ian convinced me to give this kid a ring, so I went back to my broadcast spot, unpacked my equipment, hooked it up to the telephone, and made the call to Theo, who was in Russell, Manitoba, his hometown, at the time.

I'll never forget in the interview how grateful he was to the Flames for drafting him. He'd been eligible for the draft the previous year and was bypassed by everyone.

The feeling among NHL teams, of course, was that he was too small to survive, let alone thrive.

While Ian was convinced he'd eventually become an NHL player, I'm not so sure that many—if any—other people in the Flames' hierarchy felt the same way. The general consensus was that he may be a good player for the farm team, help to sell tickets in Salt Lake City. Nothing more.

Theo Fleury turned out to be much, much more than that.

I met him face to face at his first training camp that fall and it sure didn't take him long to get noticed.

Maybe a week or even less into it, a number of the veteran players were already complaining about him: "He's out there sticking us, cross-checking us, spearing us, hooking us."

Exactly what he had to do to get himself noticed.

By the end of that training camp, even though he did go back to play junior that season, he'd made an indelible impression.

Theo opened the next season in Salt Lake of the old International Hockey League and quickly became a standout there.

After the Flames had played a game on New Year's Eve, as 1989 dawned, they were in what I would call the only slump they experienced through that Stanley Cup championship season.

So the call was made to Salt Lake City to have Theo join them, maybe intended solely as a wake-up call.

He never left.

Over the course of his career, he'd record 16 hat tricks, 15 as a Flame and one as a New York Ranger. His only four-goal game arrived in the playoffs—Theo always was known as a big-moment guy—in 1995 against the San Jose Sharks.

Theo is one of only 39 players in NHL history to play more than 1,000 games and average over a point per game, with 1,088 points in 1,084 games. He's also one of only 26 players to play in 75 or more playoff games and average over a point per game (79 in 77).

As the years passed, the economics of the game changed and the great players exited, one by one—Gilmour, Nieuwendyk, MacInnis, Vernon, etc.—and Theo graduated from supporting player to focal point to leader to face of the franchise.

He'd blossom into a 100-point player, a 50-goal man, and the overtime goal he scored in Game 6 of the playoff series against the Oilers in 1991 has become the stuff of legend, replayed endlessly on TV ever since.

After stealing the puck from Mark Messier in OT he slipped the puck past Grant Fuhr and went off on a celebration for the ages, sliding down the ice at Northlands Coliseum, diving, twisting, arms pumping. Just raw emotion. But then, that was Theo.

I remember him saying afterward, "I felt I had to do *something*. I hadn't picked up a goal in the playoffs to that point."

Unfortunately, the Flames lost Game 7 at home.

I'll never forget the day Theo was traded. Over the years, as his stature in the game grew, he'd gone through a few contract battles with the team, confiding in me about calls he'd receive from the NHL Players Association, upset that he'd signed for less than they felt appropriate.

Well, the dam broke in 1999.

Theoren Fleury: Not just a great small hockey player but a great player, period.
(AP Images)

Theo, coming up on a contract again, this time steadfastly refused to take the proverbial hometown discount. So Al Coates, general manager at the time, dealt him away to the Colorado Avalanche just prior to the deadline.

That Sunday morning he was traded, I drove down to the Saddledome and met him there. We had a live broadcast that day, set up our equipment as we do usually after a game, and were able to interview Theo right there due to the trade.

He was in tears doing the interview and he had me in tears, too, realizing the business of the game had brought about his trade from a city, an organization, he felt such a kinship to.

He clearly didn't want to leave Calgary, where he had made such an impact on the community as well as on the on-ice product. But it was done, so he left for Denver, harbouring a real hope that he could lift the Stanley Cup a second time.

With Joe Sakic, Peter Forsberg, Patrick Roy, and the rest, the Avs did have one of the stronger teams but Theo's Cup dream didn't materialize and he wound up being a free agent that summer and signing on with the New York Rangers.

With me, Theo was always accessible, his interviews often insightful. This was a guy, regardless of the situation, who'd stand up and be accountable.

After moving on to Chicago, he was involved in a brawl in a bar in Columbus after a game. After getting involved with a bouncer, his face was swollen, an eye blackened.

Soon after, the Blackhawks came to Calgary for a game and he was there in the morning and made himself available to all the media people. He even came to our own Hot Stove Lounge for an interview.

The inner demons that had been most of his adult life, since being abused by his junior coach, Graham James, began to affect his professional life.

In April 2003, he was suspended a second time by the league for violations of its substance abuse program. That looked to be the end.

A sad day for him and his scores of fans in Calgary and across the hockey spectrum.

Harley Hotchkiss, late former owner of the Flames, continued to work very hard as the NHL's chairman of the board of governors to have Theo reinstated by the league. A very influential, balanced person, Harley managed to get it done.

So the little guy hired a trainer, worked himself into shape, and landed a tryout at the Flames' training camp in 2009, hoping to revive his career, or maybe just prove something to himself.

Considering how long he'd been away from the NHL level, his play was extraordinary.

That first exhibition game at the Dome and the great response he received from the fans was amazing.

He ended the evening being the hero as he scored the only goal in the shootout to give the Flames the victory.

To mark the occasion, welcoming back an old favorite, it's the only time I ever bellowed out my "Yeah baby!" call in a preseason game.

He'd play another game in the Dome, chipping in another a goal and an assist.

Despite four points in four preseason games, though, the Flames decided not to sign him. He was a luxury the team couldn't afford.

I know Theo was upset not to be able to get his career going again but he had to feel proud of the way he'd played and in reconnecting with the Saddledome crowd.

A dignified way to exit.

He's stayed very active in the community since that swan song. It's always a pleasure chatting with him and finding out how things are going in his world.

A world he's happy with now. Which makes everyone who knows him happy, too.

Mr. Hockey

I'm no different than anybody else. I admired Gordie Howe tremendously.

Back in the 1979–80 season it was such a great personal thrill when four franchises from the World Hockey Association were incorporated into the NHL, one, of course, being the Hartford Whalers.

A thrill because that meant I'd be calling games involving Gordie Howe.

I'll never forget my first broadcast involving Gordie. I was still calling Leafs games at the time and the Whalers were playing home games in Springfield because of problems with the roof on the building in Hartford.

To this day, I can remember the puck going into the right corner in the Maple Leafs' zone, and Gordie giving chase. One of the linesmen was inadvertently impeding him. So with one arm, Gordie just reached out pushed the linesman out of the way, skated into the corner, won the puck back, passed to a teammate, and then scored on a return pass.

So I can say I called a Gordie Howe goal. One of the highlights of my career.

Another special memory is the night he came back to Toronto and the tremendous ovation he received at the old Gardens.

He'd done a lot of damage to the Leafs over the years, of course, but every time he was on the ice the fans serenaded him, out of respect.

One of the great things about having Doug Barkley and Mike Rogers as my colour commentators over the years in Calgary is that they'd both been teammates of Gordie's. In fact, Doug was a roommate of Gordie's for a time in Detroit. He also coached him with the Red Wings. Mike played alongside Gordie in Hartford, in both the WHA and NHL.

So whenever we'd be in Detroit or whenever we'd bump into Gordie on our travels, they'd get together and reminisce. That allowed me to hang out and get to know Gordie a little bit. In the Alumni Room at Joe Louis, we'd sit around—Doug or Mike, Gordie, the Wings' former broadcaster Budd Lynch—have a brew and I'd just absorb the conversation.

At one point an article was written in *Sports Illustrated* about Gordie and the guy writing it mentioned my name. I'm pretty sure he was referring to Doug and my name got put in by mistake.

But I'll take it.

You don't utter a peep of complaint when you're in an article in *Sports Illustrated* written about Gordie Howe.

He was such a gentleman. I believe it was the first year Jarome Iginla scored 50 goals and the Flames were playing in Detroit, late in the season. I'd come down after the game and there was Gordie standing in the hallway outside the visitors' dressing room. I asked him what he was doing and he replied, "Waiting for Mr. Iginla to come out. I'd like to meet him and shake his hand." I said, "Gordie, you can go in the dressing room. I'm pretty sure no one would throw you out." I mean, this is Gordie Howe we're talking about…

But he said, no, he was fine waiting.

Eventually Jarome came out of the room and I'm sure he was surprised and thrilled to see who'd been standing there, waiting for him.

Unfortunately, as everyone knows, Gordie had health issues and we lost him in the late spring of 2016. Just a very special man along with being one the greatest players ever.

Mr. Hockey. The nickname says it all.

Mr. Hockey. This picture with Gordie Howe was taken at a fund-raising event we both spoke at in Calgary.

Production from the Back

A defenceman has never led the Flames in point production over the course of a regular season, although twice a Calgary blueliner has been the NHL's top scorer at his position.

Among defencemen blessed with offensive punch, Al MacInnis, of course, immediately pops to mind, armed with that cannon of a shot from the point (although he had other outstanding attributes, as proven throughout his Hall of Fame career).

With the Flames, Al ranks as the No. 3 all-time leading career scorer with 822 points in 803 games, tucked in behind two pretty dynamic players in Jarome Iginla and Theo Fleury.

Yet the best he could do in the regular season was finish second in team scoring twice, in both 1990–91 and 1991–92.

The 1990–91 campaign, I think it's safe to say, was Al's best as a Flame. He was magnificent, breaking the 100-point plateau (103), ultra-rare for a defenceman, finishing one point behind Theo on the team scoring list and first among players at his position.

A year later, his 77 points ranked behind only the 90 of Gary Roberts on the Calgary charts.

Al's power play sidekick Gary Suter, meanwhile, sits fifth all time in Flames scoring, at 565 points in 617 regular season games.

His highest finish in team scoring was fourth in the 1987–88 campaign, registering 91 points.

Yet Suter led all NHL defencemen in scoring during that season.

Somewhat surprisingly, neither of those guys won a Norris Trophy as a member of the Flames. Theirs, remember, was also the era of Ray Bourque, Chris Chelios, and Paul Coffey. So some pretty tough competition.

But certainly Suter and MacInnis were great players for the organization, both offensively and defensively.

Scotty

Scotty Bowman, of course, is a legend. The NHL's all-time winningest coach, a nine-time Stanley Cup winner whose NHL career lasted an astounding 35 years.

He's also an extremely interesting guy.

I first got to know Scotty when he was between jobs in the NHL, working as a colour commentator on some of the mid-week broadcasts I did for Toronto Maple Leaf games.

When he was back coaching the Red Wings, I remember one morning at Joe Louis Arena in Detroit. Of course, we in the media have an obsession with getting the forward lines and defence pairings out to our listening audience. So you'd attend the morning skate and religiously copy down the numbers, who was playing or paired with who, on the main cheat sheet, along with information on different players.

This particular game, I stood at the Flames' bench as the Red Wings were running their line drills and defence pairings when Scotty skated by and very politely told me, "Peter, don't bother. I'm going to change things around three minutes into the game." And, of course, that's what he did.

Scotty, as everyone knows, had a tremendous hockey mind and infallible memory, big reasons he enjoyed unparalleled success behind the bench.

An example: The first year Mike Rogers came aboard as my colour commentator on Flames broadcasts, Scotty invited me into his office for a friendly chat and on-air interview during our first trip to Detroit that season.

During the conversation he asked about Doug Barkley retiring after 21 seasons as my sidekick and who'd been chosen to replace him.

When I told him Mike Rogers, he unhesitatingly said, "Mike Rogers? He played on those great Calgary Centennials lines in the 1970s with Danny Gare and Jerry Holland."

I was absolutely amazed that he could scroll that far back and remember a forward line on a Calgary junior team.

But that's Scotty. No detail too small. An encyclopedia of the game.

The Sutter Connection, Part I

First Brian.

Followed by Darryl.

And then Brent.

Over the years, the Sutter brothers and the Flames have become synonymous. And not simply due to proximity, Calgary being 350 kilometres away from the family homestead in Viking.

Interestingly, two of the most impactful players of an era—Jarome Iginla and Robyn Regehr—would play for all three of hockey's most famous family during their long careers at the Saddledome.

And both, post-Flames, would be L.A. Kings, brought there by Darryl.

During the summer of 2017, the entire Sutter family, the seven boys as well as their parents, Grace and Louis, were enshrined in the Alberta Hockey Hall of Fame, located in Red Deer.

It's always been a contention of mine that they should all be enshrined in the Hockey Hall of Fame, as well, for contributions as players and coaches and, well, as parents, but I'm still waiting on that one.

Louis passed away in Viking back in February of 2005 and I was fortunate enough to attend the funeral.

Louis was quite a guy.

Then again, that's quite the family.

So let's start with Brian Sutter, the first of the brothers to coach the Flames, who I got to know while he was the heart-and-soul captain of the St. Louis Blues in the early 1980s.

The Sutter clan. They were inducted as a group into the Alberta Hockey Hall of Fame in 2017. A similar Hockey HOF tribute would be appropriate. (AP Images)

The first time I met Brian was prior to a game in St. Louis. The Flames had played the night before so there was no morning skate and interviews needed to be conducted before the game.

I wasn't sure how that was all going to work out.

I'd sent a message to the Blues' media relations man but he wasn't around when I arrived at the dressing room.

The first player to emerge was Brian Sutter. I introduced myself and told him who I was and asked him if he'd be available for a chat. He complied, gave a very good interview, and later, when I got to know him better and gleaned just how intense he was, I wondered how I'd had the intestinal fortitude to ask him to talk so close to puck-drop all those years ago.

Simply put, Brian lived and breathed the game.

One of the very few players to immediately transition into head coaching duties with no minor-league prep or time spent as an NHL assistant learning the ropes.

Following his four-season tenure behind the Blues' bench, he had a stint in Boston before Flames GM Al Coates brought Brian in to coach the Flames in 1997.

An Alberta boy, from just 45 minutes north, renowned for his intensity, the oldest of the hockey-playing boys of the game's most famous family.

The fit seemed ideal.

Brian's time in charge, however, coincided with a real rough patch for the franchise. He inherited a rebuilding situation, many star players having moved on. Salaries were increasing exponentially, the Canadian dollar was hurting badly, and the Flames had become a low-budget team, required to pay players in U.S. dollars.

Undaunted, Brian pushed them to the max, but the team was unable to reach the playoffs in any of his three seasons.

During Brian's era, we saw the exit of Theo Fleury, traded to Colorado, but also the emergence of Jarome Iginla to prominence. A little-known (at the time) winger named Martin St. Louis joined the team as a U.S. college free agent and Brian appeared to be laying the groundwork for a long stay. He had Marty playing more of a defensive role in the early going, wanting him to learn that part of the game. Brian always felt St. Louis had tremendous upside on the offensive side of things, too.

But unfortunately, after the third season, both Brian and Al Coates were fired and St. Louis was let go.

So he went on to become a superstar in Tampa Bay. Not in Calgary.

Brian, like all Sutters, loathed losing. A hard-driving guy, he pushed the players and certainly wasn't shy about being critical of them, whether on the ice, in the dressing room, or on the bench. As quickly as he was to fire off a salvo, however, he could give out praise every bit as fast.

His players got to know very quickly that he was demanding but fair.

This was a very caring guy. He really did want his players to be better, as hockey players and as people.

But there were an awful lot of quiet bus rides. That I can vouch for.

My broadcast partner Doug Barkley and I would sit pretty much behind Brian on those trips to airports and back to hotels from arenas, and he certainly took losses very, very hard.

Away from the game, after moving to Sylvan Lake in the Red Deer area, he became very involved in the Sutter Fund charities, and remains a big part of those initiatives.

Brian's still coaching, too. That's in his blood. He's currently in charge of the Innisfail Eagles senior team and its quest for the Allan Cup.

His son Sean would eventually go on to be drafted by the Flames after playing part of his junior hockey career for Western Hockey League's Calgary Hitmen.

At that time my son, Jeff, was an assistant coach with the Hitmen.

I remember how Jeff would talk about how Sean Sutter was playing through very serious injuries, problems that would have kept others on the sidelines and out of games.

But toughness—in mind and body—is another Sutter family trait, isn't it?

Gary is the oldest of the family. I got to know him later on through the golf tournaments in Red Deer, and from what I understood many believed he was the most talented of all the Sutter brothers.

The only one of the brothers who didn't go on to play pro, he stayed put and worked on the family farm in Viking.

The Sutter Connection, Part II

Of the three Sutters to pilot the Flames, Darryl was the brother who enjoyed the most success.

His contribution to putting the organization back on the right track cannot be underestimated.

He was hired on December 28, 2002, about a month after being fired following five years-plus as head coach of the San Jose Sharks.

Prior to that, he'd coached with the Chicago Blackhawks for three seasons, after apprenticing by winning the International Hockey League's Turner Cup with the Hawks' top farm team, the Indianapolis Ice.

When hired by the Flames, the team's coaching situation was in a state of flux. Greg Gilbert had been let go and Al MacNeil was brought in on an interim basis.

Initially, it was thought that Al would coach three or four games, but complications developed and he wound up handling the team for 11 games before team president Ken King very quietly made his way to San Jose and met with Darryl.

Darryl would come in and coach his first game one day after being hired. The team won four of the first five games he coached and another ended in a tie.

He finished the 2002–03 season with the Flames securing points in 14 of the final 20 games, including 11 wins.

Upon taking over, Darryl realized more than half a season would be required to change the culture of a team that had missed the playoffs for six years running.

They were on the outside looking in again, going 19–18–8–1 under their new boss.

But Darryl's arrival added a stability to the coaching ranks that had been lacking since his older brother Brian held sway.

At the conclusion of the 2002–03 season, he added the title of general manager to his portfolio and during the off-season made a trade—little heralded at the time—that would positively impact the team, picking up stay-at-home defenceman Rhett Warrener from the Buffalo Sabres.

Undoubtedly the most significant trade he'd ever make came in November of the next season, when he scooped up Miikka Kiprusoff in a trade with his old employers from San Jose.

Of course, he had formed a relationship with the silent Finn during his time with the Sharks.

Kiprusoff arrived and the Flames' fortunes shifted just about immediately. They were near the bottom of the standings, but the goaltending was so good, and the players' growing belief in Kiprsuoff's ability to win games so high, that soon they were challenging for their first playoff berth in eight seasons.

Even when their new meal-ticket goalie was sidelined via injury for a month, Darryl's gang continued to pile up the victories using backup goaltenders Roman Turek and Jamie McLennan.

Darryl as a coach certainly got the maximum out of his players; he realized that with the personnel at his disposal success could only be achieved through hard work, buying in, and winning all the battles in the tough areas.

Sure he had a couple of stars in Jarome Iginla and Kiprusoff, but the bulk of his roster was made up of lunch-bucket guys all committed to a common cause.

He certainly wasn't shy about pushing his players.

That elusive playoff berth achieved, they upset three first-place teams in their respective conferences, Vancouver, Detroit, and San Jose, respectively, before ultimately losing out to Tampa Bay.

The team ran into a lot of injures, especially on defence, during that playoff run but the call-ups came into the lineup and Darryl was able to get a lot out of those guys with his very intense coaching style. He wasn't a lot of fun to be around when he was unhappy or dissatisfied.

The players definitely heard from him on a number of occasions and maybe they weren't exactly infatuated with him on a lot of days.

But all of them, to a man, praised his coaching acumen.

Before Darryl arrived, plans had already been finalized for the first Flames Fathers Trip, an initiative started by other teams a couple of years earlier to get proud dads out on the road with their sons. A little bonding time, a thank-you to the fathers, and a bit of a break from a long, gruelling schedule.

The GM at the time, Craig Button, had approved the endeavour for games on back-to-back nights in Phoenix and Dallas, January 27–29.

I'm not sure Darryl would've endorsed the idea then anyway, but as things turned out the timing couldn't have been worse.

For starters, Darryl was hit in the face by a puck while behind the bench during the game immediately prior to the Fathers Trip, against the Detroit Red Wings. The damage was extensive enough that it required surgery by team dentist Bill Blair.

Already in a bad mood, he arrived the day of the game in Phoenix, which turned out to be a 4–3 loss to the Coyotes. The next night, the Stars inflicted a 4–1 beating on the Flames in Dallas.

After which Darryl was heard to comment tersely, "There'll be no more Daddys Trips!"

I'm not quite sure what the fathers had to do with a puck in the face or two losses on the ice, but the initiative wasn't picked up again until after he'd departed the organization.

Darryl could never be considered anything approaching a media darling. I'd gotten to know him a little bit from his days coaching days in Chicago and San Jose, and when he came to Calgary he wasn't all that crazy about meeting up with the media, especially on a daily basis.

Often his comments would be short, some would be curt, though there were times when he would have some pretty good insights to pass along.

Later, when he would move on to Los Angeles to coach the Kings, he became a bit more media friendly in an area where they needed all the coverage they could get.

The media there loved some of that homespun humour he'd inject into his comments. And he certainly had that in him. We just didn't get to see it very often in Calgary.

I'll not forget in 2006, the year I was honoured by the Hockey Hall of Fame, he was there in Toronto for the festivities and made a point of attending the party we'd had the day before.

There were a number of people from Flames management in attendance, but he emphasized the fact that he was there to represent the Sutter family.

I really appreciated that.

I also remember at that same soirée, my family members—brothers, Allan and Noonan, as well as sisters, Nancy and Wendy—just raving about the time they spent with Darryl, how polite he'd been, how attentive and interesting he was.

I also got to know Darryl's son Chris, a fantastic little guy, born with Down Syndrome. He'd be hanging around the dressing room quite a bit. A lot of nights after the game, he'd come into our studio at the Saddledome and take a seat, put the headset on, wanting to be part of our postgame discussion.

From time to time, I'd ask for a comment and Chris always had something colourful to add.

When the family shifted to Los Angeles and Darryl began a very successful, two-Cup run with the Kings, Chris was a bit older and very popular with both the players and the fans at the Staples Centre.

He'd be up in the stands dancing when there was a stoppage in play and be shown on the JumboTron.

Of course, he was on hand the nights the Kings won their two Stanley Cups with Darryl at the helm and I still recall the pictures of Chris raising the Cup in delight. Seeing those, you just can't help smiling.

The Sutter Connection, Part III

The third and final Sutter coaching instalment involves Brent, who came on board prior to the 2009–10 season and stayed for three years.

As a player, Brent might've been the best of the clan, his career covering 18 seasons, first with the New York Islanders and finally the Chicago Blackhawks.

On Long Island, he was a part of two Stanley Cup winners during their dynastic days and helped Canada to three Canada Cup titles.

Brent had enjoyed great junior success as a coach, piloting the team he owned, the Red Deer Rebels, to a Memorial Cup championship. He was also in charge of Canadian teams that collected World Junior gold in back-to-back years, 2005 and 2006.

Before coming to coach the Flames, he had two seasons behind the bench with the New Jersey Devils after being hired by Lou Lamoriello, qualifying for the playoffs both years.

After the second of a three-season deal, brother Darryl, the GM of Flames and in the market for a coach, approached him.

After a lot of contemplation, Brent went to Lou and asked to be let out of the final year of his contract.

That created some controversy in New Jersey, but Brent, Lou, and Darryl made arrangements so that Brent could return to his Alberta roots.

The Flames had qualified for the playoffs five years in a row so there was instant pressure to keep that string going, but unfortunately in his three seasons, despite two campaigns of 40 wins, there would be no post-season appearances.

It was a tough, tough chore for Brent, for a number of reasons. The playoff mandate, obviously. But also working for Darryl, who had quite a record of success during his time coaching the team.

During Brent's first year, Darryl up and traded Dion Phaneuf, an outstanding defenceman who had played on Brent's teams in Red Deer.

On December 28, 2010, halfway through Brent's stint as coach, Darryl was fired, exactly six years to the day after he'd been hired by the organization, and replaced by former Tampa Bay general manager Jay Feaster.

Following the season, Brent was let go, returning to the Rebels in Red Deer.

I'll always remember that when things were tough, Darryl would do a lot of pacing on the flights, down the centre aisle, not saying much, walking back and forth, back and forth.

Not much of that from Brent as coach in the tough times, but you would always see him on planes, on buses, suffering in silence.

Of the three brothers, Brent was probably the most media friendly. The media in Calgary knew he was always available the morning of games and after games to talk about his team's fortunes, whether they be good, bad, or indifferent.

I think some of the people in the media kind of felt of bad for Brent, as the Flames struggled valiantly only to keep falling just short of the playoffs.

Mike Rogers and I would sometimes chat with Brent and he'd confide in us, letting off some steam. Brent's son Brandon would go on to play in the NHL with Carolina and later the Vancouver Canucks.

The remaining three brothers who gained fame in the NHL have ties the Flames, as well.

Duane, like Brent, a multiple Cup winner with the Islanders, would do some scouting for the organization and is currently with the rival Edmonton Oilers.

Ron still works for the Flames, while twin brother Rich is now involved in between-periods commentary on the team's games on Sportsnet.

Robyn Regehr

I often wonder whether Robyn Regehr's contributions as a Calgary Flame are celebrated enough.

Quietly effective, he enjoyed a long run with the team after being acquired in the Theo Fleury trade with Colorado.

Robyn was playing junior hockey in Kamloops when that trade was made, and would finish that season with the Western Hockey League team.

Then during the summer, he was involved in a horrific automobile accident in which he sustained multiple injuries, including two broken legs.

At one point there was very real concern that perhaps he might not be able to pursue an NHL career at all.

But Robyn worked diligently with his rehab and showed up at the Flames' training camp in 1999. He didn't make the team right away, but spent only five games in the AHL with Saint John before beginning what would be a distinguished career modelling the Flaming C.

At 19, he'd become the youngest nominee for the Bill Masterton Memorial Trophy in NHL history.

Okay, so he wasn't Al MacInnis or Gary Suter offensively from the back end, scoring only 39 goals, regular season and playoffs, over his tenure with the Flames.

What a lot of people don't realize is that he played the second-most career games for the franchise, 826, the highest total by a defenceman and trailing only Jarome Iginla.

Regehr was an outstanding defensive defenceman, arguably the best the organization's ever had.

Born in Recife, Brazil (his parents both worked there as Mennonite missionaries), Robyn's often cited as being the finest hockey player ever to come out of the land of samba, caipirinhas, and soccer (granted, he doesn't have a lot of competition).

This was an exceptionally hard-hitter along the blueline, a good shutdown guy, and was very much an integral part of the Flames' run to the Stanley Cup Final in 2004.

Incidentally, during that 2003–04 season, he displayed his durability, playing in every game that year, regular season as well as playoffs, a total of 108.

Only Iginla matched him.

Despite his modest goal and point totals, Regehr actually possessed a good shot from the point, even though he didn't use it as much as people in the organization would have liked.

Nonetheless, the coaches loved having a guy like him, dependable and difficult to play against.

An interesting note is that during their history the Flames can boast three Sutters as coach: first Brian, then Darryl, followed by Brent. Robyn's one of only two players—the inevitable Iginla being the other—to have been with the Flames for all three of the Sutter regimes.

Interestingly, as his career progressed, Darryl, by then coach of Kings, thought so highly of Robyn that he acquired him in a trade with Buffalo.

Following the crushing disappointment of the seven-game 2004 Final loss to the Tampa Bay Lightning as a Flame, a decade later Regehr had the opportunity to be part of a Stanley Cup team with the Kings.

Over the course of his career, he played in 1,089 regular season games for three clubs, hanging up his skates after the 2015–16 NHL season owing to a number of injuries. To my knowledge, to this point in time he holds the distinction of being the only player to sign a one-day contract after announcing his retirement so that he could say he exited as a member of the Flames.

Certainly, he's a big benefit to Calgary, where he returned with his family following retirement to be involved in business, serve as an active member of the Flames Alumni, and throw his energies into a lot of charity work.

He also had the chance to play alongside brother Rich on the Flames, however briefly, which must have been a highlight.

Robyn's a guy I always enjoyed interviewing. He rarely held back, had very candid comments when you'd talk to him.

Clearly a bit underrated when you consider how much he contributed over 11 seasons in Calgary.

Rhett Warrener

The news that the Flames had acquired Rhett Warrener from the Buffalo Sabres barely caused a ripple on July 3, 2003.

But he helped change the culture of the team.

A good omen: The day newly installed GM Darryl Sutter swung the deal, Rhett was actually attending the Calgary Stampede.

Being born in Shaunovon, Saskatoon, and raised in Saskatoon, this was a guy with a definite country-western flavour to him.

As things turned out, a seamless fit.

The deal along also brought centre Steve Reinprecht to Calgary, Chris Drury and Steve Begin heading the other way in return.

Warrener arrived at a time the franchise had gone seven straight seasons without reaching the playoffs. Over the four full seasons he spent in the Flaming C, they never missed the postseason.

Coincidence? Hardly.

Granted, Jarome Iginla was at the peak of his powers back then, as was goaltender Miikka Kiprusoff. Darryl's arrival had provided direction and focus, setting an unstinting tone, first as the coach and then in the dual coach/GM role.

Nonetheless, Rhett was a team-first guy. His contributions to the 2004 Stanley Cup run and playoff qualification each and every year were underpublicized but immense.

A solid, uncompromising defenceman of the old school. An "off-the-glass-and-out" style. A guy who was always ready to battle when the puck dropped. Very good at defending. His forte was inside his own blueline, certainly, but he could be handy at the offensive end, as well.

During his three NHL stops—Florida, Buffalo, and Calgary—Rhett scored 24 goals, including six game-winners, one I particularly remember in OT against Nashville at Calgary in 2007 to complete a comeback.

Of the 11 goals he scored as a Flame, three came shorthanded, tying him for second among defencemen career-wise.

Rhett certainly knew when to have a good time, and those times included most, if not all, of his teammates. His outgoing personality helped knit that team together and he generally came to be considered the off-ice captain.

The 2004 seven-game Final loss to Tampa Bay obviously hit everyone in the organization hard but one no was more gutted than Rhett Warrener. That trip marked the third time he'd reached the final round, playing for three different teams, but he never had the chance to lift the Stanley Cup.

Twice those series were beset by controversy. With Buffalo, the (in)famous Brett Hull game-winning goal, in triple-overtime, off Brett's skate for the Dallas Stars in 1999.

Five years later, also in a Game 6, more heartache, this time at the Dome and the Martin Gelinas no-goal during the third period that fans in Calgary are, to this day, still convinced should've ended the series and propelled the Flames to their second Stanley Cup triumph.

Instead, the Bolts took the series back to Florida on a Martin St. Louis goal and won Game 7 by a 2–1 score.

Denied again.

Rhett had to be gutted. Still, on the long flight home from Tampa, he came to Mike Rogers and me apologizing for not winning the Cup. We assured him no apology was required.

He was never the greatest interview as a player, I found, but after retiring he settled in as a broadcaster, to my surprise, working the morning show on the Flames' flagship station, The Fan 960.

Before that, he worked as a scout for the Flames but eventually left the role and dabbled in colour commentary on the mid-week games on Sportsnet.

I remember well when he told me the morning show was going to be a full-time gig. I told him, "Rhett, you're never gonna last at this. You've gotta get into work at 7:00 AM, get up around 5:30, and, well, you like to have some late nights."

Shows what I know. Four or five years later, Rhett's still on there and continues to be a great success.

He was also involved in a music video alongside country-and-western star Paul Brandt, called Convoy. Brandt did the singing, fortunately. Rhett and fellow defenceman Mike Commodore played truck drivers.

There were certainly no shortage of interesting characters on the team between 2003 and 2008. Rhett was definitely in that group.

He was also one of those unsung glue-guys who maybe don't generate headlines but are vital to on-ice success nonetheless.

Great Player, Good Guy

Swedish centreman Peter Forsberg is, as everyone knows, one of the greatest players of his era. A two-time Stanley Cup winner with the Colorado Avalanche, double Olympic gold medalist for Sweden, Hart Trophy recipient, and in 2017 named one of the 100 Greatest NHL players by the league during its centenary.

An unfortunate string of injuries kept him from reaching even greater heights.

He also always seemed to have big games against the Flames. An interesting guy that I had a chance to interview from time to time.

One of those chats I won't forget. I believe it was during the 1999–2000 season, when Forsberg had missed about 20 or 25 games due to an injury.

His first game back happened to be in Colorado against the Flames.

Following the morning skate that day, I was in the Avalanche dressing room and following Peter's media scrum, I asked him if he wouldn't mind doing a one-on-one taped interview for that night on the pregame show. He agreed. As we were talking, the media relations guy for the Avalanche, Jean Martineau, came up and just pulled him away.

There was no advanced signal. I soon learned that he had gone to do an interview with *Hockey Night in Canada.*

So I figured that would be the end of that and I best look around to see if I could get another suitable candidate.

Unfortunately, everybody had left.

But to my surprise, Forsberg came back looking for me, asking that we finish the interview we had started earlier.

Not very often does that happen, especially with a player other than a Flame.

The interview got to air and he would turn out to be the number-one star of that game.

Jean Martineau, well known for being a great protector of his players, didn't exactly make my Christmas card list.

But in 2006, when I was named to the NHL Hall of Fame, Jean was among those who reached out to congratulate me.

Jim Playfair

Jim Playfair's stint as head coach of the Flames would last only one season.

Coach/GM Darryl Sutter had decided to concentrate solely on managerial duties and elevated his trusted assistant to the top job.

The 2006–07 season turned out to be a fairly successful regular campaign, the Flames finishing third in a difficult Northwest Division with a 43–29–10 record for 96 points.

I always felt Jim inherited a really tough assignment, following Darryl, who'd helped resurrect the franchise and masterminded the 2004 push to the Stanley Cup Final.

A seven-game first-round loss to the Anaheim Ducks in the spring of 2006 convinced Darryl to step aside, probably believing the players needed a different voice inside the dressing room.

The organization, naturally, was still chomping at the bit to duplicate, and hopefully surpass, what it had accomplished two years earlier and felt it had the pieces in place to do precisely that.

During the years Darryl held the coaching reins, Jim had been being groomed as an assistant coach. In that role, particularly given Darryl's blunt style, there were times he had to step in and soothe dampened spirits after someone had received a rather stern lecture from the boss.

In the blink of an eye, now Jim was the one having to act like the tough guy and put some noses distinctly out of joint.

That's often an uneasy transition.

Jim had developed a very good coaching résumé before receiving the assignment, coaching the Flames' American League farm team for three years, highlighted by the 2001 Calder Cup championship. For that accomplishment, he was selected minor-league coach of the year by *The Hockey News.*

Two seasons later, when Greg Gilbert was replaced as Flames coach, he was considered a leading candidate for the job but Greg's firing coincided with the San Jose Sharks relieving Darryl of his responsibilities in the Silicon Valley, and the Flames hired the Alberta boy with a proven NHL track record.

Darryl, recognizing Jim's potential, brought him up to act as one of his right-hand men.

Certainly a very good teacher and strategist, in his roles as both an assistant and head coach, Jim was nevertheless replaced following a first-round playoff exit to the Detroit Red Wings in his first, and only, season in charge.

His replacement? Veteran Mike Keenan.

Darryl, however, was still keen for Jim to remain in the organization and offered him a co-coaching title as incentive not to seek out other opportunities.

Keenan stayed on for two seasons, with Jim involved in a lot of the strategizing.

He'd then move on to Phoenix to become part of Dave Tippett's staff for a number of seasons in the Arizona desert.

I often wonder under different circumstances if Jim's tenure in charge of the Flames wouldn't have been considerably longer.

Rich Preston

No one served as an assistant coach for the organization longer than Rich Preston.

Rich, of course, enjoyed a solid playing career, first in the WHA for five years and then for eight more in the NHL, splitting time between New Jersey and Chicago.

During his WHA days, he helped both the Houston Aeros and later the Winnipeg Jets to Avco Cup triumphs. In 1979, the league's final year of operation, he was named MVP of the playoffs.

Sporting roots run deep in the Preston family. His father, Ken, had played in the Canadian Football League and would go on to become general manager of the Saskatchewan Roughriders from 1958 to 1978.

Rich continues to follow football very closely and remains a lifelong, avid member of Rider Nation, often on the golf course wearing a Rider cap.

A real fun character, very well suited to the role of assistant coach, marrying his knowledge of the game with that winning personality.

First joining the Flames in 1997 as part of Brian Sutter's staff, he held that position through 2000 before heading to San Jose to join Brian's brother Darryl.

When Darryl joined the Flames, Rich followed him back, lasting through the coaching regimes of not only Darryl, but Jim Playfair and then Mike Keenan. Rich was familiar with Keenan, having spent time as an assistant coach with the Blackhawks, under both Mike and Darryl.

He's also worked in the Western Hockey League in both Lethbridge and Regina.

So, no shortage of experience.

Highlighting his Calgary tenure, of course, was 2004 and that incredible run to the seventh game of the Stanley Cup Final.

This is someone, as I mentioned, who really understood his role. He could loosen guys up when needed but also had a serious professional side to him. Working with Darryl, who could be a prickly sort regarding his players, someone like Rich, able to smooth troubled water, proved invaluable. Same with Mike.

On long bus rides to hotels after long plane trips, Rich would often lighten the mood. He had a wonderful knack for that. Many of the buses were equipped with a microphone/public address system and he'd seize the opportunity to grab the mic and tell stories or jokes in a slow-moving but wry way, usually eliciting catcalls or sarcastic applause from the back of the bus where the players sat.

A great storyteller, a lifelong hockey man, and just a joy to be around, Rich continues to live in Calgary while currently serving as an assistant coach for the Anaheim Ducks.

The Kipper Coup

Of the scores of trades made by the organization over the course of more than three decades, none can match November 16, 2003, for immediate and lasting impact.

That was the day Miikka Kiprusoff was acquired by then general manager/coach Darryl Sutter from the San Jose Sharks.

From the moment he arrived, and through the nine seasons he'd remain a Flame, Kiprusoff was a decisive factor in the successes of the club.

Very, very durable and someone capable of logging an awful lot of minutes. Really, only in that first year did injury manage to keep Kipper out of the lineup for any discernible length of time, four weeks, after hurting a knee.

When Sutter took a gamble on a guy he knew from his days in San Jose, the team was languishing near the bottom of the standings.

The arrival of Miikka Kiprusoff in November 2003 in a trade from San Jose helped transform the Flames from a non-playoff team into a Stanley Cup contender. (AP Images)

He quickly earned everyone's trust, posting a victory in his first start for his new team. By the time he was done, he'd tack on 304 more to shoot to the top of the franchise goaltending wins list.

No coincidence that his arrival dovetailed into a run to the Stanley Cup Final. Over 38 regular season starts, he won 24 games, and both his goals-against average (1.69) and save percentage (.933) were spectacular. That was followed up by a 1.85 GAA, five-shutout turn through 25 playoff games.

The Final, of course, ended in seventh-game heartbreak at Tampa for the Flames but a new star had introduced himself to NHL fans.

For seven straight seasons after that he'd be called upon 70 or more times, twice playing in 76 games. Three times he won 40 or more games, capturing the Vezina Trophy in the 2005–06 season for nailing down 42 wins.

Kipper's spectacular feats earned him a tremendous number of fans, naturally. One, in particular, remains memorable—a youngster seated in the Saddledome stands, who'd be christened Kipper Kid, and would arrive at games all decked out in miniature Kiprusoff gear, imitating the moves and saves his hero would be supplying in net that night.

Over the course of his Calgary career he'd establish all sorts of goaltending records for the club, smashing marks that had been set by Mike Vernon—including games played minutes played, wins, goals-against average, and shutouts.

Kipper could even take his brilliance outside. At the Heritage Classic played at McMahon Stadium in 2011 against the Montreal Canadiens, he was named first star in a 4–0 victory. Later that year he'd stop two penalty shots in the same game against Columbus, a real rarity in the NHL.

Miikka was a calm, relaxed, controlled guy, at least outwardly, and that translated into his unflappability on the ice, no matter how tense the situation. From a media standpoint, not the greatest interview, obviously.

Someone who very much wanted to be at the top of his profession but remain as under-the-radar as humanly possible.

In at least one of those ambitions he succeeded.

The man of few words we in the media dealt with was in direct contrast to the person his teammates remember, who by all accounts was very talkative on the ice, directing defencemen when the puck would enter the zone, forever yelling instructions or calling attention to situations.

Socially, we hear, a really funny guy to be around, too, always cracking jokes and firing off one-liners.

The 2012–13 season would be Kipper's last. He'd play only 23 games that year, shortened by a work stoppage. An 8–14–1 record in 24 games would be the only time he didn't post a winning record as a Flame.

I remember after a game in Nashville one night that year, being with him in the back of Tootsie's bar and him confiding in me that this would, in fact, be his final season. That was even though he had a year remaining on a six-year contract—the first time I can recall the Flames handing out what was a largely front-loaded deal, meaning the majority of the salary was owed him over the first few seasons of the agreement.

As I remember, he'd only have pulled in a little over $1 million U.S. had he stuck around to play out the contract.

Interest in his services remained high, though. There were indications the Toronto Maple Leafs had made overtures to the Flames to acquire the then 33-year-old, but he refused to waive his no-trade clause to allow a deal. The Leafs, we heard, had let him know through various sources that they were willing to offer him a contract extension if he'd agree to the trade.

But Kipper would not be swayed.

His final game at the Saddledome was typically him: A fantastic performance, named the game's first star and richly deserving of the accompanying standing ovation after a 32-save, 3–1 triumph over Anaheim.

In true Kiprusoff fashion, he didn't even attend his formal retirement announcement on September 9. Vintage Miikka.

He stayed around Calgary for a year before heading back to Finland, living in nearby DeWinton and watching and supporting his son play minor hockey. He'd catch up with his former teammates from time to time but other public appearances—including a reported celebration of his career at the Saddledome—never happened.

That was just the way the guy happened to be built.

The Bearcat

An added bonus to my gaining entry into the Alberta Sports Hall of Fame in the year of 2015 is that Jim "Bearcat" Murray was part of my induction class.

That's mighty good company.

The Bearcat and I became great friends over his long tenure as trainer of the Flames.

Eventually, he'd also be inducted into the Professional Hockey Athletic Trainers Society Hall of Fame.

No one has ever been more richly deserving.

Bearcat was already a legend in town before I ever met him, for his years with the Calgary Centennials and Wranglers junior teams as well as the Calgary Cowboys of the by-then defunct World Hockey Association.

A true character as well as a very effective trainer.

He certainly wasn't as formally educated as the athletic therapists teams now employ and wasn't privy to the high-tech kinds of equipment used today.

Bearcat was a self-taught guy, an incredibly hard worker. He looked after those players as if they were his own kids and even produced some remedies for me when I was plagued by colds or a sore throat.

When I needed treating to help me get through a broadcast, he always came through.

Bearcat became famous for cruising around concourses, hallways, and corridors on roller skates, getting a workout while the team practiced in foreign rinks. But he was on hand instantly should one of the players needed anything. He even inspired his own fan club, to my knowledge the only one for a trainer in any sport.

That craziness started when a bunch of hockey fans in Boston happened to be tuned in the night Bearcat waded into the crowd at Northlands Coliseum in Edmonton in search of his son, assistant trainer Al "Alleycat" Murray, who himself had gone off in search of a stick stolen from defenceman Gary Suter by Oilers fans.

Impressed by Bearcat's paternal instincts, they immediately adopted him as their hero and would meet at the Penalty Box Pub, kitty corner to the old Boston Garden.

The first time the Flames visited Beantown after the incident in Edmonton, these guys, well fuelled with liquid refreshments, showed up to the game outfitted in skull caps, moustaches, and fan club T-shirts in honour of the Cat.

Bear was stunned, as were we all. Flames TV host Grant Pollock of 2&7 followed the group, including Bearcat, after the game to relay the story back to Calgary.

Their appearance at Calgary-Boston games became something of a ritual for a number of years after that. Bear would always find time, if possible, to share a few brews with them in gratitude afterward. The fan club would from time to time travel, too, and show up unexpectedly at games in Montreal and other spots.

Bear also gained notoriety during a playoff game in 1989, rushing to the aid of fallen goaltender Mike Vernon. When Vernon went down, Bearcat hot-footed it onto the ice while the play was still going on. The Flames wound up scoring a goal in the confusion.

Turned out, Mike wasn't injured at all but he had to fake being hurt to bail himself, and Bearcat, out of what could've been a very serious jam. There was a lot of complaining by the Kings, Wayne Gretzky in particular, over Bearcat's presence and the goal. Los Angeles claimed the Flames should've been assessed a penalty for having too many "players" on the ice.

Away from the game, Bearcat and I became close friends. My long-time colour commentator Doug Barkley had been a pal of Bear's long before I arrived in Calgary, from his time coaching and playing in Calgary.

The three of us played a whole whack of charity golf tournaments together. I'd be willing to bet that Bearcat holds the worldwide record for participation in charity golf tourneys. Any given summer, he'd tee it up in 80 or 90 such events, although now in his early eighties, he's cut down on that number a little bit.

With both of us fighting receding hairlines, we became known as bookend buddies at those tournaments.

In fact, Flames equipment manager Bobby Stewart was in reality Bear's real bookend buddy. Those two gentlemen did an awful lot of work that went unnoticed by hockey fans in order for things to run smoothly behind the scenes.

I've always said the trainers and equipment people have the toughest job in the game.

They're at the arena long before the players arrive and long after the players leave, home game or on the road. When the team reaches a city, while the players, coaches, and media types head straight for the hotel and dinner afterward, they're off to the arena to hang up gear.

Even following late-night charters on, say, back-to-back games, they'd be trooping over to the rink until 3:00 or 4:00 in the morning and have to be back by 8:00 AM.

In addition to Bearcat, athletic therapists such as Terry Kane and Morris Boyer and equipment guys like Les Jarvis, Mark DePasquale, Corey Osmak, and Brian Patafie were such a great help to me over the years.

Those guys are the best.

Iron Mike

Of all the coaches to assume the reins down at the Saddledome, none had a finer résumé than Mike Keenan.

Terry Crisp would exit with a Stanley Cup title and two President's Trophies and Darryl Sutter would head south and collect two Stanley Cup rings while in command of the Los Angeles Kings after leaving the organization.

But only Keenan arrived already armed with a Stanley Cup, captured with the NY Rangers in 1994.

Among his other achievements he could count three additional trips to the Final and as many President's Trophies.

Mike had also piloted Canada to a pair of Canada Cups, in 1987 and 1991, had an American Hockey League championship to look back on, had a Canadian college title, and was the recipient of the Jack Adams Trophy as NHL coach of the year in 1984–85 with the Philadelphia Flyers.

He'd been away from coaching for three years before Darryl brought him to Calgary to assume command of his eighth NHL team. The connection there was Darryl having worked as an assistant to Mike in Chicago for a couple seasons in the 1990s.

Getting to know Mike during his tenure here, he was justifiably proud of his coaching record, particularly the Stanley Cup year in Manhattan, ending a 54-year Cup famine.

His reputation for working his No. 1 goalie a great deal preceded him and proved to be only too true. Miikka Kiprusoff would make 76 appearances in each year of Mike's reign. Mike was also legendary about being quick with the hook on his goalies and more than a few times received a real sour look from Kiprusoff after being yanked from games.

But that had always been Mike's way of operating.

Like all coaches, he had his moments. During his first year, for instance, the Flames lost the second-to-last game of the regular season, in Minnesota, missing out on a chance to clinch a playoff spot.

None too pleased, on the bus and the ensuing charter flight, Mike let his players know in no uncertain terms just how unhappy he was.

About halfway through a four-hour flight to Vancouver, though, he received information from the airline crew that Edmonton had lost its later start, and therefore the Flames were assured a postseason position.

Mike's mood changed instantly and he started high-fiving players and everyone else on the plane, the next night hosting a dinner for the travelling crew, including the flight crew and us broadcasters.

Mike's regular seasons—42 wins and 94 points, followed by 46 wins and 96 points—were certainly solid enough.

But after falling in the first round two years running, to San Jose in seven games and Chicago in six, respectively, he was relieved of his duties and eventually replaced by Brent Sutter.

Until now, though, he remains the last coach to propel the Flames into the postseason party in back-to-back springs. He would later go on to coach Metallurg Magnitogorsk to a Gagarin Cup, a Kontinental Hockey League championship trophy in Russia.

Craig Conroy

Craig Conroy was so valuable that three different Calgary Flames general managers have come after his services.

Al Coates tried unsuccessfully to pry him out of St. Louis in his final season as GM in 2000. Craig Button was able to secure him a year later in a trade. Then Darryl Sutter lost Conroy in 2005 but was able to retrieve him in 2007.

Craig's so valuable that he's still a member of the Flames organization, now in the role of assistant general manager.

A positive, talkative, smiling, upbeat guy, Craig was very popular with the media and fans during his playing days and I certainly had the opportunity to interview him a lot.

He always made himself available, whether it was after a win or a loss, and always provided good insights.

Such a fun guy and a great teammate.

It's difficult to believe that at his first NHL training camp in 1994, the very first day that he was on the ice with the team that drafted him, the Montreal Canadiens, he ended up in a fight with goaltending great Patrick Roy after Conroy took a snapshot at Patrick in practice. Certainly an interesting way to start things off.

He turned pro after four years of playing hockey at Clarkson University in his hometown of Potsdam, New York. He was a sixth-round draft pick in 1990, only playing in 13 games with the Canadiens before moving on to St. Louis, where he became a solid two-way centreman.

On one occasion, he was a finalist for the Selke Trophy as the top defensive forward. The Flames would get him in exchange for one of their top scorers, Cory Stillman, in a trade at the deadline in 2001, and in his first full season with the team, Conroy would become centreman for Jarome Iginla.

Ever-popular Craig Conroy meeting my daughter, Tricia, and granddaughter Haylee, then two and a half, after the team parade and Olympic Plaza rally following the 2004 run to the Stanley Cup Final.

Jarome responded by coming through with the first of his 50-goal seasons.

Craig was a finalist that season for the Selke Trophy as well, as he notched 27 goals and picked up 75 points.

He wore the C for the Flames for a time, sharing the captaincy with Bob Boughner in the 2001–02 season and then taking over as sole captain the next year before eventually relinquishing the role to Iginla at the beginning of the 2003–04 campaign.

Craig, never forget, was the Flames' second-leading scorer in that run to the Stanley Cup Final in the unforgettable spring of 2004.

However, it was during that off-season that he signed as a free agent with Los Angeles. I remember chatting with him at the time. It was clearly a very tough decision for him to make.

He liked the Flames and they liked him. However, with a work stoppage pending, the Kings offered a guaranteed contract, so Conroy accepted.

Sutter was able to get him back in January of 2007 when he sent Jamie Lundmark and two draft picks to L.A.

Craig made his first game back as a Flame memorable, scoring two goals against the Kings. Then, early in the 2010–11 season, I well remember the organization honouring his 1,000th NHL game played. He and his wife and family were on the ice at the Saddledome and received a standing ovation from the crowd.

At age 39, he became the second-oldest NHL player to play in his 1,000th game. But after being in and out of the Flames' lineup, he announced his retirement as a player on February 4, 2011. An emotional day.

The Flames valued him so much that they immediately named him a special assistant to general manager Jay Feaster. That proved to be, initially at least, a tough adjustment for Craig. I recall talking to him early on and he was noting how difficult it was for him to attend meetings with coaches and management personnel when they would be critical of some players. Of course, these players all had been teammates and pals of his right up until he got his new position.

Eventually he adjusted and in June of 2014 was named assistant general manager to Brad Treliving and continues in that role.

As a player, he won two team awards, the Ralph Scurfield Humanitarian and also the Bud McCaig Leadership Award.

I couldn't help but think if the Peter Maher Good Guy Award had been around when he played, Craig certainly would have won that on a few occasions given the relationship he had with the Calgary media.

Hartley-Feaster

Jay Feaster was general manager of the Flames between 2010 and 2013, and in that time he brought in a coach with a Stanley Cup pedigree from his past in Bob Hartley.

Jay came in as an assistant to Darryl Sutter and when Darryl was let go the former Tampa Bay GM was elevated to the top position.

He guided the organization through some very interesting times.

Jay, of course, was in command of the Lightning team that beat the Flames to the Stanley Cup by a nose, in seven games, in 2004.

His time in Calgary saw the trading of both Jarome Iginla and Jay Bouwmeester, two outstanding players, signalling the beginning of the team's rebuild.

Also on Jay's watch, Brian Burke arrived as president of hockey operations (Brian would assume the GM's role briefly after Jay was let go).

The drafts that Feaster oversaw included, in 2010, Micheal Ferland, currently on the Flames' top line; Sven Baertschi and Markus Grunland a year later, who were later dealt away to Vancouver and developed into NHL regulars; as well as, of course, Johnny Gaudreau.

In 2012, Jay's first draft pick, 21st overall, was quite controversial at the time. But Mark Jankowski, after playing four years of college hockey, has emerged now as an NHL player with a big upside.

Recently talking to Jay on the phone, he said he knew when Mark was drafted that it would take him time to develop. A rangy centreman now, Mark was actually quite small back then, playing high school hockey in Quebec. He needed to fill out, which he did, and develop his skills.

Jay said they saw the great potential in him.

Jay hired Bob Hartley to coach the Flames before the 2012–13 season.

They had a history together when Jay was working as manager and Bob was the coach at Hershey of the American Hockey League.

Eventually, Bob won a Calder Cup in the AHL in 1997 before being bumped up to take the reins in Colorado. He'd pilot the Avalanche to a Stanley Cup in 2001.

Following a five-year tenure in Denver that included four first-place divisional finishes, Bob was let go and moved on to coach the Atlanta Thrashers.

Prior to going pro, he'd enjoyed success coaching in Hawksbury, his hometown, in Tier II junior hockey, and then Laval of the Quebec major junior league before moving on to coach the Quebec Nordiques' AHL farm team in Cornwall, first as an assistant and then moving on to the top spot. He would then move on to Hershey when the Nords moved to Colorado and their farm team shifted, as well.

To this point, Hartley has the distinction of being the only Calgary Flames coach to win the Jack Adams Trophy as the NHL coach of the year, for his outstanding work in 2014–15.

He guided the Flames for four seasons, becoming the second-longest-tenured coach in franchise history in the process.

Bob Johnson holds the record, being at the helm for five years in the 1980s.

Hartley's teams usually started slowly and then improved as things went along. That was the case with the Flames in his first year, as they finished five games under the .500 mark. The next year it was five under .500 once again. But then the team really came on in the 2014–15 campaign, when they not only made the playoffs with a record 15 games over .500, but would also win the opening round of the playoffs against Vancouver.

They bowed out in the second round to Anaheim but it certainly was a surprise finish.

Unfortunately, they fell back the next year and after that season Bob was relieved of his duties.

During his time behind the Flames' bench, he saw the departure of some top players like Iginla and Bouwmeester, as well as Mike Cammalleri, but also was on hand for the arrival of Sean Monahan and Gaudreau.

Getting to know Bob, I found him to be extremely personable with the media. By then, he'd worked some on Quebec television and also with RDS as an analyst between coaching assignments.

He always had lot of time for us, very accessible, and he always would come up with a humorous line virtually every day. That made for good material for broadcasters and writers.

That outgoing personality seemed quite different from when he was in Colorado, at least from a visiting media standpoint.

In those days, when the Flames would play the Avalanche, he would be made available after morning skates and after games, but on all those occasions it would invariably turn out to be for a frustratingly short time.

So, much different by the time he reached Calgary and his training in the broadcast business certainly could've been a factor in his longer availability.

As a coach, Bob pushed his players to the max, from what I could gather, but that makes for a short shelf life sometimes for coaches, which is maybe why Bob didn't last longer with the Flames.

The Presidents

To this point in their history, the Flames have had four presidents/CEOs.

The man in the chair the longest is Ken King, who took over in 2001, now in his 17th year at the helm. Ken came in with a strong business background after a career in the newspaper business, as publisher of both the *Calgary Sun* and *Calgary Herald*, and was very familiar with the Calgary market and the Flames.

He took over at a time just after the franchise had undergone a couple of "Save the Flames" campaigns, and under King's guidance the team's fortunes improved. He brought in Jim Peplinski and Rollie Cyr, among others, on the sales end of the operation. Attendance got larger, and the season ticket base grew back to previous highs. Ken made an astute move in December of 2002, bringing in Darryl Sutter to coach, the team's fortunes improving a year and a half later with a trip to the Stanley Cup Final.

Attendance at the Saddledome began to pick up about midseason in 2003–04, and a string of sellout crowds of 19,289 began and ran for several years and has carried on through today.

Ken also presided over the Flames' purchase of the Canadian Football League's Calgary Stampeders and the National Lacrosse League's Calgary Roughnecks, bringing about the formation of the Calgary Sports and Entertainment Corporation.

The Flames' Foundation for Life and Charity wing increased its contributions into the $3 million to $4 million a year range under his charge.

Cliff Fletcher was the team's first president and also the only one to hold the dual role of president and general manager, holding both positions from the time the team arrived from Atlanta until he departed for Toronto to guide the Maple Leafs in 1991.

Bill Hay, who would later be inducted into the Hockey Hall of Fame as a builder, replaced Cliff. Bill had played eight years in the NHL back in the 1960s, winning the Calder Trophy as rookie of the year in 1960 and a year later helping the Chicago Blackhawks win the Stanley Cup, centring the "Million Dollar Line" of Hay, Bobby Hull, and Murray Balfour.

After retiring as a player, Bill built an impressive résumé in the oil patch, involved in business with Doc and B.J. Seaman, part of the Flames' ownership group. He was also very active with Hockey Canada, acting as president and CEO there as well as in various roles with the Hockey Hall of Fame from 1980 through until 2012.

Bill's tenure as CEO ended in 1995 and he oversaw the renovation of the Saddledome. A dedicated worker and a humorous guy to be around, filled with great stories of his Blackhawks days as a teammate of Hull, Stan Mikita, Glenn Hall, and company.

Ron Bremner succeeded Bill in 1996, arriving from Vancouver to take the reins of the Flames following a highly successful career in broadcasting sales and management. In 2000, he was inducted into the Canadian Broadcasting Hall of Fame.

A decreased Canadian dollar and a drop in season ticket sales during Ron's tenure in Calgary, combined with a drop in on-ice fortunes at a time when salaries were exploding in the NHL, made it extremely difficult for the team to be as competitive as everyone would've liked.

Ron later returned to Ontario where he now works in public speaking and mentoring high-profile Canadian executives.

Remembering Johnny

It was very sad news, hearing of the passing of legendary Toronto Maple Leafs goaltender Johnny Bower on December 26, 2017, at age 93 after a short battle with pneumonia.

That day, I recalled the time I'd spent in Johnny's company. He'd long retired before I started broadcasting NHL games, of course, but I got to know him a little bit during the three years I called Maple Leafs games. He was working in a scouting capacity with the team then.

I had coffee with him a few times at the old Gardens coffee shop and found him to be a most generous, amiable guy. He offered me great insight into the game and during my early years could be considered a great mentor, helping me meet many people in the NHL world.

As a kid, I was a goalie and a Leafs fan so, naturally, Johnny was one of my idols. Watching him play without a mask and winning those four Stanley Cups was pretty impressive.

In 1980, I almost got a chance to call a game he played in. The Leafs' two regular goalkeepers, Mike Palmateer and Paul Harrison, were sick and the team wasn't sure if replacement callup Vincent Tremblay would make it in in time for the game. So, Johnny—55 years old at the time— was hurriedly signed to a one-day contract, just in case.

Tremblay, as it turned out, made it in time to suit up and I missed my chance.

But Johnny was willing to play in a pinch.

An inspiration to anyone who knew or met him.

CHAPTER 3
THE MOMENTS AND THE MEMORIES

The Only Bet

The only time I ever bet on a hockey game was back on May 15, 1979, Game 2 of that year's Stanley Cup Final and my first opportunity to cover one. The Montreal Canadiens were playing the New York Rangers.

The Rangers had won the first game at the old Montreal Forum 6–2. Not a very good night for Canadiens goaltender Ken Dryden.

As usual, a bunch of media types gathered at the old Winston Churchill pub in Montreal for a few cold ones on the off day between games. During the course of the evening, I got into a conversation with former broadcaster Dan Kelly. The subject of who would start in goal for Montreal in Game 2 came up.

I said the Habs would stick with Dryden, he said Montreal's backup, Michel "Bunny" Larocque, would get the call.

We made a $10 bet.

What I didn't know is that before Dan arrived at the pub, he'd been out for dinner with Canadiens coach Scotty Bowman. Bowman had told him confidentially that Larocque would start.

The next night, Larocque was indeed scheduled to start. But during the pregame warmup, he took a shot in the throat from Doug Risebrough and was unable to play. So Dryden started.

After the game, I went to collect my $10 since Dryden had, indeed, started.

Dan jokingly refused to pay, insisting Larocque was supposed to be the starting goaltender.

(As an aside, the Canadiens won that night and would sweep the next three to claim the Cup.)

As fate would have it, a number of years later Dan was in Moncton, New Brunswick, for a charity golf tournament as guest speaker. I was the master of ceremonies.

After dinner, during his address, he mentioned our long-ago bet and asked the crowd—a New Brunswick crowd, my home province—who they thought had actually won the wager.

The reaction was, of course, overwhelmingly in my favour. So Dan came over and presented me with my $10.

I bought a number of drinks later on for Dan, so it didn't take long for that $10 to evaporate.

The next year, I heard the news that he was battling lung cancer. When the Flames were in St. Louis for a game I went to visit him in the hospital, only two or three weeks before he passed away. I'll never forget him asking me, "Do you know anyone who smokes? Tell them to stop. That's why I'm here and in the condition I'm in."

From then on, I made sure that whenever I was in the company with a friend who smoked, I'd deliver Dan's message.

Dan Kelly, a great guy and an outstanding broadcaster.

First Game at the Dome

The night of October 15, 1983.

The first game to be played at the then Olympic Saddledome. The atmosphere was absolutely electric.

The Flames had started their season with three games on the road and it was only fitting that the Edmonton Oilers would provide the opposition.

A thrilling night and a real change of pace after three years of the claustrophobic confines of the Corral, just across the street. Nice, roomy press box to work in. The dressing rooms seemed cavernous after the cramped quarters in the 33-year-old Corral. Big-league scoreclock.

At the time it opened, the Dome was absolutely state of the art. One of the finest facilities anywhere in North America.

The Corral had been very intimate and the Flames had enjoyed no small measure of success in there, but the trappings of the team's new $97.7 million home were impossible to ignore (that's $216 million when adjusted to today's dollar).

Reggie Lemelin started in goal for the Flames, Grant Fuhr for the Oilers. Kent Nilsson, the Magic Man, didn't play that night because of a back injury sustained in Minnesota three nights earlier.

Prime minister Pierre Elliott Trudeau, to a resounding chorus of boos, handled the opening faceoff duties.

The Oilers, about to embark on a run of four Stanley Cups in five years, would prevail 4–3. But all in all, still a thrilling night.

The first goal in the new building came via the Oilers' Finnish future Hall of Fame sniper Jari Kurri, with Wayne Gretzky and Paul Coffey picking up the assists at 1:51.

Arguably the most popular Flame ever, Lanny McDonald, holds the distinction of netting the first home goal at the Dome.

Gretzky's first snipe in the new building occurred early in the second period. It was already No. 99's seventh goal of the season, playing in only his fourth game.

The flow of play was disrupted numerous times, I remember, due to Plexiglass issues, the glass either shattering or breaking loose.

Colour commentator Doug Barkley and I had to fill a lot of open air time due to the stoppages.

Attendance was 16,605 owing to the upper loge area not being open that night, or indeed for most of the first season. When the Winter Olympics arrived in 1988, capacity in the building swelled to over 20,000.

And tickets, to no one's surprise, proved virtually impossible to find.

Hallowed Ground

There are certain arenas and buildings that possess a sort of indefinable, magical quality.

The old Montreal Forum tops them all.

Being born and growing up in New Brunswick, the Canadiens always held that magical allure to me. Those famous names. The history. All the banners hanging from the rafters.

The Canadiens weren't actually my team—I cheered for the Toronto Maple Leafs—but there was something regal, majestic about them and the way they played.

I saw my first NHL game live at the old Forum after the eight-hour train ride from my hometown to Montreal. My dad and I.

Rocket Richard, in the twilight of his Hall of Fame career, scored a goal that night. A special moment, for sure.

As I got older, friends and I took several weekend pilgrimages to the big city, departing Friday evening, game Saturday night, and the train home Sunday morning.

A lot of things don't live up to expectations. The atmosphere at the Forum did. We'd head off to Toe Blake's Tavern for a beer or two before games, which only added to the experience.

So many memories of that place. Being on hand in 1976 for the final game of the Canada Cup, Darryl Sittler's goal winning the tournament for Canada against the Czechs. Or broadcasting my first game there on my 29th birthday and getting to see, for the first time, behind the scenes at the Forum with Danny Gallivan acting as tour guide, no less.

That was the first time I met Scotty Bowman. Beside us up in the press box, Danny and Dick Irvin were doing their broadcast and beside them Rene Lecavalier, the French-language play-by-play man, someone else I'd listened to growing up.

Rubbing shoulders with those fellows was a thrill, let me tell you.

The broadcast location in the Forum was one of the good ones in those days, with one caveat, at least for me. It was one of the few buildings where I had to stand up to call the game, in order to see the entire ice surface.

Any time in Montreal for a game was a special event, though.

Fitting, then, that the Flames would lift their only Stanley Cup on May 25, 1989.

So when the announcement arrived that the Canadiens would vacate the Forum and move to the Bell Centre to open the 1996–97 season, I felt a wave of sadness and nostalgia. As I'm sure millions of other hockey fans did, too.

The march of time stops for no one, for nothing, of course, but this one really stung.

In the fall of 2011, the Flames, in Montreal to play at the Bell Centre, had a rare complete day off. So I decided to step back in time, walking from the hotel over to the Forum on Atwater Street and taking a real tour of the area I'd grown to know so well over the years.

The building from the outside hadn't changed much but inside there were stores, theatres. I was happy to find the famous hockey stick–themed escalators from the old days were still in commission, though, moving people from floor to floor.

An exhibit to commemorate had also been installed as you entered the building, with seats from the old Forum.

A great trip down memory lane.

Dick Irvin and Golf

Dick Irvin is one of the greatest hosts, colour commentators, and historians the game in general, and *Hockey Night in Canada* in particular, has ever known.

What I didn't know until I started my NHL play-by-play career was that Dick was play-by-play voice of the Montreal Canadiens on a local Montreal radio station when not involved in TV broadcasts.

I only got to know Dick well when he became an annual visitor to the Flames' charity golf tournament—one of, if not the, first big-time events of the kind in and around Calgary.

To this day that tournament continues, growing and growing, part of the proceeds being allocated to the Flames Foundation for Life, which annually donates millions of dollars to local charities.

Candice Goudie and her staff do an outstanding job there, going about the business of raising an enormous amount of money for those charitable endeavours.

The golf tournament has been an annual tradition for 37 years. Bill Creighton of Canyon Meadows Golf Club and Al Coates, then heading up the PR and media relations arm of the Flames, came up with the idea for the event and nurtured it through its first two decades.

The tournament always took place a day or two before the opening of training camp and involved current and former players and coaches in a Texas Scramble format.

It's now expanded to 36 holes at Country Hills and 18 holes at the Hamptons.

The night before tee-off, a draft is staged for teams to select a Flame player.

Dick and Red Storey would annually arrive to be after-golf speakers. The day before, Dick and Red partnered with me and colour man Doug Barkley, respectively, for a personal 18-hole match at Canyon Meadows.

As time went on, I'd often meet up with Dick in either Montreal or Calgary. We worked together on the NHL Broadcaster's Association for a number of years.

Such a good mentor for me in the early years of my career. I was honoured that Dick attended when I went into the Hockey Hall of Fame's media wing in 2006.

He, of course, had been presented with the same Foster Hewitt Award many years before that.

I certainly owe the Flames' charity golf tournament for initiating, and strengthening, my friendship with Dick Irvin.

The 1985–86 Regular Season

Even given the customary ups and downs, oddities, and crazy happenings of any long, gruelling NHL campaign, the 1985–86 regular season certainly produced more than its fair share of peculiarities.

For starters, the team suffered through a franchise-worst 11-game losing streak, a record that stands to this day.

Then there was the game of goaltending Snakes & Ladders.

The guy who started the season as No. 3, Mike Vernon, would, by the opening of the postseason, have elevated himself to the role of starter.

Reggie Lemelin opened as the consensus No. 1 between the wickets and the man pencilled in by most to be his successor, the future of the organization at the most critical position, Marc D'Amour, experienced dehydration issues causing cramps during games and would ultimately tumble down the depth chart and out of the organization.

All kinds of crazy goings-on.

One night Lemelin had his goal stick measured—a rare occurrence— during the course of a game against the Winnipeg Jets to ascertain if it did, in fact, conform to league standards. On February 9, at the Fabulous Forum in L.A., the Flames went on a power play rampage, scoring three times in the span of 48 seconds during the third period to establish a club record, counting six on the PP in total, tying a franchise high.

There were injuries to key personnel, triggering a series of influential acquisitions by general manager Cliff Fletcher: Sniper Joey Mullen from St. Louis, adding old Oilers killer John Tonelli from the New York Islanders, and enforcer Nick Fotiu from the New York Rangers.

Fotiu was certainly an interesting guy, one of the toughest players of his era. His physical presence and reputation turned out to be a largely unheralded but quietly important factor in the unexpected run to the Final.

After Nick left the Flames and later retired, working as an assistant coach, I remember meeting him one day and he told me, kind of half-jokingly, "Well, you couldn't beat the Oilers until I got there, we beat 'em, then I left, and you haven't beaten 'em since."

Bringing in the all-energy Tonelli certainly helped, too, given his vast experience and familiarity with winning, collecting four Stanley Cup rings as a vital component of the Islanders' dynasty.

That 11-game losing streak I spoke of began, oddly enough, immediately following a shutout victory, 4–0 over Los Angeles, with Lemelin in net. The next game, on December 14, began a run of frustration that would stretch until January 7.

Five of the first six games of that string were one-goal losses; in the middle of it, the team was committed to an exhibition game against touring Moscow Dynamo.

To plug in that night, Vernon was called up from Moncton, home of the American League farm team. They'd beat the Russian touring team, but the euphoria was short-lived; it didn't help improve their NHL form any.

The stretch culminated with an embarrassing 9–1 loss at the Saddledome to the Hartford Whalers, the worst beating they'd absorbed.

Desperate to change their luck, the team turned to Vernon again and he'd be the goaltender of record on January 9, versus the Vancouver Canucks on home ice, the game that would end the agony.

Nothing, obviously, was coming easy at that point, and the Flames were forced to go to overtime before prevailing, 5–4.

The number 13 is supposedly unlucky, but Jim Peplinski scored his 13th goal of the season at the 13-second mark of overtime.

The idyll was temporary, though, and after losing two of the next three, Vernon would be shipped back to the minors. The veteran Lemelin then going on a hot streak, the club lost only one game of its next seven.

A significant moment for what was to come that season and the future fortunes of the franchise, that really didn't have any significance with regards to standings, was the second-to-last date of the regular season against the mighty Oilers at the Dome.

Calgary hadn't managed to beat the Stanley Cup champs all year. But that night, the Flames breezed past their provincial rivals 9–3 and it had to serve as a mammoth boost from a mental standpoint for the second round of the playoffs, when they would face the Oilers.

Gary Suter, the Flames' young defender, set a team record by ringing up four assists in one period and he also tied a club record with six in the game.

Battle Lines Drawn

Among the many great instalments of the Battle of Alberta I was lucky enough to call, one stands out in particular: The playoff series in 1986.

The Oilers, of course, had Gretzky, Coffey, Fuhr, Kurri, and Messier, for starters.

A powerhouse. Unbeatable, in the minds of most.

Coming off back-to-back Stanley Cups, they'd won the President's Trophy, finishing with 119 points, 30 more than the Flames.

As everyone remembers, that series went the distance and was decided by one goal.

That goal.

The Steve Smith goal.

The game couldn't have been tighter, 2–2 heading into the third period. The fans at Northlands Coliseum were growing increasingly uneasy, as the Oilers were unable to put their arch-rivals away.

Then, out of nothing, nowhere, the break the Flames needed. Winger Perry Berezan actually shot the puck into the corner in the Oilers' zone and headed to the bench.

Oilers rookie defenceman Smith then inadvertently banked a diagonal pass attempt off goaltender Grant Fuhr's left leg and into the Edmonton net.

It was crazy. Time seemed to stop.

Perry was stunned. The Flames were stunned. The crowd was stunned. The Oilers were stunned. I was stunned.

The image remains etched in memory: Smith, on his knees, head down, inconsolable.

Looking back, perhaps that was the best way for the Flames to score the go-ahead goal, considering there were nearly 15 minutes left to go, because there was no huge celebration.

It was such a freak occurrence.

I'll always remember the end of that game, with four seconds left and the faceoff in the Flames' zone. The tension in the building was off the charts.

The Oilers actually won the draw but the ensuing shot went wide of the net. Let the celebration begin.

That marked, in fact, the first time I would yell out, "Yeah baby!" which would become my play-by-play calling card.

That series teemed with fascinating battles.

I even found myself embroiled in a minor one after Game 4 in Calgary.

On the morning of Game 5, back up north, I was standing in the area outside the Oilers' dressing room as they trooped off the ice after their morning skate. I was looking for a player for a pre-recorded interview.

Five or six Oilers went by and all of them gave me a rejection slip.

In fact, few of them would even speak to me.

When I sought an explanation, Bill Tuele, then director of media relations for the Oilers, told me, "We're not talking to you today."

I asked why.

He said: "Well, the other night when we were playing you were calling Wayne a whiner." Confused, I said, "I beg your pardon?"

Bill told me that they had it from "good sources" that I'd been using that term during the broadcast. I hadn't. I never would.

I said, "Look, to clear this up, if you'd like I'll get you a tape recording of that game and you can listen to it. That term may have been yelled by many fans in the stands that night at the Saddledome, but it certainly didn't come from me or anyone on our broadcast."

So he got me Charlie Huddy to interview but I still had to get things settled with Wayne.

He emerged from the room and I said, "I understand you have a problem with something that was perceived that I said during the broadcast of the game the other night. If you'd like, I'll send Bill a tape of the game, he can listen to it and let you know that I didn't say anything like that about you. I've always admired your play..." And so on.

"Yeah, we heard that you said that," Wayne said. "It wasn't quite believable because I'd heard broadcasts of your games sometimes when I'm driving around Edmonton on a night when the Flames are playing and I find you a very fair broadcaster. So it was kind of shocking for me to hear."

I assured him I felt I was fair and repeated the offer to send the tape. That ended that discussion and we never had another problem.

I always found Wayne good to deal with. In fact, he'd break Oilers' rules to do an interview with media people he respected.

He'd always remember my name—even when he went to Los Angeles, I'd see him and it was always "Hi, Peter." Even later on, as a coach with the Phoenix Coyotes, he'd go out of his way to engage in conversation.

I've always felt Wayne was the most talented player ever to grace the NHL and I consider him as graceful off the ice as on it.

Beating the Blues in 1986

In sitting down and analyzing the 1986 Stanley Cup Final loss to Montreal, I keep coming back to the semifinal series against the St. Louis Blues.

I'm certainly not alone in that regard.

The Flames would dearly regret a missed opportunity to eliminate the Blues in Game 6 and give themselves a bit of a breather before tackling the Habs and their arsenal of tradition.

And the whole thing was so avoidable.

Scroll back to May 12, 1986: Calgary is cruising in St. Louis, leading 5–2 with only 13 minutes left, and a ticket to the Final assured.

At least, apparently.

So when future Calgary coach Brian Sutter scores to whittle the Blues' deficit to two, no one seems to pay it much heed.

But then, unbelievably, Greg Paslawski counts back-to-back goals, the second with 68 seconds to play, sending the game in OT.

The Flames are reeling.

Almost as if it were fated, Blues centreman Doug Wickenheiser then scores against Mike Vernon 7:30 into overtime to bring the Blues all the way back from the abyss and force a tension-filled Game 7 back at the Saddledome.

Bob Johnson's crew would prevail in that deciding clash 2–1, but the extra game unnecessarily required to eliminate the Blues, coupled with a ridiculously short time between the opening of that Final against Montreal—all of one, yes, *one*, day—conspired against the Flames.

Such a short break before a Final would never be permitted today.

A couple of other things stand out for me from that Blues series. First, Mr. Goalie, Glenn Hall, then worked for the Flames as a goaltending coach. He'd spent the final four seasons of his Hall of Fame career in St. Louis, of course, when the Blues were an expansion franchise trying to find its footing.

Thanks in major part to the puck-stopping prowess of a pair of legends, Glenn and Jacques Plante, the Blues reached back-to-back Stanley Cup Finals in 1969 and '70.

So Glenn had wonderful memories of his time in STL.

And he was extremely unhappy with the way the old building was—or more accurately wasn't—being kept up by the owner of the Blues at the time, Harry Ornest.

Glenn couldn't believe the lack of paint and all the garbage around the old building and certainly made his feelings known to everyone within earshot, including Harry himself.

I also remember Blues GM Ron Caron, a very boisterous guy, had a seat next to our broadcast location. His booth had an open window and often the air was blue with Caron's rage, either yelling at a member of the Flames or at an official who he felt missed a call.

Being right next door, my colour commentator Doug Barkley and I had to constantly keep talking so that none of the four-letter words would escape over the broadcast air.

Ron would also hammer on the desk and that would reverberate into our booth, shaking everything.

If Ron had a tendency to vent his frustration during games, then in the aftermath of the Game 7 disappointment, owner Ornest could best be described as downright livid.

Seems he had had chartered an aircraft to take his triumphant team out east to Montreal to begin the Stanley Cup Final.

Well, he wasn't in a particularly jolly mood after losing at the Dome and having his plans so rudely scuttled. So he promptly cancelled the charter, having made no contingencies for them to return to St. Louis, and left players to scrounge around and find their own commercial flights back home the next day.

Brian Sutter, I'm told, was one of the key guys in making those arrangements and actually spent some of his own money, with his own credit card, to get some of the guys back to St. Louis.

That's only a small part of why Brian was considered one of the great captains of any era.

The 1986 Stanley Cup Final

One day. Twenty-four hours. That's all the time the Flames had, as I mentioned, to regroup between winning the Campbell Conference Final against the St. Louis Blues and starting their first bid to lift the Stanley Cup.

Against the Montreal Canadiens, armed with all that history.

One day of grace. It seems impossible now.

And I believe such a ridiculously tiny window of rest and preparation time played a large part in the outcome of that series.

The Flames started strongly, winning Game 1 at the Saddledome 5–2 but the tide shifted in Game 2. Trailing 2–0 early in the second period, the Canadiens fought back to tie it 2–2 and force overtime.

Then came the backbreaker, one of those goals that turns the tide of a series: Brian Skrudland of the Habs scoring nine seconds into OT—the fastest goal in overtime history.

Right off the opening faceoff.

So instead of 2–0 Calgary, the Canadiens had only a foothold heading back to Montreal.

Any time I'd see Brian after that, and particularly when he was traded to the Flames later on his career, one or the other of us would mention that goal.

Understandably, he didn't want to talk about it too much in public in Calgary.

The Canadiens seized their advantage after Skrudland's dramatic goal, taking Games 3 and 4 at the Forum, 5–3 and 1–0. Back in Calgary for the fifth game, the chance to clinch the series and hoist the Stanley Cup for the 23rd time, they roared out to a 4–1 lead and took that apparently insurmountable advantage into the third period.

But—and this is the thing I'll never forget about that series—somehow the Flames clawed back on goals by Steve Bozek and Joey Mullen in the final four minutes and then pressed like crazy over the final 43 seconds to tie the game, send it to overtime, and maybe extend the series.

But it was not to be.

What continues to stick with me is the reaction of fans at the Dome, though. They had to be deeply disappointed but they were great, cheering the Canadiens as they celebrated. And even more amazing, those 19,000-plus fans serenaded their team off the ice, chanting "Thank you, Flames! Thank you, Flames!"

An interesting sidelight: That summer Flames GM Cliff Fletcher campaigned the NHL, hard, to guarantee teams at least two days off between the conference finals and Stanley Cup Final.

He made his point. A lot of people around the NHL referred to it as The Cliff Fletcher Rule.

The Other Rival

While games against the Edmonton Oilers were the ones circled on everyone's calendars in those days, the mid-1980s produced another memorable rival for the Flames: The Winnipeg Jets.

The Jets had a pretty good team in those days, but weren't quite in the same class as the Flames or Oilers.

Nonetheless, the matchup—they played each other a lot, both being in the Smythe Division—produced some hammer-and-tong battles.

How could it be any other way? Gentle John Ferguson, one of the toughest, give-no-quarter people in the game's history, was Winnipeg's GM at the time.

Fergie certainly wasn't one to hide his emotions. At the old Winnipeg Arena, John had his regular spot in the media area right next to the visiting broadcast booth.

He was, let's say, a very rambunctious guy up there. You could hear him through the walls, yelling and screaming at officials and players. When things weren't going good he'd bang the wall so hard our whole room shook.

I can only imagine what listeners thought was going on.

But that was John, very much someone who took everything very much to heart and an incredibly strong competitor.

I remember his playing days in Montreal, watching those games on television and how hard he battled. He fought everyone, was justifiably considered the heavyweight champ of the NHL on those highly successful Canadiens teams back in the 1960s.

As a manager, Gentle John was no less intense.

On one trip into the Manitoba capital before the morning of the game, Fergie had instructed all his personnel, players, coaching staff, et al, not to talk to anybody in the media from Calgary, figuring that this was a way that could change the outcome of the game.

I recall going into the Jets' dressing room, not being able to talk to anybody and then seeing the coach at the time, Barry Long. "I understand you can't talk to any of the people from Calgary today," I teased Barry, "but I'd really like to get an interview for our pregame show." So Barry—a very genial guy—graciously allowed me to interview him. We started the interview, had gotten three or four minutes into it, just about ready to wrap up, when Fergie came by and he saw the two of us chatting.

He was not pleased, gave us a bit of a look. A pretty good signal for me to wrap things up.

That night, the Flames went out and won. Later on, Barry and I would have a pretty good laugh but I thanked him for doing what he did on that particular day.

Unfortunately, Barry Long was fired late in the 1985–86 regular season. As fate would have it, the Flames faced the Jets—sweeping them in three straight—in the opening round of playoffs.

Their coach by then? Fergie.

During his time in Winnipeg, John never really spoke too much to me. I was from Calgary and he, of course, was the Jets' guy.

Nothing personal. That was the competitor in him. He had only one allegiance: To his team.

So I was a bit surprised on one particular occasion when he stopped me prior to the start of a game to shake my hand. He said, "You know, I've seen you many, many times but I've never really had the opportunity to hear your broadcast. But I happened to be watching one of the Maple Leafs games that you were doing the play-by-play for and I was very, very impressed with your work. You're an outstanding broadcaster."

In my mind, the highest of compliments, coming from Fergie.

Champions

My recollections of the touchstone moment the Flames lifted the Stanley Cup actually begin two nights before the clincher, following Game 5 at the Saddledome in a 3–2 victory that had left them just one win from the ultimate prize.

After finishing up in the dressing room postgame, GM Cliff Fletcher came by accidentally-on-purpose and reminded me to make sure Doug Barkley, my long-time colour commentator, and I made absolutely sure we were on the bus heading to the Forum for Game 6.

The reason?

Superstition.

Neither Doug nor I had been on the bus for Game 3 in Montreal, a 4–3 loss in double-overtime.

Cliff didn't want to leave anything to chance.

With that in mind, and certainly not wanting to incur Cliff's wrath, I took the red-eye flight that went from Calgary to Toronto and then on to Montreal—I had stayed behind to go to my son's graduation—to get in at 10:00 in the morning.

I wasn't going to miss that bus.

The media hotel located in downtown Montreal back then was the Sheraton, away from the players, so Doug and I taxied over to the team hotel and got on the bus.

But—and this is where superstition really kicks in—Ian McKenzie, the chief scout who didn't travel much with the team throughout the year, was in my accustomed seat, third row on the aisle, door side.

I politely mentioned to Ian—unfamiliar with protocol—that he'd taken my seat. Could he please move? Well, he pointed to another seat both in the row behind and the row in front. I told him I *had* to sit in that particular seat but couldn't tell him why, because if you divulge the superstition it can sometimes sabotage the good you're trying to do.

After some badgering, I was finally able to convince a perplexed Ian to get up from the seat he was, I must say, quite comfortable in.

When we arrived at the Forum, the players, management, and Doug all went directly inside. I, on the other hand, snuck across the street to a mall that had a liquor store and purchased three small bottles of champagne so that in the event of a Flames win, Doug, myself, and my brother Noonan, who had come in from New Brunswick for the game, could have a little sip of the bubbly in the broadcast booth to celebrate.

I'll admit that it kind of counteracted the other superstitions we'd been so keen to adhere to, but I made the purchase anyway and stowed the bottles in my attaché case.

After Doug Gilmour had scored the empty-net goal to make it a 4–2 game and clinched the Cup, I hollered my "Yeah baby!"s and then brought out the champagne. While Doug and I chatted in the post-game segment, my brother opened the bottles and we had a bit of the bubbly.

After that, Doug stayed up in the booth, my brother and I went down to the dressing room. Noonan's job was to snare Flames players and other team personnel and bring them out in the hallway, where we had a live microphone and would be conducting interviews.

Noonan was very diligent in getting me guests to talk to and his reward was being able to drink out of the Stanley Cup before I did!

At one point I threw the broadcast back to Doug and as I was listening in he had the usual script in front of him and said, out of habit, "Now it's time for the out-of-town scoreboard…"

But, of course, there were no other games.

We had a bit of a laugh about that.

What was kind of interesting is during that summer, at the NHL draft, they showed the video highlights of the 1988–89 season, and when they were showing the Flames' post-Cup-clinching celebrations, there was Noonan in the background. He managed to get himself into three shots.

After finishing our interviews and wrapping things up, we got onto the team bus and the players realized they didn't have any beer for the trip from the Forum to the airport, which was quite a drive, 45 minutes to an hour.

I remember when the bus pulled out, Joe Nieuwendyk's mother was out there, directing traffic so that cars would stop and allow the bus to get out.

We went down St. Catherine's Street, maybe two or three blocks, and then pulled off to the side once again and Ric Nattress and a couple of other players went into a tavern and came back lugging cases of beer.

On the charter flight home, no end of excitement, as you'd imagine.

General manager Cliff Fletcher had arranged for the wives and girlfriends to be in Montreal in case the Flames won, so they could be part of the celebration.

At the beginning of the flight, the Cup was nowhere to be found. Somehow, it had been stored in the baggage compartment.

To the rescue, assistant trainer Al Murray, son of Bearcat. Alley Cat, as he was called, figured out a way to get down into the compartment and retrieve what everyone was clamouring for.

That was the first time I had the opportunity to drink from the Stanley Cup. And the sensation lived up to expectations.

The party went on, unabated, but after a third beer, I went to the front of the plane, signalling the end of my celebration. I'd committed to being part of CTV's *Canada AM* show, a live hit from the Saddledome that would take place at 5:00 in the morning Calgary time, so I wanted to be in full command of my faculties.

As the plane landed, I immediately trooped down to the Dome and went on live, and then caught up with the rest of the crew at Honey's Bar in downtown Calgary.

A moment with the Cup in 1989: (clockwise) Broadcast partner Doug Barkley, sports psychologist Max Offenberger, then Flames assistant to the president Al Coates, Dan Kennelly, yours truly, and coach Terry Crisp.

I was well behind them when it came to the drinking. But if recollection serves me well, I think I caught up to them a little while later.

On Saturday, the city held a parade for the Stanley Cup champions and I had the good fortune of being master of ceremonies for the reception at Olympic Plaza, introducing the players to thousands of Calgarians who had gathered to salute this amazing collection of athletes.

It culminated four days of unprecedented excitement.

The Friendship Tour

The very first time I covered NHL games overseas was in September of 1989, months after the Flames had captured the Stanley Cup.

The initiative, called The Friendship Tour, also included the Washington Capitals, and had been planned well in advance of the Final. But it certainly didn't hurt having the champions involved.

The Flames began the junket in Czechoslovakia for two dates and then moved on to play four games in the Soviet Union. Back before everything changed.

There were no play-by-play broadcasts of games, but I did get to make the trip and send back reports.

One thing immediately stood out for me—lots of people were heavy-duty smokers. For a non-smoker like myself, this presented a bit of a problem, dealing with the clouds of smoke that seemed to be everywhere.

On the first leg of the tour, interest centred around Flames forward Jiri Hrdina, who'd been a great star in Czechoslovakia before shifting to the NHL in 1988. While we were in Prague, I vividly recall Jiri hosting a dinner for everyone in our travelling party at one of the top restaurants in the capital, a night to be remembered. Prague is a very pretty city, a joy to walk in. Many sights, lots of water. There were also bullet holes in some buildings, reminders of past conflicts.

The first two games were against the Czech national team and the Flames lost both, 4–1 and 4–2. An interesting sidelight in the second game was the call-up of three young players by the Czechs—Robert Reichel, a Calgary draftee, an undrafted Jaromir Jagr, and Bobby Holik, another future long-time NHLer.

Jagr would register an assist in the second game. After he arrived in Calgary for his brief stint as a Flame in the 2017–18 season, I asked him about that long-ago chance, his first against NHL competition, and he still held fond memories of the game. The big things that stood out for him were the size of the opposition and Flames enforcer Tim Hunter, a big, scary guy to play against in Jagr's recollection.

Another of the Czech players of that time was Leo Gudas, a big, tough defenceman whose often questionable tactics drew the ire of the Flames. His son Radko would go on to play in the NHL, currently with the Philadelphia Flyers.

After their time in the Czech Republic, the Flames moved on to the Soviet Union for four games against club teams, including Central Red Army.

The biggest draw was undeniably Sergei Makarov. He'd been a megastar with both Red Army and the USSR national team for a decade, of course, and been released by the Soviet Hockey Federation to play for the Flames that summer.

Sergei's presence always drew a crowd. Military officers at the various buildings we'd visit would salute him out of respect and recognition and yell out his name in the streets, as did fans. That was enlightening, to see how popular he was in his home country.

I remember cobblestone streets in the various cities we visited, a lot of churches, and a lot of castles. Going around on the bus, we'd see people out on the streets shovelling coal into buildings, an eye-opener for us North Americans. Our group did a lot of bartering on the streets

A fun moment with Jim Peplinski and a military guard during sightseeing portion of Friendship Tour to Czechoslovakia and Soviet Union in September 1989.

for distinctly Russian items, offering pins and such, which was fun and novel for us.

A big concern was the food. Sometimes we'd wonder what was being put in front of us but none of our group ever had any serious ailments. The team, of course, had brought a whole bunch of food on its own, just in case.

The hotels the team stayed in at that time were certainly not up to North American standards. The walls, I recall, were almost paper thin. My room in Moscow was next door to one being shared by Brad McCrimmon and another player. When I'd do my reports back to

Calgary over the phone, they could hear me through the walls. Given the time difference, I'd be doing the afternoon report early in the morning and vice-versa.

Before getting on the elevator to reach your room, you had to pass through security, and when you got off it, someone would be waiting to double-check that you should be there. Some of the guys wondered whether or not they were being monitored by cameras and that sort of thing. So there were all sorts of little intrigues going on.

The Flames would play, and win, a game in Leningrad (since renamed St. Petersberg) before moving on play in Kiev, where they also won, 5–2. Then it was off to Moscow for a pair of games, both played in the Luzhniki Sports Palace, site of Paul Henderson's unforgettable series-winning goal for Canada against the Russians during the 1972 Summit Series. An iconic arena in Moscow, and certainly an interesting stop on the trip.

The final game before heading home came against Red Army, losing 2–1 to the perennial Soviet champions.

The First to Know

During my time as a play-by-play broadcaster, only two players called me to notify me that they'd been traded before an announcement was formally made.

One of them with massive repercussions for the organization.

It's very unusual for any player to let any member of the media know ahead of the organizational announcement, but I had a special relationship with the two guys who did phone me.

One of them was Perry Berezan, when he was offloaded to Minnesota in 1989. The other was Doug Gilmour, key component to the 1989 Cup team, when he was dealt away in 1992 to the Toronto Maple Leafs.

Perry was a member of the 1988–89 Flames team that would make history. He confided in me about a week or so before he was shipped out that he'd approached GM Cliff Fletcher very quietly, asking if he would deal him to another team.

Perry was frustrated over a lack of playing time on a powerhouse team that sat atop the NHL standings.

So Cliff eventually was able to engineer a trade with the North Stars to acquire winger Brian MacLellan—now general manager of the Washington Capitals.

I was at the radio station and was just preparing to go on for the afternoon sports run when Perry called to give me the news first.

Given that he himself initiated the move, you have to wonder now if he had second thoughts about asking for the trade. He'd ultimately get to play in the Stanley Cup Final with the North Stars when they played Pittsburgh, only to lose that series in 1991.

I gave him a good-luck call just as that Final was getting underway that year. I guess it didn't do the trick.

In Doug Gilmour's situation, I received a call in the morning on the second day of 1992, although I'd known for a couple of weeks that he was far from happy, as sometimes happens after a salary arbitration hearing.

Back in those days the hearings were held during the season—today they're scheduled during the summer months.

Doug's case was heard in Calgary in late November of 1991, a day after a game in which the arbitrator was in attendance. During the contest, Doug looked and saw someone sitting with Flames general manager Doug Risebrough in his suite. After the game, Gilmour learned that person was the arbitrator.

He wasn't amused.

The process plus rumours that Risebrough was looking to trade him left Gilmour unhappy. He confided as much to me in early December of 1991 and said he was considering leaving the Flames.

In the 1991 New Year's Eve game, Gilmour delivered star a performance in a 3–2 overtime win against the Montreal Canadiens, the team he had helped defeat in the Stanley Cup Final only a couple of years earlier.

It would be Doug Gilmour's final game as a Flame.

He scored a shorthanded goal which gave the Flames a 2–1 lead in the second period, then at 2:33 of overtime set up Paul Ranheim for the decider.

He was announced as one of the game's stars and I interviewed him in the Flames' dressing room afterward discussing the win and his performance.

When the radio microphone was turned off, he told me in confidence that he was through with the Flames.

He let Risebrough know the next morning. For the next 24 hours the GM worked the phones looking to make a trade with no public awareness of the situation. Some of Gilmour's teammates knew, since he had told them at a New Year's Eve dinner after the game.

On New Year's Day evening we talked on the phone but Gilmour had heard nothing regarding a trade and was planning to practice with Team Canada, which was headquartered in Calgary.

The next morning around 9:00, while I was having breakfast at home, he called to tell me he'd been traded to Toronto. At the time he didn't know any details of the transaction, such as who was going with him or whom the Flames were getting in return.

Soon enough, the magnitude of the 10-player swap would be known. It had a resounding impact.

While Flames fans watched from a distance, Gilmour would go on to have his greatest seasons with the Maple Leafs, twice leading them to the Campbell Conference Final.

He'd later go on to play with Chicago, New Jersey, Buffalo, and Montreal before returning to the Leafs at the 2003 trade deadline.

As fate would have it, Doug played just one game in his return to the Leafs and it would be in Calgary on March 13. That night, he accidentally collided with Dave Lowry on his second shift of the game, tearing an ACL.

After 1,474 games, Doug Gilmour was done.

I went to the visitors' dressing room in the Saddledome after the game but Doug had already departed.

The Snowstorm Game

Among the most interesting nights of my career, as well as in Flames franchise history, had to be January 22, 1987.

Anyone who was there—and there weren't a lot us—talks about it to this day.

The morning started off as a normal game day in New Jersey. No problems getting to the Brendan Byrne Arena—as it was called at the time—for the morning skate.

The Devils were there, too, using ice time before the Flames. No issues.

At about 2:00 PM I'm sitting in the hotel room and I receive a phone call from assistant general manager Al Coates telling me the bus time had moved up, would leave early.

He explained that a storm was on its way and instead of a 5:00 departure, the team would be taking off at 4:00.

I looked outside and at that point it was still a bright, sunny afternoon.

Leaving at 4:00, it didn't take us any longer to get to the arena than usual. We arrived at 4:30, three hours before the game was scheduled to start. So there was a lot of time to fill.

We didn't know it then, but the storm was starting to pick up steam.

As time passed, the New Jersey players started trickling in. Slowly. In some cases, we found out later, it took players five hours to reach the rink.

The officials working the game were staying at a hotel across the turnpike and some of them braved the elements, walking over in the blowing snow and biting wind.

By game time, the building was virtually deserted. There'd been 11,247 tickets sold for that game but only 334 fans were actually there.

The game eventually started two hours late, just after 9:30.

During the lengthy delay, the Flames would go on the ice three different times for warmups. We all just sat around and waited.

So at the broadcast location, located in the crowd right at centre ice, our job—Doug Barkley's and mine—was to fill time. Lots of time.

We asked anyone who was around to come on for a few minutes and give us a hand.

One of our guests turned out to be the wife of Flames coach Bob Johnson, Martha. Like Bob, she was a pretty good talker. I remember enjoying our chat until one of the announcements over the public address system—providing updates on the progress of getting things started—promised free gifts for anyone who'd braved the storm to attend the game.

Right away, Martha says, "I've got to go. I've got to get one of those gifts."

So off she went, mid-interview.

We heard later that Bob had been down by the dressing rooms, counting the Devils players as they arrived. Once they had 16 or 17, as stated in league rules, that meant there were enough to get the game going.

But the Devils were waiting for some of their key individuals, like Patrik Sundstrom, who as it turned out was one of the last to arrive.

That stalling tactic really irked Bob.

Officials kept checking the room to get a head count but apparently the Devils were hiding some guys so they wouldn't be noticed as they awaited the arrival of Sundstrom. A bit of cloak and dagger there, for sure.

No cell phones at the time, of course, so everyone was pretty much in the dark about who was where and when anyone still outside thought they might reach the arena.

Finally, they got the game started. An interesting sidelight: Doug Dadswell had been called up from the minors by the Flames to play goal that night. He'd been battling a bad flu bug, but kept quiet about it, not wanting to miss his first start in the NHL. So he sat around, feeling lousy, nervous.

The Flames lost 7–5. The big gunner for New Jersey turned out to be Doug Sulliman with three goals and an assist. He wasn't even supposed to play, nursing a mild injury, but all the absences due to the snowstorm left the Devils no choice. He played.

A lousy day and a lousy result. So the worry on the Flames' bus heading back to the hotel afterward was whether or not the kitchen would still be open in the restaurant.

That, at least, worked out.

But you really had to feel for Dadswell.

A loss. The flu. And 334 as an announced attendance on your big night.

Not a debut he's likely to forget. Or a crazy night the rest of us will, either.

The Nieuwendyk Deal

December 19, 1995. A day, actually a night, of great significance for the franchise:

The trading of captain Joe Nieuwendyk, a future Hall of Famer, to the Dallas Stars. Coming back in the deal, a future captain, and a Hall of Famer in waiting, Jarome Iginla.

Nieuwendyk had not played a game that year, leaving the team during the preseason over a contract dispute with the general manager at the time, Doug Risebrough.

Compounding the Flames' woes, another of their top players, Gary Roberts, Nieuwendyk's boyhood pal from Whitby, Ontario, had been sidelined due to injury.

In early November, with the team languishing near the bottom of the Western Conference, Al Coates replaced Risebrough as GM. A tough position for Al to be put in: A struggling team with two of its best players—including its leading scorer and captain—not there to help right the ship.

As the holiday trade deadline neared, the Flames found themselves on a long road trip. They'd won the first game and tied the second before losing 6–3 in Boston.

At practice the next day the tension that had been building blew up.

Practice lasted all of one minute.

Three players—Phil Housley, Dean Evason, and Steve Chiasson—were perhaps a minute late getting on to the ice, so coach Pierre Page ordered everybody to head for the dressing room.

Things didn't get any better next game.

The Flames were beaten two nights later 7–1 by the Penguins, with Mario Lemieux, Jaromir Jagr, and Ron Francis padding their stats.

The enormity of that loss, the way the team was sinking, convinced Coates to make the deal to move Nieuwendyk to the Stars.

Joe Nieuwendyk, the only Flame to score 50 goals in each of his first two NHL seasons.
(Getty Images)

The team was on the bus on the way to the Pittsburgh airport and a charter flight to Hartford and the second of back-to-back games.

The mood was gloomy, silent, as you'd expect. But en route the bus made an unscheduled stop at a Holiday Inn hotel. No one was quite sure what was happening. Page and assistant coach Guy Lapointe got off. They got back on but before we reached the airport the bus stopped again, this time at a Denny's restaurant. Again, Page and Lapointe got off, and got on again.

Turns out, Page and Coates were on the phone. The deadline of 10:00 PM Calgary time, midnight out east, was approaching.

After the plane had taken off for Hartford, Page informed the media and players that a trade had been made: Nieuwendyk to Dallas in exchange for centre Corey Millen and the Stars' top draft pick, Iginla.

A controversial deal, at least at the outset.

Nieuwendyk hadn't been playing, of course, but Corey Millen, a handy, versatile forward, certainly wasn't considered an adequate replacement. And the other guy, the young guy, in the deal, no one knew a lot about.

But the ace in the equation turned out to be Iginla, of course, playing then for Kamloops of the Western Hockey League. He'd been thoroughly scouted by Coates and the Stars were very, very high on his prospects.

The funny part about the whole situation? A team that had been second-to-last in the conference came on strong after the burden of the Nieuwendyk situation—Will he come back? Will he be traded?—had been lifted actually qualified for the playoffs that year.

Jarome would make his Flames debut during a playoff series against Chicago, after his junior team had been eliminated from postseason contention. And thus began his long, successful career in the organization.

Shut 'Er Down

Over decades of travel, you have to endure your share of bad weather. Snow, rain, sleet, the tedium of waiting for airplane wings to be de-iced. They're all occupational hazards.

But December 21, 2006, we experienced something that had never happened before in franchise history, and hasn't happened since: A game involving the Flames was postponed.

It was the second-to-last stop of a long six-city road trip that began in Vancouver, went to Phoenix, then Anaheim-L.A. on back-to-back nights before moving on to Denver.

San Jose was scheduled for two days following the game against the Avalanche at the Pepsi Center.

Our charter flight arrived in Denver early in the morning, around 1:00 AM, and had no problems reaching the team hotel, the Westin Tabor Center.

But we'd already heard the forecast of a large storm approaching— you hear that a lot over the course of a season on the road, and most of the time everything works out, somehow.

Sure enough, everyone awoke to heavy snowfall.

Coach Jim Playfair and some of the players managed to reach a suburban rink to practice that afternoon but the intensity of the storm continued to increase.

By nightfall, everything was shut down, nothing whatsoever was moving downtown, and an announcement of a postponement seemed imminent.

Interestingly, the NBA's Phoenix Suns were also in the hotel, scheduled to play that night against the Denver Nuggets. So the Flames and Suns players, including Canadian Steve Nash, a hockey fan, spent the evening in the restaurant, telling stories and comparing notes.

The next morning, more snow, and a biting wind. Offices, schools, and malls all closed. The airport hadn't been in operation for a couple of days, stranding somewhere in the vicinity of 4,500 passengers.

We learned later that the blizzard had dropped a half-metre of snow on the city.

The Colorado governor declared a state of emergency. Given hectic travel schedules of teams and arena availability, every possibility is explored in ensuring games are played on their scheduled dates.

Finally, though, this one had to be postponed. There was no other option.

Those two days in Denver felt like a week and everyone naturally started becoming concerned about getting out of there and home in time for Christmas.

On the Friday, thankfully, the snowfall had subsided and we were able to leave the downtown hotel and reach the airport, taking a charter flight to San Jose.

The only postponed game in franchise history was rescheduled to April 8, and the Avalanche won 6–3.

Tip of the Hat

Only once in Flames history has the team strung together a string of hat tricks over four consecutive games.

The rarity occurred in the early part of the 1992–93 season, beginning in a home game on October 31 against the old Minnesota North Stars.

That night, Soviet legend Sergei Makarov notched the three-goal performance, connecting for a goal in the first period and two more in the second, each at even strength.

As a follow-up, on November 2, a 5–3 victory over the Vancouver Canucks, Makarov's linemate Joe Nieuwendyk was the one to connect for three: Two goals in the first, one via power play, and then another PP goal in the second.

The next game, November 4, a rematch at Pacific Coliseum in Vancouver, it was Theo Fleury's turn. The three-goal barrage the next night came via Gary Leeman, with the Flames back home to face the Ottawa Senators.

And they came within a whisker, one shot, of extending the streak even further.

On November 8 against the Quebec Nordiques, left winger Gary Roberts connected for a pair of goals, otherwise the run would've reached five.

Columbus

When the Blue Jackets entered the NHL in 2000, it generated a lot of excitement in a city that had previously been known for Ohio State Buckeyes football.

Their rink, Nationwide Arena, was ideally situated in the city's downtown and bordered by a practice facility.

Indeed a welcome addition to the NHL's expanding community.

But three situations stand out for me from my visits to Columbus. None of them particularly pleasant.

Only once in my entire career was I around a player when he received word that he'd been traded—in Columbus, March 13, 2001.

After practicing in the arena that day, trade deadline day, the players were gathered in the dressing room watching TSN's coverage of the final half hour on a cluster of TV monitors inside the dressing room.

I wound up sitting among a group that included Cory Stillman, a couple of perches down from me.

Suddenly, like a bolt out of the blue, news flashed that Cory had been shipped to the St. Louis Blues in exchange for Craig Conroy and a seventh-round draft pick (which would turn out to be David Moss).

The room went silent.

Cory had no idea. No inkling it was coming.

No one in management had uttered a word of warning to him. We had no idea what to say.

A number of players went over to shake Cory's hand, remarking it was a terrible way for anyone to learn he'd been traded.

Soon after, Flames media relations director Peter Hanlon came in and said that he had been in touch with general manager Craig Button and that the trade was not yet official.

Apparently, there's the trade call after two teams agree to a deal, but because this was agreed upon as the deadline was fast approaching, there were probably a bunch of transactions lined up in the NHL office, waiting to be approved.

At this point, a lawyer designated by the league sits down with representatives of each team involved in a trade and goes over the contracts of the players involved.

That part of the exercise hadn't been completed so the Flames didn't want to announce anything until it had been. It certainly created quite a furor in the dressing room.

Ultimately, the deal went through.

Stillman would move on and have a pretty good career after his six seasons in Calgary, playing for two different Stanley Cup winners, including the Tampa Bay Lightning that defeated the Flames in 2004 and then with Carolina in 2006.

Conroy, of course, would ultimately become a very popular player in Calgary. Twice, actually.

He moved on to Los Angeles but Calgary GM Darryl Sutter would bring him back to conclude his NHL career as a Flame, and he'd ultimately become assistant GM following his retirement.

As if the mix-up involving Cory wasn't enough, the day following the confusing Stillman trade, coach Don Hay was fired.

The team was still in Columbus.

The morning of that game, Hay was in control of the team's skate but later, when the team was departing from the hotel, Don wasn't on the bus.

Odd.

Not until the team reached the rink did we hear of a hastily called media conference involving GM Craig Button. We learned then that Don had been relieved of his coaching duties and replaced by Greg Gilbert.

The night before, as chance would have it, I'd gone to dinner with Don. The team was struggling so we had quite a discussion about the problems and, naturally, the Conroy trade. Don expressed a bit of concern about his job but I don't think he had an idea of what would happen the next day.

The next season on a Flames visit, the unthinkable occurred. March 16, 2002, a shot was deflected off a stick up into about the 15th row of the seating area in the Columbus end, striking a young girl, Brittanie Cecil.

The puck hit the 13-year-old on the left temple. She was conscious when taken out of the building. I remember noting on the broadcast that she was helped out with her parents.

She was taken to a nearby hospital and three days later would die from the injury. Apparently, soon after she got to the hospital, she lapsed into unconsciousness and never recovered.

Brittanie passed away the day before her 14th birthday.

A tragedy difficult for anyone to come to grips with.

The following year the NHL made it mandatory for all buildings throughout the league to install the netting we now see to prevent another such terrible incident from occurring.

At first when the netting was brought in, a whole lot of fans thought it impeded their view of the game.

Their protests quickly quieted. No would could complain long about implementing something that added to the safety of the game.

Point Streaks

Calgary's franchise record for points in consecutive games is 16 and is shared by three players.

I vividly recall those streaks and in particular how they ended.

The record was originally set by defenceman Gary Suter during the 1987–88 season, between March 3 and April 3.

During the run, Gary piled up 25 points, a large number for a defenceman.

Two more conventional runs would follow: Left winger Gary Roberts, 27 points, and all-time franchise point leader Jarome Iginla, 26.

Given his position, Suter's ranks as the most impressive in my mind.

In nine of those 16 games, he only collected one point. Interestingly, Gary's streak was pieced together during the final 16 games of the season. In the 80th and final fixture of the regular season, he didn't collect a point until late in proceedings, picking up an assist on Hakan Loob's 50th goal of the season (historically significant as it would turn out, as Loob is still the only Swedish-born player to connect for 50).

Gary would sail into the playoffs and collect points in the first two games of the first-round series against the Los Angeles Kings before being held off the scoresheet.

Playoff points, however, don't count in streaks from the regular season so he ended up with 16.

Gary would start the next season picking up two points in the first two games to extend it to 18, but, again, the league didn't allow for carryover.

The streak Gary Roberts put together, unsurprisingly was during the 1991–92 campaign when he'd score 53 times, the second-most in franchise history behind Lanny McDonald's out-of-sight total of 66.

As with Suter's steak, Roberts' roll came to an end with the games running out, March 3 to April 16, and was actually interrupted for a week as the NHL went on strike late in the season.

That stoppage, however, didn't stop the streak, and Gary was able to pick up where he left off.

During the run, 17 of his 27 points were goals: One hat trick and five two-goal games.

In the 16th game, Roberts registered an assist on a goal by Sergei Makarov with 5:17 left in regulation time to tie Suter's record.

That Flames team failed to qualify for the playoffs. The next season, Roberts would start by picking up points in the first three games, but once again the carryover was not allowed.

So his streak ended in the neutral-site game in Saskatoon, against Minnesota.

Iginla, meanwhile, equalled the record in a season that was far from his most productive. In fact, he didn't even lead the Flames in scoring that year, a pretty commonplace occurrence during Jarome's great seasons with the organization.

His 29 goals that season placed second on the team to Val Bure, who had 35.

The Iginla streak stretched from January 29 to March 5 and consisted of 12 sniped and 14 assists.

It started with a goal with 45 seconds left in the game, after the Flames, down one, had pulled their goaltender. During the streak, he had two-goal games on two occasions as well as seven games with one point.

The record-tying run ended against Colorado, the Flames falling 8–3.

The Suter, Roberts, and Iginla point streaks all arrived during regular season play. Al MacInnis delivered a superb 17-game run during the 1989 Stanley Cup playoff push. Al, who won the Conn Smythe Trophy as playoff MVP, of course, started the streak on April 13 in Game 6 of the first round against Vancouver, scoring the first goal for the Flames in a 6–3 loss.

Over the totality of the streak, he scored seven goals and added 19 assists.

Japan and the Sharks

At the start of the 1998–99 season, the Flames played their first two regular season games in Tokyo, Japan.

The games pitted them against the San Jose Sharks and followed the Olympics held in Nagano a year earlier, as the NHL wanted to continue to increase its profile in Japan.

After a long, tiring journey—I'd never been on a plane that long— we arrived in Tokyo.

The two games were contested in the Yoyogi Arena in Tokyo, with a seating capacity of 8,400.

Both games were sold out.

One of the interesting things about that building was that the ice surface was reconstructed from a swimming pool and you could hear the hollow from the skates swishing on the ice, even from as far away as our broadcast location.

Culturally, Tokyo was quite the experience. The lights, the constant mass of people really jumped out at me, and I'd visited New York City more than a few times by then.

The high-speed trains were fabulous and another thing that stood out were the number of cell phones being used on the streets. This was 20 years ago, remember, but everyone seemed to own one.

The games featured a brother vs. brother coaching matchup—Brian Sutter for the Flames and Darryl for the Sharks. To add to the promotional value, it was in the first of these games that the Flames introduced their third jersey, the flaming horse on a black background.

The first clash wound up in a 3–3 tie, Jason Wiemer having the distinction of collecting the first goal. The Flames took a 2–1 lead into the third period before Mike Ricci would score the game-tying goal with 2:18 left.

Ken Wregget was in goal for the Flames; he'd been acquired in the off-season and was making his Calgary debut and was named the number-one star for outduelling former Flame Mike Vernon.

The game had a five-minute overtime period, neither team scoring.

The Flames proved victorious in the second contest, skating away with a 5–3 triumph in a game where the teams combined for 27 power play chances.

Theoren Fleury—immensely popular with the Japanese fans—led the way with a hat trick, scoring once in each period.

The Flames would return home and have five days off to try to get their body clocks back in sync.

Unsurprisingly, they didn't start off so well, losing the first three games back in North America. That would seem to be a signal for the year as the club did not make the playoffs.

They used an awful lot of players, 42, including a team-record six goaltenders.

Late in that season, just before the trade deadline, they traded away Theo Fleury, the heart and soul of the franchise and an upcoming UFA.

Another time of transition had begun, with general manager Al Coates executing 10 deals before and during the 1998–99 season.

The Importance of 2004

The Flames' long-odds 2004 run to the Stanley Cup Final was more than a tremendous party, an unlikely storyline, and a long-awaited return to relevance.

I believe it may have saved the franchise in Calgary.

The team had run into some awfully hard times on the ice, seven consecutive years without postseason play stretching back to 1996 and a four-game sweep by the Chicago Blackhawks.

Crowds were dwindling in the Saddledome, the automatic sell-outs of the early years a thing of the past. Tickets were easy to obtain, a lot of empty seats in the building. Adding to the misery, the Canadian dollar was taking a tremendous hit and salaries were being paid in U.S. greenbacks.

The compounding factors all had a draining effect on the organization.

You can be sure people at the ownership level were quite concerned about the viability of the franchise at that point.

There were rumbles of them losing money some of those seasons, also rumbles about the possibility of other cities making bids to purchase the team.

To its credit, the ownership group held fast despite all of those difficulties over that period.

Whatever misgivings there might have been about hanging tough vanished in the spring of 2004 and that dramatic run to the Stanley Cup Final.

Beating, in order, favoured Vancouver, Detroit, and then San Jose, pushing Tampa Bay to the brink in an exhaustive seven-game series, jolted the franchise into relevance, and to life again.

The buzz was back.

By mid-January the building was full again and triggered a run of sellouts that went to more than 200 games in succession. The C of Red returned, fiercer than ever. In 2004, everyone in the city was wearing red or Flames gear to salute what was going on with their upstart darlings.

If that team hadn't surpassed all expectations, it would have been eight straight campaigns without playoffs in Calgary.

The next season brought another NHL work stoppage, owners locking out the players for the entire season.

Without the wonders of springtime 2004, I'm not at all convinced fans would have come rushing back to the Dome after a full year abandoned in the work-stoppage wilderness.

Tough Guy Shout-Out

Some awfully tough gentlemen have worn the Flaming C down through the years. Tim Hunter, Nick Fotiu.

Only one, however, has ever been the recipient of a "Yeah baby!" shout-out.

Brian McGrattan.

The occasion was a Gordie Howe hat trick—goal, assist, fight—on October 16, 2009, against the Vancouver Canucks.

Brian enjoyed two tours as a Flame and gained quite a following among Saddledome fans.

They just *loved* him.

At the conclusion of his fights, much to their delight, he'd salute them.

That became his trademark.

On the night in question, just 3:32 in, he dropped the gloves with Vancouver's Darcy Hordichuk. In the second period, at 9:16, he assisted on a Dustin Boyd goal that would turn out to be the game-winner.

Just over two minutes later, the big man was back, scoring himself—assists to Boyd and Brandon Prust—to stake the Flames to a 5–0 lead (the final score would read 5–3).

So when he scored the goal to complete the Gordie Howe hat trick I couldn't help myself. I bellowed, "Yeah baby!"

I'd gotten to know Brian only a little bit at that point, hanging around the dressing room and travelling on the road with the team.

He always remembered the "Yeah baby!" and was greatly appreciative of it. Both with the Flames and when he'd moved to another team.

And Brian was able to repay the favour. When I announced my retirement as a play-by-play broadcaster in 2014, one of the phone calls I received was from Brian and he started the conversation by yelling, "Yeah baby!" as his recognition of my career.

A wonderful gesture by a great guy.

As an aside: By my count, Jarome Iginla had seven Gordie Howe hat tricks during his career but I never cut loose with my signature phrase in his honour on any of them.

Jarome was at the height of his powers at the time, arguably the game's best player. And I remember telling him once, half-jokingly, during a postgame interview that I felt the goal-assist-fight should be re-named the Jarome Iginla Hat Trick after hearing from historians that Gordie actually had only two or three over the course of his unparalleled career (probably because after a certain amount of time, no one in their right mind wanted to fight Gordie).

Jarome, characteristically, was having none of it.

"No, no, no. Gordie Howe is the legend. I'm just happy to be able to have a few during my career and be mentioned in the same sentence," he said.

Travel Woes

When I started in Toronto, the Maple Leafs would charter a small plane owner Harold Ballard dubbed "The Windmill" on short-haul trips, to Montreal, for example, and some of the eastern U.S. trips.

The rest of the time, we'd travel the conventional way.

When I moved to Calgary, the flights were, at least at the beginning, almost exclusively commercial, too.

Playoffs would be the only time the team would charter to different cities.

By the late 1980s and into the 1990s, charters would be used for back-to-back regular season games. After 9/11, the league mandated that all teams charter.

But those early days sure were interesting. The commercial flights made for some long journeys and grumpy players (and broadcasters). Layovers. Delays. Connecting flights. Usually the team would be able to secure window and aisle seats but those stuck in the middle were not very happy.

Often, one of the assistant coaches would be appointed travel manager, and had to arrive early at airports to try and sort through various issues. Those poor fellows weren't very popular when a whole slew of players would arrive at the airport to find they'd been assigned those dreaded middle seats—which were invariably assigned to the youngsters.

Age and experience had its perks.

What we used to go through seems unreal now when teams charter exclusively, and fly in style. But in the old days, a big guy like Joel Otto might be crammed into a middle seat for three or four hours and then get off the plane and be called on to play a game.

One trip from 1984 stands out. The Flames had just played in St. Louis and were on their way to Detroit for a game the next night. A late Jim Peplinski goal earned them a 2–2 tie at the old Arena—no overtime in those days—and the team was forced to stay overnight in St. Louis as there were no commercial flights out late.

We went back to the hotel and had a 5:00 AM wake-up call to take the bus at 5:15, because at the time there was a stipulation that if teams didn't charter they were obliged to take the first commercial flight out on a game day.

The flight was supposed to leave at 7:00 AM, but a snowstorm had begun pummelling the Detroit area. We sat around the airport for hours, waiting for an all-clear on the flight. Finally we arrived in Detroit roughly two and a half hours before game time. The airport is a ways out there so the bus picked us up and took us straight to Joe Louis Arena.

Amazingly, the Flames won that game 4–2 on two goals each in the first and second periods. A fast start, given the fatigue factor, was imperative, and they held on. Hakan Loob scored twice that night, I remember, and goaltender Reggie Lemelin, who'd stopped 30 saves the night before in St. Louis, blocked 26 playing in the back-to-back situation.

Sometimes, later flights from one city to another would be late, or delayed, for whatever reason, and the bus would be sitting on the tarmac. There were nights the players, bored, would be out there playing soccor or volleyball, using a string of equipment bags as a net, just killing time.

The connecting flights were, as you'd guess, always popular. We'd have to fly to Chicago, change planes and then fly to our destination.

Charters, naturally, were much more expensive but much more convenient, making luring free agents easier.

As charter flights became standard, the playing field in that area became more even.

By comparison, today, full-time charter, ample leg room to stretch out, is first-class, gold-star, all-the-bells-and-whistles luxury.

They don't realize how lucky they've got it.

And the Three Stars Are...

In 2017, as part of its centenary anniversary, the NHL named its Top 100 players, making for lively debate.

One featured Wayne Gretzky, Bobby Orr, and Mario Lemieux together to discuss who should be hailed as No. 1.

Significantly, all three without hesitation named Gordie Howe as the greatest player they ever saw.

Pretty difficult to argue with.

Selecting a greatest this or a best-ever that is always tricky, of course. Whenever I'm asked the question, I always choose three different players in three categories.

I label Howe the Greatest All-Around Player. He had so many ways to impact outcomes. Great knowledge of the game, great skills with or without the puck, could play tough, as everyone knows. He could score goals and set them up. He rallied his teammates, possessed that aura, the charisma, that all of the truly great ones do.

In short, he had every feature you could ask for in a player. Nobody even comes close in terms of variety of game-changing skills.

I call Gretzky the Smartest Player Ever. Most people do. It's fashionable these days to talk about players having a high hockey IQ. Nobody before or since approaches No. 99 in the way he worked a game.

I broadcasted many, many games he was involved in, of course, and he just seemed 10 steps ahead in his thinking, the way he read the game. He wasn't the fastest player on the ice, the largest, or the toughest, but he could pick teams apart night after night after night. Goodness knows he did it often enough against the Flames through the 1980s and early 1990s.

I used to say the only thing wrong with Gretzky is that he played for Edmonton.

My third category, Most Thrilling Player, is a pretty easy call, too: No. 4, Bobby Orr. I was so fortunate to see him on television and a few times live, perhaps most memorably at the Canada Cup of 1976.

Wayne Gretzky had the highest hockey IQ of any player I ever saw. Here we get together at a Team Canada training camp.

He did things at such a high speed. It was a marvel to see him spin, twist, and turn. He was so colourful, so mesmerizing. The old saying "worth the price of admission" gets overused. Only a very few gifted players actually qualify in that category. Bobby Orr was one of them.

Guy Lafleur was a forward who generated the same type of excitement. Again, someone capable of astonishing feats at top speed.

Living in New Brunswick into my early adult years, when Orr and Lafleur were in their primes, my friends and I would plan our annual pilgrimage to Montreal for a Bruins-Canadiens game. What a show. Wonderful times.

I never did get the chance to broadcast one of Orr's games before his unfortunate, premature retirement at the age of 30 due to recurring knee problems. I did, however, think I'd get that chance once. November 8, 1978. I was working Leafs games at the time and the team was in Chicago to face the Blackhawks. My opportunity to call a game with Bobby Orr playing.

But in the morning at the old Stadium we received word that Orr, after a six-game return following a year away, was scheduled to announce his retirement at noon.

The reason: His performances weren't up to the dizzying standard he'd set.

I remember the press conference being very emotional, and it hurt seeing such a fantastic player in tears, robbed of the back half of his prime playing years.

Playing in the modern era, with the advancement in medical technology, maybe he could've continued thrilling us all for seasons to come. We'll never know.

Gordie, Wayne, and Bobby.

My personal three stars of the game.

Boot Trick

In the mid- to late 1980s, the sales group at what was known then as QR 77—which owned Flames broadcast rights—came up with kind of a novel idea for what we commonly refer to as the hat trick.

They developed a promotion with a boot company in Calgary, Alberta Boot, to have a "boot trick," honouring any player scoring three goals in a Flames game or a goaltender recording a shutout with a pair of cowboy boots.

It became a very popular promotion. And in those free-scoring days, the boots were flying off the shelves

Theo Fleury, for instance, had five in one season, keeping him in Calgary Stampede–applicable footwear for years.

Hakan Loob had five, too. Guys like Joey Mullen, Joe Nieuwendyk, Gary Roberts, and Lanny McDonald would be frequent winners of boots and it became an interesting topic of discussion in the dressing room.

Unlike their teammates, goaltenders didn't get involved too frequently, as shutouts weren't such a common thing at that time.

The players had a little deal going on with Bob Johnson and later Terry Crisp, because the coaches wanted to get in on the action, too.

Robert Reichel was an interesting guy from the Czech Republic. Back home, cowboy boots weren't exactly the norm, so Robert would sell the boots he won to people for cash.

It was a very popular promotion.

Goaltending Carousel

The 1998–99 season won't ever be confused with one of the more successful campaigns in Calgary's history.

What does sets it apart, however, is the number of different goaltenders that strapped on the pads on behalf of the Flames.

Over a stretch of 30 games, a close-to-unbelievable eight men.

Not unbelievably, that number continues to stand as a record for the most goaltenders used in a single season.

The general manger that year was Al Coates, the coach was Brian Sutter, and the campaign opened with a trip to Tokyo, Japan, for the first two regular season games of the season.

The opposition: Brian Sutter's baby brother Darryl and his San Jose Sharks.

The club carried three puck-stoppers on that Asia trip: Veteran Ken Wregget, who had been acquired in an off-season in a deal from Toronto; Tyler Moss; and J.S. Giguere.

The third goaltender was tagging along as a just-in-case insurance policy.

As it turned out, Wregget started and finished both of the games in Japan and would continue to carry the load when the team returned to North America, called upon through the next nine starts (in the final one of that particular spell, he was involved in a scoreless duel against the Washington Capitals, the first scoreless tie to ever be contested in the Saddledome).

Two games later, Wregget suffered a back injury, a pretty serious one that put him on the sideline for a lengthy spell.

Enter Tyler Moss, called upon to mop up. Giguere was immediately called up from the farm team in Saint John to back up Moss.

Moss started one more game before Giguere made his NHL debut, 13 games into the season, gaining a 3–1 victory.

That tandem lasted a while before Moss went down—beginning to sound familiar?—due to an injury in Game 27. That brought Ty Garner into the ranks on an emergency basis.

Garner was a Flames draft pick who'd been sent back to junior to play with Oshawa in the OHL during training camp. He served as the backup for the next several games, until Giguere suffered a hamstring injury.

The crisis was mounting, forcing Coates to engineer a deal with the Chicago Blackhawks and acquire another goalie, Andre Trefilov.

Trefilov, in fact, had been with the Flames earlier in his career. The Russian started a couple of times but in his third appearance was pulled in the second period, providing Garner the chance to make his NHL bow.

The rotten luck continued, Trefilov tweaking his groin in Boston at the front end of back-to-backs, meaning Garner received the start 24 hours later in Pittsburgh, a 5–1 loss to Mario Lemieux and the Penguins.

An interesting situation developed in getting a backup goaltender in for that game at the Igloo.

Igor Karpenko, one of the goalies down on the farm in Saint John, was summoned—the Flames were getting used to this routine by now—to hopefully arrive in time to caddy for Garner.

Flight complications intervened, however, so a call was placed to Johnstown of the East Coast league, located just down the road from Pittsburgh, to have Pavel Nestak on hand, just in case his services might be required.

A native of the Czech Republic, Nestak made the drive up for the game and actually put the gear on for warmups as everyone waited with bated breath for Karpenko to arrive.

Well, Karpenko arrived and while in the taxi heading to the arena, he signed an NHL contract, and sat on the end of the bench.

It was a strange scene in the dressing room afterward, with Karpenko, an extremely excited guy, overjoyed at having been able to live out a dream and put on NHL duds for the first time, even though he didn't actually dress for the game.

In a jovial mood, Karpenko actually danced around room, getting autographs from his one-night teammates.

While that craziness was going on, the Flames were in the process of bringing in yet another goalie, Fred Brathwaite. Freddie had been a part of the Edmonton organization earlier in his career but at the moment didn't have an NHL job and was keeping sharp with the Canadian National Team stationed in Calgary.

Brathwaite had gone over to Europe to play in the Spengler Cup and his outstanding performance there for Canada caught the eye of Coates.

The Flames signed him to a contract, and he was originally slated to head down to Saint John and play for the farm team.

But when Trefilov's injury cropped up, Brathwaite then became the Flames' next goaltender to actually play in a game, No. 40 on the season, January 8 at home against the Dallas Stars.

And he made it an introduction to remember, blanking Dallas 1–0 to end an eight-game losing streak.

Brathwaite took over and played a number of games and Giguere returned from his injury, so Garner was returned to Oshawa.

Trefilov, when healthy, moved back to play with Chicago in the International League.

Eventually, the No. 1 to start the season, Wregget returned, but by that time Brathwaite was putting on a pretty strong show, and would play in 14 consecutive games.

Brathwaite, in fact, would play in only 28 games that entire season, but also would win the Molson Cup for most three-star selections, following Theo Fleury's trade to Colorado.

Brathwaite would continue to play another couple of strong years in the Flames net.

But quite the game of goaltending musical chairs.

Winter Olympics

When Calgary hosted the 1988 Winter Olympics, the Saddledome ice surface was converted to international size and the Flames hit the road for three separate trips. Following the Flames was my job, but I have to admit I was disappointed not to have the chance to experience such a major sports event.

However, 22 years later I'd get my chance when I was asked to be the play-by-play broadcaster for Team Canada's men's games on the Sportsnet Canada-wide radio network from the 2010 Games in Vancouver.

The night after the last Flames game before the Olympics, I was on a flight with star right winger Jarome Iginla to the West Coast. And, as it turned out, Jarome played a major role in one of the highlight goals I'd call in my career.

In Vancouver, I joined our radio broadcast team with former NHL goalie John Garrett, long-time color commentator on *Hockey Night in Canada*; Vancouver Canucks game host Dan Dunleavy, now play-by-play broadcaster for the Buffalo Sabres; and interviewer Howard Berger, who had the same role with the Toronto Maple Leafs.

It was awesome, the two-week excitement in Vancouver topped off with the Canada-USA game for the gold medal on February 28, a Sunday afternoon.

Canada ultimately won 3–2 in overtime but the contest had plenty of drama. A broadcaster's delight.

When the U.S. tied the game with 24.4 seconds remaining in the third period, the largely pro-Canadian crowd was briefly silenced. The tension could be felt throughout the intermission before OT. From my standpoint, I wanted Canada to win and hoped it would be a clean goal, easy to identify.

It took 7:40 of extra time before the two players on Team Canada who I personally knew best collaborated for the marker that touched off tremendous celebrations across Canada.

It was Iginla winning a corner battle in the U.S. zone before making a perfect pass to Sidney Crosby, who I'd met a few times at summer charity events in the Maritimes. Crosby fired a low, hard shot into the American net and I let loose with my best "Yeah baby!" roar.

I will admit that Chris Cuthbert, calling the game on Canadian television, had the best citation, calling it "the Golden Goal."

Broadcasting Olympic hockey was a thrill in itself, but having such a historic finish made everything even more incredible.

Trading Iginla

Given the lockout that shut the league down, pushing NHL opening night back to January 13 and condensing the schedule to 48 games, the 2012–13 season already felt odd.

But the weird feeling got ratcheted up a whole other level on March 27.

I'd actually heard possibilities a few days beforehand, a couple of Flames confiding in me, that Jarome Iginla—captain, icon, all-time franchise-leading scorer, beacon of hope during a series of bleak seasons—had been asked by the team to waive his no-trade clause.

Jarome was then 35, in the final year of his contract, and the organization had finally decided to commit to a rebuild. The chances of him fulfilling his Stanley Cup dream on a team committed to the future seemed remote, at best.

So, checking his options, he'd finally given GM Jay Feaster a list of teams he'd waive the clause to join. Jay got busy working the phones.

On the afternoon of March 27, news broke that Iginla would be held out of the game that night at the Scotiabank Saddledome against the Colorado Avalanche.

A deal was close—Chicago, Boston, Pittsburgh, and L.A. reportedly in the discussions—and the Flames didn't want to risk an injury.

The city was, naturally, engulfed in Iginla trade talk.

Since I had my NHL Insider show at 5:00 that night, I, like Jay, had been working the phones. Unsurprisingly, team management, Jarome himself, and his agent Don Meehan weren't returning calls.

But a pretty good source was telling me that Jarome's designation would be the Bruins. The Iginla-to-Boston chatter began to pick up in intensity prior to game time and throughout the evening.

The outcome itself had become nothing more than an afterthought, especially after the Flames announced a press conference after the game in the Ed Whalen Media Lounge.

Midway through the second period, Feaster, assistant GM John Weisbrod, team owner Murray Edwards, and president Ken King left their spot in the press box and began walking over the catwalk to the elevators which would take them down to the Flames offices.

The antennae immediately went up.

That intermission was filled with whispers about a potential Boston trade and when the game ended, colour commentator Mike Rogers, Pat Steinberg, and I adjourned to our postgame Hot Stove Lounge studio, which was directly across the hall from the media lounge.

On the bottom of our TV screen in the lounge flashed the news: Iginla traded to Boston.

So, done deal.

But then, one last twist: At the podium in the media lounge shortly thereafter, Feaster shocked everyone by announcing that Iginla had, in fact, been dealt to Pittsburgh.

In the transaction, the Flames got the Pens' first-round draft pick in 2013, plus college prospects Ben Hanowski and Kenny Agostino.

Hanowski and Agostino did get to play a little bit with the Flames but didn't develop into NHLers.

Rumours were that the Flames preferred the Boston deal, but Iginla had the final say and his desire was to play alongside Sidney Crosby. The two men had teamed up on the winning goal in OT against the U.S. at the 2010 Olympics in Vancouver, a moment etched forever in the memory bank of every hockey-mad Canadian.

The hope was that they could be part of a Stanley Cup winner together, too.

The Bruins were livid, believing they had reached a deal, and Bruins GM Peter Chiarelli went public the next day to voice his dissatisfaction.

As fate would have it, Boston swiftly swept aside the Penguins in the playoffs that spring and Bruins players afterward admitted that Iginla spurning them had added incentive.

An interesting side note from my point of view: Later that year, July 1, with Iginla becoming a free agent, I was back in New Brunswick for some golfing with my brother Noonan and friends.

We returned to Noonan's house from the course and as we were sitting on the deck in late afternoon, somebody asked where I thought Iginla would sign.

I said I had no idea but that it *definitely* wouldn't be Calgary or Boston.

The TV was on with live coverage of the signing frenzy inside the house and when Noonan returned with a few beers, he reported that Jarome Iginla had just signed a one-year deal with Boston.

I was stunned that the Bruins would take him after being so displeased after he turned them down just two and a half months before.

Goalie First Wins/First Games

That first NHL victory is a keepsake moment for any goaltender. It's especially sweet should it arrive in someone's first start.

Two of the more well-known goalies in franchise annals, Mike Vernon and Trevor Kidd, for instance, didn't notch a victory in their first tries.

Only two men, in fact, accomplished that feat during my time calling games. The first was Tyler Moss, who came over from Tampa in a 1997 trade. He'd been the Lightning's second-round pick, 29th overall, four years earlier.

Moss had put together a great junior season with Kingston of the Ontario Hockey League. He'd only play 17 games over two seasons as a Flame, winning five of those, but had the distinction on October 28, 1997, of becoming the first goalie in franchise history to win his first NHL start as a member of the organization.

Rick Tabaracci started nine of the first 11 games that year, with Dwayne Roloson in charge of the other two. But on the heels of a four-game losing string, Moss was summoned from the AHL Saint John Flames.

One of his quirks, at least in my eyes, is that he was the second Flames netminder in my experience to wear the catching glove on his right hand (the other being Pat Riggin in the early 1980s).

Talking to shooters used to facing left-handed-catching goaltenders, they admitted there was a difference, and I wondered if that might help Tyler in solidifying an NHL career.

The beginning of that first game certainly didn't go well, the Pittsburgh Penguins scoring three times on their first seven shots by the nine-minute mark.

But Moss settled down, not allowing a goal on the next 22 shots, the Flames roaring from behind to win 6–3 on the strength of two goals each from Jarome Iginla and Marty McInnis.

Moss also won his second game, 4–2 over Phoenix, then a 3–3 tie at Colorado, facing 43 shots in a goaltending duel against a future Hall of Famer, Patrick Roy.

Those three games would be the only ones Moss took points out of and soon he was back in the AHL, playing three more games for the Flames that year, all losses, before moving on to other NHL locales and then Europe.

Following his playing career, he returned to Calgary and worked in the oil patch. I'd see him from time to time and we'd often reminisce about his little slice of franchise history—being the first Flames goalie to win his first start.

The second goalie to win in his first opportunity was Henrik Karlsson, a 6-foot-5 undrafted free agent signed by the San Jose Sharks before being traded to the Flames in June of 2010.

Karlsson arrived to understudy for Miikka Kiprusoff. Kiprusoff was accustomed to a lot of work, of course, and started the first six games of the year.

But on the second end of a back-to-back situation on the road, in Columbus on October 22, the lanky Swede received his chance.

And he made the most of it, stopping 20 shots in a 6–2 victory over the Blue Jackets, also notable for a Rene Bourque hat trick.

Karlsson then lost his second start and wound up with five wins in 26 starts for the team.

Two more goalies would join them in the select first start/first win club, starting with Swiss-born Reto Berra, who came to Calgary in the Jay Bouwmeester swap with St. Louis.

On November 3, 2013, he won an overtime game in a difficult building, Chicago's United Center, 3–2.

Highly regarded Jon Gillies notched his first NHL win in his first start, 4–1 over the Los Angeles Kings on April 4, 2017, after I'd retired.

Gillies' Stockton battery mate, David Rittich, would later notch his first win but in his first start, not his first taste of NHL action.

Giving No. 1 man Mike Smith a breather, Rittich started the second end of back-to-back games at the Pepsi Centre in Denver, producing 24 saves in a 4–1 victory over the Avalanche on November 26, 2017.

Rittich had actually made his NHL debut against the San Jose Sharks in the third period of the 2016–17 season finale, but that appearance had been in relief.

Dressed for Success

The Flames have modelled a number of different uniform designs and colours over the years, of course.

Fans often ask me which one of the varying array I personally liked best. Well, the one that stands out for me is the highly accented red with gold and white trim, all-white numbers and nameplate on the back of the jersey.

To me, those are the classics.

Not coincidentally, the ones they were wearing at the Montreal Forum on May 25, 1989, Stanley Cup night.

Which is, I must admit, a big, big reason for my preference. Another reason, more practical, is that for a play-by-by announcer, it's important to be able to pick out the numbers on the sweaters from quite a distance away.

The white numerals on the red background jumped out at you on that design. They also boasted larger numbers on the back and, importantly, numbers on the sleeves, as well.

There are other ways to help identify players, of course—skating style, physique, helmet, etc.

But the old-fashioned one, numbers, is always the best.

The organization has introduced a variety of different schemes since, and I must admit I've liked the look of a lot of them. But that 1980s version remains tops in my mind. It still makes a reappearance from time-to-time.

An interesting note: In those days the home team wore white jerseys, the visiting team the dark. Now it's been flipped.

It'll change in the next decade or so, I'm sure, because the NHL likes to alter the uniform pattern every so often.

Women's Olympic Hockey

When the NHL began its Olympic participation at the 1998 Winter Games in Nagano, Japan, it afforded those of us in the day-to-day a bit of a break.

Other than 2010, when I was calling the men's games in Vancouver, that meant some welcome time off to be a fan again.

And, I must say, the Canadian women's team has provided me with the most emotional moments over the years.

In 2002 at Salt Lake City, the men's team—led by Mario Lemieux, Joe Sakic, Al MacInnis, and Jarome Iginla—would end a lengthy gold-medal drought, beating the U.S. 5–2.

The whole of Canada, from tip to tip, was tuned into that one.

I remember that Sunday afternoon well, all of my family gathering at my house. My granddaughter Haylee, who at the time was just over a year old, all decked out in Maple Leafs gear and cheering on the Canadian team capturing the gold medal that afternoon. An amazing moment.

But it was actually the women's final that made the most impact on me.

I was watching that game alone in my home, in disbelief at some of the calls that went against the Canadians and in the Americans' favour.

But in the end, our girls came back from behind to pull off a major victory and collect the gold medal. For their perseverance and resolve they had at least one old play-by-play announcer in tears when they received their medals.

In 2006, the year the Olympics were held in Turin, Italy.

My father was quite ill at the time so I flew home to Moncton to spend time with him and, of course, watch hockey.

As it turned out, the very last game I shared with my father was the women's gold medal final. My dad was kind of in and out of it that afternoon and how much focus he actually had on the game is debatable.

But for me, sitting there, with him, brought back such wonderful memories of when I was a kid watching NHL games, many of those in front of black-and-white TVs, with him.

It was quite emotional seeing the girls come through to reclaim gold, 4–1 over Sweden, and sharing it with my dad, who passed away only a month later.

Following those Olympics, I was attending a function in Calgary and Hayley Wickenheiser, one of the stars from the Canadian women's team, was there.

She had her gold medal with her. Luckily, I'd brought Haylee, who at the time was five years old, and they had a grand chat.

A Hayley and a Haylee, talking hockey.

Four years later, in 2010, I'd been assigned to broadcast the Canadian men's games on Sportsnet's national radio network.

I wasn't working the women's tournament but I wouldn't have missed the women's championship game for anything and made sure I was at Rogers Arena early. I cheered them on in a 2–0 victory.

The men's gold-medal clash against the U.S. was scheduled to follow three days later.

An interesting sidelight: I was sitting in the stands conducting an interview back to our radio station, The Fan 960, when the women made their way back onto the ice to continue their celebration, drinking Molson Canadian beer and champagne.

I didn't make mention of that on the radio show—not thinking it was appropriate—but the ongoing festivities were picked up by the worldwide media.

The ladies created a major furor.

Lucky 13

The second-year San Jose Sharks could've been forgiven for feeling pretty good about themselves when Johan Garpenlov opened the scoring at 2:54 of the first period at the Saddledome on February 10, 1993.

Never in their most disturbing nightmares could have they imagined surrendering the next 13.

It remains the highest-scoring output ever by a Flames team. One crazy note in a game when you singe the opposition for that many goals: None of Calgary's 13 goals came via the power play (the only PP goal of the game was that opener from San Jose).

Dave King's crew needed 10 minutes following Garpenlov's opening strike to tie matters, but after following it up with a second only 13 seconds later, the barrage was well and truly on.

With starter Mike Vernon given the night off, backup Jeff Reese got the call and responded with three assists, which remains a single-game NHL record for points by a goalie.

Where do you start in trying to wrap your head around such a game?

Both Robert Reichel and Ronnie Stern notched hat tricks. Reichel and Theo Fleury each padded their point totals by six. Defenceman Gary Suter finished just a shade behind, at five.

Fleury—with arguably the most incredible stat of an incredible night—wound up a +9, the second-highest in history. Only Philly's Tom Bladon, at +10 back in 1977, can top it.

Newly acquired Brian Skrudland, who arrived from the Montreal Canadiens in exchange for winger Gary Leeman a week earlier, scored his first goal as a Flame, the final one of a one-sided evening, establishing the club record.

Another oddity: One of the Flames' top scorers, winger Sergei Makarov, was an injury scratch. Otherwise the damage inflicted could've been worse.

Among the franchise records established:

- Most goals in a game.
- The fastest three goals (in 36 seconds) and fastest four goals (in 81 seconds), eclipsing the standards they had set seven years and a day earlier, versus the Los Angeles Kings.
- Largest margin of victory.
- Most assists by a goaltender in game (3), by Reese.
- Fastest three goals from the start of a period (53 seconds), in the third.
- Most consecutive goals (13).
- Highest plus-minus in a single game (Fleury).

One last footnote: Leeman would go on to help the Canadiens win the 1993 Stanley Cup and not much later the Flames would, much to their surprise, lose Skrudland in the expansion draft to the new boys on the NHL block, the Florida Panthers.

Goals, Goals, Goals

Looking back at the volume of high-scoring games I broadcast back in the 1980s and into the 1990s, I wonder now about the workout I gave my vocal chords.

Two of the wildest games came against the Quebec Nordiques.

February 23, 1991, delivered the highest-scoring game ever to involve the Flames. They and the Nords ran riot, scoring 18 goals between them in a 10–8 Calgary victory at the Saddledome.

Perhaps we should've had a hint as to what lay in store because in the previous four games, the Flames and their opponents had combined for 39 goals.

The Nordiques were a very different affair, arriving in town having delivered only five goals over the opening four games of a five-game road swing.

The tone was set early, Quebec on top 2–0 by the 1:18 mark of the first period. After shaving the deficit to one on an Al MacInnis power play howitzer, the first of four on the night by the PP, the combatants shared eight goals in the second period, the Flames grabbing a 6–5 lead.

The third-period highlight was a penalty shot awarded to Theo Fleury, who scored (he went three-for-three during his career) on his way to a three-goal, two-assist outing. MacInnis also rang up five points.

Another high-scoring Calgary-Quebec affair had occurred a year before at le Colisée, October 17, 1989, less than five months after the Flames claimed the Stanley Cup.

Notable on a number of fronts, not the least of which was an 8–8 scoreline. The contest was played on the same night as a magnitude 6.9 earthquake struck the Bay City area, near San Francisco, postponing Game 3 of the World Series between the Giants and Oakland A's.

The Flames would stage their greatest comeback, scoring five goals in a space of six minutes and 22 seconds to tie after falling behind 8–3.

Hard enough to take for the Nordiques that Gary Roberts ignited the Calgary comeback by scoring twice in 16 seconds, followed by a Jim Peplinski snipe 11 seconds later to shave the deficit to 8–6.

But for anyone there in the building that evening, the dramatic manner in which the invaders counted goals 7 and 8 simply defied logic.

Scored in a span of four seconds. Both—believe it or not—shorthanded.

The rabble-rousing Roberts found himself sitting out thanks to an unsportsmanlike conduct penalty with time winding down when first Doug Gilmour, at 19:45, beat Nords rookie goaltender Stephane Fiset, and then, directly off a faceoff win at centre ice, Paul Ranheim accepted a pass from Gilmour and zipped the puck past Fiset to equalize.

The Nordiques were stunned. The Colisée crowd was stunned. I was stunned. So stunned I forget to bellow, "Yeah baby!"

Everyone was stunned.

Somehow, the rattled Nordiques collected themselves well enough to escape overtime without conceding a winner.

The two goals erased a record the Flames themselves had set a couple seasons earlier when Hakan Loob and Perry Berezan had counted twice while a man down in eight seconds.

Against? You guessed it. The Quebec Nordiques.

Shorthanded situations back then were specialty of the Flames, it seems. Theo Fleury, in March of 1991, incredibly scored three times shorthanded in one game, in St. Louis.

Calling the Game (Off the Ice)

Broadcasters have no bearing on whether a team wins, loses, or, in the old days, ties.

But it makes the job much easier when the team you're associated with is winning.

You spend late fall, winter, and hopefully some spring around the players, coaches, and staff, so when the on-ice result is positive, it makes the broadcasters' work a bit easier.

A broadcaster isn't part of the team, but there is that attachment with management, coaches, players, trainers, media relations people, and the travel coordinators. You're around them at rinks for practices and games, on buses, planes, hotels, and so on.

Interviews are much better after a team has gained two points; it puts everybody in a better frame of mind and a little more discussion can be generated.

After losses, sometimes you get very short answers from coaches and players. Alas, I was not the play-by-play man for either of the longest winning streaks in franchise history, which were a pair of 10-game successes separated by almost 40 years.

The first was October 14 through November of 1978, while the team was in Atlanta. At the time, Jiggs McDonald was the radio broadcaster. The second came between February 21 and March 13 of 2017, when my successor Derek Wills called the plays.

The longest Flames win streak while I was behind the mike were three eight-game stretches; the first was in the Stanley Cup season of 1988–89. But for a break here or there, it could have been longer as it was all part of an 11-game unbeaten string during a season that also produced a club-record 13-game undefeated run.

That eight-game streak started in Los Angeles on January 31, 1989, with an 8–5 triumph over the Kings. Two nights earlier, a two-game win streak ended in a 4–4 tie in Vancouver. The string of eight wins ended with a 4–3 loss at home to Boston when the Bruins overcame a 3–2 deficit, scoring twice late in the game.

The second eight-gamer also commenced after a tie game that was preceded by a win. The first win of the run was on December 14, 1992, the first of 3–0 shutouts on back-to-back nights by Mike Vernon. The streak of 164 minutes and 40 seconds of shutout play by Vernon still stands as the Flames record, by the way.

The closest the Flames came to losing during that stretch was December 21 in the Saddledome when Edmonton took the game into overtime before Gary Roberts connected. The streak ended with a 4–2 setback against Winnipeg.

It would be a while before the next eight-game winning run would arrive. That was from November 1 to November 16, 2005. This run had seven of the eight triumphs coming on home ice, beginning with a 3–0 Miikka Kiprusoff whitewashing of the San Jose Sharks.

Kiprusoff also earned a shutout in the third game of that streak, 1–0 over Vancouver. The seventh win saw the Flames come back from a 2–0 deficit to topple Minnesota 3–2. The string ended with a 5–2 home-ice loss to Chicago.

The longest undefeated streak in franchise history lasted 13 games, from November 10 to December 8, 1988, the lone blemish a 3–3 tie against the Canucks on November 28 after falling behind 2–0 in the first period. They won the other 12 games in an incredible run which saw the Flames lose only once over 18 games and just twice in a 22-game stretch.

That 13-game streak featured no shutouts with four of the wins by a single goal, including the night it started in Philadelphia with a 3–2 overtime triumph, Joe Nieuwendyk notching the decisive goal.

Joe would score 12 times during those 13 games.

Calling the Game (On the Ice)

I know they sometimes absorb a lot of flak but I have always had a profound respect for the on-ice officials in the NHL, the referees and linesmen.

That may have had to do with an early introduction to officials when I began broadcasting games in my hometown of Campbelltown, New

Brunswick, calling games of the team there in Dalhousie. I'd travel with Bill Payne, a local referee who, if there'd been more franchises in the NHL during that time, might've worked his way to that level.

Bill had a regular job and refereed nights and was considered the best ref in New Brunswick, if not the entire Maritimes.

In travelling with him to games, I learned many principles I tried to incorporate into my own career—fairness, class, balance, that type of thing.

During my formative days broadcasting the NHL, I got to know a lot of its officials, too. I found them to be great guys. Early on, when the teams travelled on commercial flights, there'd often be referees and linesmen on the same plane, so we'd have the chance to chat with them, pick their brains and learn the ins and outs, good and bad, of their jobs.

Often they'd stay at the same hotel as the team, so after games before heading out to the next assignment there'd be a lot of socializing at the hotel bar or local watering hole.

Not often did I get into discussions about on-ice calls made that night or in any other game, for that matter, but when I had questions, I found them more than willing to oblige.

When I was broadcasting Maple Leafs games in Toronto, I lived in the suburb of Milton. So did referee Bruce Hood and linesman Leon Stickle, so occasionally we'd travel down to the Gardens together. Later on, I'd also get to know Andy Van Hellemond, Ron Wicks, Bryan Lewis, Don Koharski, and Ray Scapinello.

Koharski, in particular, as he was from the Maritimes, too. So we'd bump into each other at local off-season charity golf tournaments.

In Calgary, there were also a number of officials I got to know, but most particularly Mike Cvik, another guy very, very active—now in retirement, as then—on the charity golf circuit.

I well remember Mike's last game officiating, at the Saddledome, his 1,868th regular season assignment (to go along with 90 postseason), when the Flames held a ceremony for him. Late in that game he got hit right near the bench, went down awkwardly, and stayed down for a bit. You wondered whether he'd be able to get up and continue.

But these guys are made of tough, durable stuff, especially big Mike, and although he was in a lot of discomfort, he finished his final NHL appearance.

Mike wore No. 88, recognizing the fact that his hometown of Calgary had hosted the 1988 Winter Olympic Games.

As the years rolled on, the league began to frown on officials staying in the same hotels as the teams, for whatever reasons, and we began seeing less and less of them away from the rink, maybe just the odd time on a flight. Then when charter travel took over, we wouldn't see them at all except at the rink.

So the dynamics changed exponentially in getting to better know these people who are such a big, big part of the game.

But from my experience around them over the years they were great guys, dedicated and determined to do the best job possible.

Czech Influence

Many European players have arrived to play for the Flames over the years but I'd like to reflect back on three Czech players who arrived here in the early years of the franchise.

The first of those, of course, would be Jiri Hrdina.

Drafted in the eighth round in 1984, Jiri donned the Flaming C after participating for his national team at the 1988 Olympics held in Calgary.

He joined the Flames soon after, when he received permission to make the leap, the first player trained in what was then known as Czechoslovakia to receive permission from its hockey federation to come play in the NHL.

In the 10 years Jiri played in the Czech league, he'd collected an awful lot of individual and team honours. He'd also competed at the international level at various Winter Olympics and world championships.

He was 30 years old at the time and played nine games that year. The next season, after becoming acclimatized, he made more of an impact.

At the start of the 1988–89 season, his first full campaign with the Flames, he started off strong, notching a hat trick on October 17 against Los Angeles and followed that feat with a four-goal game on November 7 versus the Hartford Whalers.

The Flames won the President's Trophy for finishing first overall during the regular season, but as the playoffs moved along, Jiri didn't play all that much. He would, in fact, only dress for four games during the run to the Stanley Cup.

But three of those games, tellingly, were the last three of the Final against the Montreal Canadiens.

After the Flames had lost the second and third games to the Habs, coach Terry Crisp inserted Hrdina back into the lineup and he was on the ice the night the Flames lifted the Cup.

Early in the 1990–91 season, he found himself traded to the Pittsburgh Penguins, where he would go on to win two more Stanley Cups.

Hrdina played four full years in the NHL and in three of them won the Stanley Cup. Not a bad return.

When he went to Pittsburgh, he proved invaluable in aiding teenager Jaromir Jagr's transition from the Czech Republic.

A top scorer in his home country, Hrdina became a solid two-way forward, extremely popular with his teammates. Just a very outgoing guy.

A lot of European players, when they first come over, are quite shy, but Jiri was quite engaging, smiled a lot, and gained the nickname Jirshi.

Sometimes they'd call him George, a rough translation of Jiri. He was a good pal of Jim Peplinski in his time in Calgary and learned the English language very, very quickly.

He was also helpful when Robert Reichel first came over from the Czech Republic, helping him transition into the NHL.

Jiri has worked for years as a scout for the Dallas Stars.

Defenceman Frank Musil was another result of Calgary's Czech connection.

Drafted by the Minnesota North Stars in the second round in 1983, Frank defected to North America in 1985 after competing in a world championship tournament.

Following a stint with the North Stars, he joined the Flames; also playing with Ottawa and Edmonton during his NHL career, a total of 797 games.

Frank was traded to the Flames in 1990–91 and left after the 1994–95 season. But not before becoming a very popular guy among his teammates and the Calgary media.

He was always smiling, always upbeat, and by the time he got to the Flames, Frank wasn't a shy guy.

While playing in Edmonton, he suffered a spinal cord injury that would eventually bring about his retirement and afterward he stayed on with the Oilers organization to scout. Always fun to run into him.

His wife, Andrea, was a world class tennis player. Another interesting aspect about Frank: While most European players would come over, play the season, and then go back home, he stayed in Calgary a lot of the summers and would actually take on jobs in the area for extra income but also to help prepare him for life after hockey.

One particular summer, he worked at a slaughterhouse.

Later, his son David would come over to North America and play in the Western Hockey League, primarily with the Vancouver Giants.

Of the players who left the Czech Republic to ply their trade here, though, none had more impact than Reichel.

This was a young guy who, when he was drafted as a teenager—a fourth-round pick in 1989—had already made quite a name for himself in his homeland (Robert also had some German descent, thus the name Reichel).

Twice, he put up 40-goal seasons for the Flames, leading the team in points with 93 during the 1993–94 campaign. The year prior, he'd finished second to Theoren Fleury.

Off the ice, he was an interesting character, a seemingly dour guy but someone you could have some fun with, and he'd smile when he was in the right mood. Frank Musil would always come over to settle Robert down when he got out of sorts, over himself or the team.

I'll never forget one time, the sales crew at the radio station handling the broadcast had made an arrangement with a men's store in Calgary, giving gift certificates to all Flames players so they could go in and buy clothing.

I can't remember how much the certificates were for, but one day Robert went to the men's store to use his.

The next day I saw him and he had that dour look on his face. He said, "That certificate they gave me, that store is so expensive, I couldn't even buy a pair of socks!"

That was the way he was, but in his own way, a fun guy to be around, as well.

He wasn't shy about doing interviews after he gained command of the English language. His wife, Karen, was a real avid listener to the broadcast, especially the postgame shows. There were times when one of the panellists might say something about Robert that was kind of negative and she would get real upset.

Of course, that would be relayed to us, even if she'd blame the wrong guy for a certain comment from time to time.

As I mentioned, he was a frugal sort. And so, after completing the 1994–95 season, he ended up in a contract dispute with the team and would ultimately leave to play a season over in Germany, where he led the league in scoring.

He returned to the Flames for the 1996–97 season, when his scoring numbers plummeted—perhaps a residue of the contract battle—and he ended up being traded to the New York Islanders.

He also spent time in Phoenix and Toronto before exiting the NHL.

As a member of the Flames, Robert certainly put up some big numbers during the regular season, but his scoring would tail off a bit in the playoffs. Unfortunately, in the five years he was with Calgary, the team never did get past the first round of the playoffs.

However, he did come through with a massive goal that sealed Canada's fate in the 1998 Olympics at Nagano, Japan.

Robert was back with the Czech team and they faced off against Canada, the winner to move on in the tournament.

The game went to a shootout and Robert scored the only goal to give the Czechs the victory and they advanced to the gold-medal game where they beat Russia, touching off a tremendous celebration back in Prague.

That was the first year the NHL players competed in the Olympics.

Overnight, Robert became a guy Canada wasn't too crazy about.

Incidentally, that was the same night on which Marc Crawford, coach of the Canadian team, did not select Wayne Gretzky for the shootout against Dominik Hasek.

New Year's Tradition

In my mind, nobody in the NHL does New Year's Eve hockey the way the Flames do.

December 31, 2017, marked the 25th time the Saddledome had hosted a game on the big night.

The tradition began back in 1987. Prior to that, the Flames had played a couple New Year's Eves on the road, in Minnesota in 1985 and Detroit in 1986. The next year marked their very first home game on New Year's Eve, and produced a 5–4 victory over the invading Philadelphia Flyers.

That started the ball rolling, although there were five subsequent occasions when the Dome didn't host a New Year's Eve date.

Work stoppages in 1994, 2004, and 2012 meant no hockey at all, while in 1999 the Y2K scare preempted the game, and then in 2011 the World Junior Championships had taken over the building.

Otherwise, hockey in Calgary has become as quintessentially New Year's Eve as noisemakers, champagne toasts, and resolutions that are quickly broken.

The Montreal Canadiens have been the most frequent opponents over those years, making seven appearances. The Edmonton Oilers are next, with six.

Calgary's record since the 1987 inaugural NYE game? Seventeen wins, six losses, and three ties (yes, there were ties back in the day).

The most one-sided result came in 1990 when the Canadiens made their first New Year's visit and were dismantled 7–2. Theo Fleury scored once and chipped in with three helpers that night.

Four of the games have gone to overtime and the Flames have won them all, with Paul Ranheim scoring in a 3–2 victory over Montreal in 1991, a Derek Morris goal silencing the Habs 5–4 in 2000, Josh Jooris providing the winning margin 4–3 in 2014 versus Edmonton, and then in 2017 the Chicago Blackhawks falling to a Mark Giordano OT goal.

The highest-scoring game can be traced back to 2005 when the Flames and Oilers combined for 11 goals, Calgary emerging 6–5 winners. Kristian Huselius sent the Dome fans off to their revels happy, scoring the winner. In 2010, the Oilers and Flames again, this time for 10 goals, a 6–4 victory for the home side on the back of Mike Cammalleri's two-goal/three-assist performance, the most individually in any of the New Year's Eve games.

Other interesting New Year's historical notes: No shutouts recorded, no hat tricks, and the longest Calgary win streak stands at six games, from 2005 to 2010, the longest losing run at three years, from 1996 to 1998.

Record Road Trip

The most impressive road trip the team has enjoyed since relocating in Calgary came somewhat unexpectedly just before Christmas in 2007.

After losing five of six games and falling two games below .500 during Mike Keenan's first season behind the bench, the team and its coach were certainly not very happy with the way things were going.

Everyone, to put it mildly, was very, very upset.

Then out of the blue, with people predicting disaster, they headed out on a six-game trip.

And wouldn't you know it? They won all six.

Half of those games, by the way, came against teams that Mike had previously worked for, including his the 600th career coaching triumph in a game at St. Louis.

The trip encompassed 10 days; Jarome Iginla scored eight goals in the six matches, including a hat trick in a 9–6 victory at Tampa. Kristian Huselius also had a hat trick in the same game, a rare time in which two players had a three-goal performance together.

Three of the wins were by one goal, including a shootout victory in Florida.

Miikka Kiprusoff was the goalie of record in all six of those wins, facing over 30 shots in all but one of the contests.

Keenan, so irked before they'd set sail on the trip, was elated after the team rose to the occasion to not only establish a Flames record for consecutive wins on a road journey but also tying an NHL record.

The 2004 Stanley Cup Run

I'm often asked to compare the 2004 and 1989 runs to the Stanley Cup Final, mostly from fans who were quite young the year the Flames lifted the Stanley Cup.

The 1986 push, which is more ways similar to 2004, isn't mentioned nearly as often.

There are, in fact, many differences between 2004 and 1989. For one thing, the city was much bigger in 2004, which translates into more people being caught up in the hysteria. The other difference is that the 1989 team was *expected* to win. Many pundits favoured them right from the start. In contrast, the 2004 squad wasn't expected to even reach the playoffs, let alone advance all the way to Game 7 of the Final.

The underdog factor always generates added excitement.

Both years, though, the Flames became a focal point for the entire city, gathering more momentum, more of a following, as they drew ever closer to the Final.

By that time it seemed that every citizen—many of whom were anything but diehard Flames fans—had been caught up in the madness.

The downtown celebration spots were different in each year: In 1989, it was Electric Avenue on 11th and in 2004 the Red Mile on 17th. Crowds at the games were different, too. In 1989, dress was business or business casual. In 2004, almost everyone wore red.

On the ice, the teams' styles were dissimilar, as well. That 1989 squad had a tremendous amount of talent; the 2004 collection had a couple of real stars in Miikka Kiprusoff and Jarome Iginla, and some guys scoring timely goals, such as Marty Gelinas and Shean Donovan.

The 2003–04 group played a grinding game, keeping the opponent off stride with a never-quit attitude. That team wasn't favoured to win any of the four series it played, whereas the 1989 group was the overwhelming pick, as I mentioned, from the start.

The 2004 team was such an underdog that during the Labour Day weekend, September of 2003, I was in Las Vegas just prior to the start of training camp and I noticed the Flames were 125-to-1 odds to win the Cup.

I put down a $20 bet taking those odds and I had that ticket in my wallet the night of Game 7 in Tampa. Unfortunately, it didn't pay off!

But I certainly came a lot closer than anyone had anticipated.

In both years, fans told me tales of being stuck in traffic on Deerfoot Trail at rush hour, especially during games played out east, and the loud, persistent honking of horns that would follow Flames goals.

In 2004, a playoff spot was clinched as late as Game 80, on March 31, with a 1–0 victory over Phoenix in the Saddledome.

That game was the team's 10th straight sellout.

Earlier in the year, they weren't close to filling the building.

Jarome Iginla—who else?—scored the only goal of that game, at 15:54 of the first period on the power play. It was the captain's 40th of the year. Miikka Kiprusoff made 27 stops to post the shutout.

At game's end, ending seven long, painful years of not reaching the playoffs, I yelled, "Playoffs! Yeah baby!" and then let the crowd take over.

Later, I learned that a company out of British Columbia had put out a licensed product in conjunction with the NHL, bottle openers and key holders, with my postgame yell.

Fans still tell me about them.

Soon after they hit the market, when my granddaughter Haylee would come by my place, she'd press the button time after time after time to hear the audio.

Iginla would end that year with those 40 goals, 24 more than the team's second-leading goal-scorer, Shean Donovan. Jarome's 73 points were 26 more than the second-place guy, Craig Conroy, the centre on his line.

Four goalies were utilized—three of them playing 18 or more games—but Kiprusoff was, indisputably, The Man. He hadn't started the season with the club and then missed a month with a knee injury, yet played in 38 games, compiling a record 1.69 goals-against average. Jamie McLennan played 26 games, including a stretch pained by a fractured sternum. Jamie ended up being traded late in the season, just before the deadline, to the New York Rangers.

Other injuries also plagued the team, but they were somehow able to overcome the problems.

They started the postseason without three regulars in the lineup and the injury toll only grew.

Their playoff run lasted exactly two months, stretching from Pacific to Atlantic, starting on April 7 in Vancouver and ending June 7 in Tampa, encompassing 28 games. Only the Vancouver games had flights under two and a half hours.

The Flames won 10 games away from home compared to just five of 12 in the Saddledome. There were close games galore, 13 of them with a one-goal differential, with the Flames coming out on top in nine of those.

Six of the games went to overtime, Calgary winning four.

The first series in 2004 was against the Vancouver Canucks, the top team in the Northwest. The series started as expected, the Canucks winning the opener at home 5–3, then the teams traded victories.

Prior to Game 4, coach Darryl Sutter publicly challenged his players to be better, and they responded with a 4–0 win. Iginla and Donovan had goals and Kiprusoff made 20 stops. It was the first of five shutouts he would collect during that playoff run.

Later, a video review would not be very kind to the Flames, but in Game 5 in Vancouver they received a positive review on Iginla's game-winner at 5:37 of the third period.

They looked to clinch in Game 6, but it turned out to be a long night as the Canucks won 5–4 in triple overtime.

Game 7 went to overtime as well, Gelinas getting the first of his series-deciding goals on a power play at 3:25 of the OT. Vancouver's Matt Cooke had tied the game with only six seconds left in regulation.

Iginla had himself a great game, scoring two goals in regulation and also assisting on the Gelinas winner.

Later, Vancouver general manager Brian Burke would say, "Iginla cost me my job."

The series took its toll on the Flames as six regulars would be sidelined to begin the second round, three defencemen and as many forwards.

But it was on to Detroit for a series against the Red Wings, No. 1 in the Central Division and President's Trophy winners with 110 points.

The Flames took the first game, but the Wings came back to capture Game 2, Steve Yzerman getting two goals in that one and Nicklas Lidstrom a goal and three assists.

They split Games 3 and 4 in Calgary and after losing the latter, the Flames got a boost for the pivotal fifth game with veteran Dave Lowry returning to the lineup for the first time since January 6, when he suffered an abdominal injury.

Kiprusoff made 31 saves and Craig Conroy scored the game's only goal in the win.

Back to the Dome for Game 6 and the teams played 79 minutes and 13 seconds before Gelinas tallied in overtime, touching off an explosion from the C of Red.

Kiprusoff made 38 saves in that one (incidentally, he was named number-one star in all four games the Flames won in that series).

A six-day break followed but still they would start a series against the San Jose Sharks, pennant winners in the Pacific Division.

The teams opened the series with a Sunday matinee. The Flames had 2–0 and 3–2 leads but needed defenceman Steve Montador's goal at 18:48 of OT to net another upset.

Another key goal from an unlikely source.

After a 4–1 win in the second game in San Jose, things certainly looked good for the Flames. Maybe too good, because they lost the next two at home.

Back in San Jose, Iginla scored a shorthanded goal early in the first period and Kiprusoff made 19 saves for a 3–0 win, making the Flames the only road team to win a game in that series.

The "C of Red" came into prominence during the 2004 run to the Stanley Cup Final.
(AP Images)

They clinched the series in Game 6 with a 3–1 triumph, the game-winner once again going to Mr. Gelinas.

The Tampa Bay Lightning were in the Stanley Cup Final after finishing first in the Southeast Division with 106 points, second-best in the NHL, under coach John Tortorella.

The Flames arrived in Tampa Bay two days ahead of the opener and unlike Calgary, where everyone seemed to have flags and signs, other than around the Forum, where the Lightning played, you couldn't have guessed that Tampa had a team playing for the Stanley Cup.

There was, however, lot of excitement around the arena on game nights, where the bars were full and there was a battalion of car flags to be seen.

The Flames stayed at a hotel across the street from a shopping mall and with the humidity and temperatures in the 30s (Celsius), team doctors advised the players to conserve energy by going outdoors as little as possible. So they spent much of their leisure time walking around the air-conditioned mall where Iginla, Kiprusoff, and the rest of the gang could stroll along without anybody recognizing them, no autograph seekers.

The Flames captured the opener 4–1, but the Lightning took the second match by an identical 4–1 scoreline after Darryl Sutter's group failed to score on four power play chances in the first period.

Back home for the third game, Kiprusoff made 21 saves in a 3–0 win with Iginla and Chris Simon both notching a goal and an assist.

Two days later, Tampa's Nikolai Khabibulin notched a 29-save 1–0 shutout.

The Lightning were equipped with a number of oxygen tanks on their bench and in the dressing room to combat Calgary's higher altitude.

Ville Nieminen smacked Tampa star Vincent Lecavalier from behind in that fourth game, leaving Sutter an awful lot of pacing on the ensuing plane ride back to Tampa.

When the team arrived in Florida, everyone learned that Nieminen had received a one-game suspension for that hit.

Prior to the fifth game, chatting with Scotty Bowman up in the media area (he has a winter home in Florida), he felt the Flames needed a boost after losing the fourth game and asked me if anyone was coming back from injury. As it happened, Toni Lydman was returning to the lineup after being out since Game 3 of the Vancouver series due to a concussion.

Jarome Iginla at Calgary City Hall joins my granddaughter Haylee and daughter, Tricia, after the team parade following the 2004 run.

The Finnish defenceman made his presence felt early, assisting on the game's first goal. Later on, Oleg Saprykin would connect in overtime to give the Flames a precious win and it was back home with an opportunity to clinch the championship.

A festive spirit was already building outside of the Saddledome in the morning.

That evening when I arrived at the rink, about 90 minutes before game time, anticipation was high.

Walking into the building, I noticed a large number of Flames family members gathered around the players' lounge and wondered if this wouldn't only add to the undeniable pressure the team was already under.

The organization had done a tremendous job looking after the requests, but still there was an awful lot of family around.

Most players bunked at a city hotel the afternoon of the games and some had even stayed the night before to avoid distraction.

In the end, though, Tampa would win that game, 33 seconds into double overtime, when former Flame Marty St. Louis scored. But not before the goal that wasn't a goal by Gelinas created quite a controversy. With 6:37 left in the third period, the game tied at 2–2, and Gelinas went hard to the Tampa net, a centering pass ricocheting off Khabibulin's blocker, then Gelinas' right foot and over the goal line.

The puck was quickly kicked out by the goaltender with his right pad.

Play went on and finally there was a stoppage.

The Flames didn't realize that it might have gone into the net, thus there was very little delay. The NHL did have a video review, in its early stages, but didn't have the number of camera angles there are today.

A review lasted about 48 seconds. ABC-TV, which was covering the series live, showed a replay with the puck in the net, detected by commentator John Davidson just after the puck had been dropped to resume play.

Nothing could be done about it. Play had resumed.

Gelinas and other players didn't realize there was a controversy until media approached them after the game. The coaches didn't want to bring it up before the overtime as it could be a distraction.

So it was packing and back to Tampa for Game 7.

The games, the travel, and the pressure fatigued both teams, perhaps affecting the Flames more, who'd been forced to travel a bit more than Tampa through the course of the playoffs.

The Flames started that game a bit sluggish, got behind 2–0, and that was the score heading into the third period. Finally, there was a spark when Conroy scored on a power play with 11:39 left in regulation time.

They pushed for a tying goal but were denied; they also got a penalty in the closing minute and a half of the game.

Afterward, inside the Flames' dressing room, there were many, many tears shed, likely the same back home among fans, coming so far and to end up losing by a single goal.

In the parking lot by the bus, Tampa's Brad Richards, who I knew from the Maritimes, had his equipment on and was talking to his pals from Prince Edward Island on his cell phone while we were waiting to get on the bus to the airport.

On the charter flight home, a couple of Flames owners mentioned to me that if they'd had an inkling the team had a shot at getting this close to the Cup, they would have given Darryl more money to bulk up the roster with additional players.

As it was, the underdog, the low-salary team, certainly made quite the impact anyway.

Taking It Outdoors

Calgary finally got to host an outdoor game, the Heritage Classic, on February 20, 2011.

We had to wait eight years after Edmonton staged the first one, with the Montreal Canadiens as the opposition, 51,167 frozen fans huddling at Commonwealth Stadium.

The Habs, as it turned out, were also the visitors to McMahon Stadium, generating a lot of buzz in town and around southern Alberta.

But in the end I was upset—with myself. And broke one of my cardinal rules in the process.

My daughter, Tricia, her husband, Ross, and granddaughters, Haylee and Sydney, went to the McMahon Stadium parking lot for the carnival-like pregame festivities.

I still have a picture of five-year-old Sydney dressed like a goaltender hanging in my office, wearing one on the special replica jerseys the Flames would be donning that afternoon.

My son, Jeff, and a bunch of his pals attended, along with my brother Noonan and New Brunswick friends Lionel Ahier, Mike Boushel, Ken Little, and Bob Reid, who flew in for the weekend.

A big party ensued.

Some of those guys were Canadiens fans so it took very little coaxing for them to make the 3,000-plus mile journey.

Two weeks prior to the festivities, Don Phelps, who was a long-time coach of the Calgary Canucks and works at McMahon, took me up to where our broadcast location would be, high atop the seats on the west seating area.

At the time, the boards were being set up and when I looked down, I knew it would be a much greater distance to the ice than it was at the Saddledome or any other NHL arena.

Still, I felt confident that I wouldn't need a big monitor screen, as had been suggested, to call the game.

All the regular games I broadcast were without the use of a monitor, other than for replays.

In hindsight, perhaps I should have asked for one.

The Saturday alumni game was filled with nostalgia. The Stanley Cup finalists from 1989 met, with the Flames honouring long-time team owner Harley Hotchkiss, who was ill and would pass away a few months later. He dropped the ceremonial first puck.

The afternoon was only a bit overcast so I had no difficulty picking out the players' numbers and I was happy with how that broadcast went with Mike Rogers and our host Rob Kerr.

The came Sunday.

Very cold, minus-10 (Celsius) for the opening faceoff, and windy.

More than 40,000 fans had gathered in the home of the CFL's Calgary Stampeders.

As the game went on, the temperature began to drop, as anyone in the crowd could attest, along with the *Hockey Night in Canada* TV crew. Their broadcast location was outdoors, near the ice surface.

As the players came on the ice for the warmup, I started my normal pregame ritual of doing a mental play-by-play. The Canadiens wore their traditional white jerseys, so IDing numbers was not a problem. The Flames, on the other hand, brought back memories of the old Calgary Tigers, a pro team that had operated in the city back in the 1920s and actually played for the Stanley Cup against Montreal in 1924.

The jerseys were a nice retro look, but from my vantage point as a broadcaster, a distinct problem.

The different colour scheme of maroon with the white numbers on the yellow background made it difficult to pick up the digits.

With the sunlight streaming into the stadium early on the game, it was darn near impossible.

Throughout my career, regardless of circumstances, I had never complained about the broadcasting nuances and didn't on this particular Sunday afternoon, either.

But I'm complaining now.

It was certainly a struggle from the start. I was able to identify the goal-scorers, but sometimes had to improvise a little bit so thus the normal flow of my call was not up to standard.

Inwardly, I was ticked off at myself.

During the intermissions, I'd go off and stew a little bit, not wanting to show anyone else the disgust I had for the way I was performing.

But I kept with my hard-and-fast rule: Don't let others know when you feel you're not having your best broadcast.

The afternoon certainly turned out great with the Flames winning 4–0 and Miikka Kiprusoff brilliant in the nets, making 39 saves.

The only outdoor game in Flames history was on a very cold February 20, 2011, afternoon at McMahon Stadium. The Flames blanked the Montreal Canadiens 4–0.
(AP Images)

But after the broadcast was completed and I got to my car, I was far from happy with myself and that's when I broke my own rule—I let my dissatisfaction show. When I met up with my brother and my pals from New Brunswick for dinner and then over to Flames Central for the post-game party, I certainly wasn't in a chipper mood.

It was obvious to those in Peter's Posse so I told them of my issues with my broadcast and apologized for my behaviour.

Despite several Coors Lights and glasses of wine, my mood didn't change, even when Flames fans dropped by to say hello, upbeat and cordial.

I felt I hadn't been a very good host for those who had come all that way.

At one point, Mike said to me, "Peter, it shows you're a true professional, not being happy with your performance."

Nice of him to say but that didn't pacify me all that much.

The next game was back in the friendly confines of the Saddledome, but I'll not forget the McMahon Stadium experience. For all the wrong reasons.

Flood Waters Rising

On June 19, 2013, the rains came to Calgary, and the waters rose. By the time the deluge had subsided, 100,000 people were evacuated and $5 billion in damages incurred.

Among those hit hard, the Scotiabank Saddledome.

The water had risen to 10 rows high in the building. Amazingly, working through the summer allowed the regular season to start on schedule, back in business only a little more than three months later.

The first photos taken in the building were truly incredible. The luxury boxes were flooded, dressing rooms had been severely damaged, one-of-a-kind memorabilia lost and equipment—including the JumboTron resting on the arena floor—ruined. Virtually everything at event level, the ice plant, ice resurfacing machines, and kitchens, a total write-off.

To think they could make that building game-ready in that short amount of time is, to this day, mind-boggling.

The first game back in the Dome was a split-squad affair between the Flames and Edmonton Oilers. Besides kicking off the season, that night served as a tremendous tribute to the many workers who put in so many hours to restore the building.

Upon first viewing of the devastation inside the building, the organization must've been immediately devising contingency plans.

I know the team had made provisions for preseason games, perhaps in Medicine Hat or Lethbridge.

The Herculean efforts to have things workable by September 14 is as great a performance as has ever been seen in an arena that's been witness to so many of them down through the years.

Jarome Iginla Retires as a Flame

Flames fans never really got to say good-bye to Jarome Iginla when he was traded to Pittsburgh on March 27, 2013, but just over five years later, on July 30, 2018, the brilliant right winger returned to the Flames family to announce his retirement after 20 NHL seasons.

The event was so massive that two national Canadian cable television stations, as well as two local radio outlets, carried the proceedings live. I was honoured to have been master of ceremonies for the news conference.

In his 16 seasons as a Flame, Jarome established team records that aren't likely to be broken. He played 1,219 regular season games, amassing 525 goals and 1,095 points—all club standards. He also produced 26 goals and 49 points in 54 playoff games with the team. He engaged in 63 fights as well, making him the ultimate power forward.

He was classy off the ice, quickly becoming extremely popular with the fans who he always had time for with his smile, and giving and caring ways. Near the end of the news conference the day after he had been traded, I took it upon myself to stand up and thank him for his thoughtfulness and availability on behalf of Flames fans and media. I'm guessing many other media types in the room wanted to thank him as well but didn't feel it would be a professional way to act. Being the most senior media guy in the room, I assessed it would be okay.

I interviewed Jarome numerous times and not once did he decline regardless of the situation. Three of the goals he scored stand out for me. On April 7, 2002, he became the first Flame in 10 years to score 50 goals in a season. With the schedule winding down, he took a four-game goal scoring streak into Chicago when he scored with a shot from the top of the right faceoff circle on a Flames power play for the milestone marker. Six years later, on April 5, 2008, he had his second 50-goal campaign when he tallied in the final game of the season on a slapshot with 7:25 left in the game at Vancouver.

While those 50th goals occurred on the road, Iginla brought the Scotiabank Saddledome fans out of their seats and got a thunderous ovation on January 7, 2012, with his monumental 500th career goal in the third period against Minnesota. He would go on to score 32 goals during that 2011–12 campaign, making him just the seventh player in NHL history to score 30 or more goals in 11 straight seasons. Later that year, the night after my 3,000th NHL broadcast, I hosted a party at a local restaurant. Out of courtesy I invited Jarome. When I handed him the written invitation I told him I didn't expect him to come but wanted to invite him. He came that Sunday evening and stayed for over an hour.

I'll not forget the evening the Flames won the Western Conference championship in 2004, winning Game 6 at home against the San Jose Sharks. When I left the Saddledome well over an hour after the game, in the parking lot, on a night for celebrating, there was Jarome signing autographs for a group of kids while taking time to ask them how they were doing in school.

In 2020, Iginla will be eligible for selection to the Hockey Hall of Fame. There's a good chance he could be selected on the first ballot. Regardless of when the HHOF calls, Jarome will accept the accolades in the same humble manner he exhibited throughout his career.

CHAPTER 4
SIGNING OFF

Family

Family's always important in a career but in a job like mine—travelling half the winter, working nights, non-stop game days—the backing and understanding of your nearest and dearest are essential.

Nancy, my wife, was so supportive. On game days, she left me pretty much alone, knowing I needed focus to prepare, and made sure the kids got to their events at various levels.

I was often asked: "Did you wife travel with you on road trips?" Well, she joined me on just two over all the years I broadcast, one to Los Angeles, another to Nashville.

Both were during days when the team flew commercial and when there was a day or two off in the cities before games, allowing for a little sightseeing.

Most trips simply didn't allow for any downtime, arriving in a city one night, playing the next, and then leaving either immediately afterward or early the next day. When charters arrived, we always left right after games, with the airline schedules tailored to the team's wishes.

I have very few regrets about my career. One has to be the number of events my kids—Jeff and Tricia—were involved in that the schedule forced me to miss.

Now, in retirement, I'm trying to make some of that up with my grandkids.

Jeff played minor hockey in Calgary, with the Buffaloes. At the 1988 Mac's Midget Tournament I made an arrangement with Ed Whalen, in those days the broadcaster for the championship game every year, to sit and do a little play-by-play if Jeff's team reached the final. Unfortunately, the Buffaloes lost in the quarterfinals that year.

They became a very strong team and went on to win the Alberta midget AAA championship, then would go on to play, and win, the Air Canada Cup in St. John's, Newfoundland. A month later, the Flames would win the Stanley Cup.

My biggest fans—my family members—were all on the ice with me on November 18, 2014, when the Flames honoured my career at the Saddledome prior to a game against Anaheim. (Left to right) Haylee, Russ Thompson, Tricia, Sydney, me, Nancy, Jeff, Kate, and Amy are indebted to the Flames and the fans for making it a most memorable evening. (© Calgary Flames)

Nancy and Tricia both flew out to watch that event but my Flames schedule—they were in the playoffs at the time—didn't permit my attending. But I did manage to watch the game on television at the old Forum in Los Angeles via satellite thanks the Kings' TV crew.

Later, Jeff would play with the Canucks in the Alberta Junior Hockey League and then move to the University of Wisconsin–Superior, combining school and hockey.

In 1994–95, the NHL was going through a work stoppage that would last almost through January, allowing me the opportunity to attend a few more of Jeff's games, and when I'd go the team's play-by-play guys wanted me to work the games. I refused—they were the young up-and-comers trying to polish their work, after all—until one night in Bemidji when Jeff scored a couple of goals, his team won, and I had the thrill of calling a game involving my son.

After his playing career ended, Jeff returned to Calgary and was an assistant coach for the midget North Stars, and helped them win a provincial championship, then moved up to the same position with the Western Hockey League's Calgary Hitmen. He held that position for five years and they won the WHL championship in 1999 and went on to play in the Memorial Cup at Ottawa. Luckily, I was able to attend that entire tournament and they reached the final before losing to the host 67's in OT.

Jeff then took on a position selling hockey equipment for CCM, Reebok, and Adidas, initially covering WHL teams before moving up to National Hockey League teams in western Canada and also getting into retail.

Tricia was into soccer as a youngster and later developed a passion for singing. For a number of years, she's been singing the national anthem prior to Calgary Hitmen games in the Scotiabank Saddledome, and once had an opportunity to sing it at a Flames game, in 2001, against the St. Louis Blues, a game that turned out to be a tie.

My favourite rendition of hers, however, has to be October 14, 2006, the night after my Hockey Hall of Fame media induction. I dropped the puck at centre ice with Flames co-owner Harley Hotchkiss, who'd been honoured by the Hall as well. The Flames won that game, 3–2 over Minnesota.

Then she sang again on November 18, 2014, the night I was honoured by the organization, a contest in which the Flames beat Anaheim.

So I like to say, for the moment at least, she's undefeated while performing the anthem at Flames games. A great mom to Haylee and Sydney and wife to husband, Russ.

Lanny McDonald; my son, Jeff; and I with the object of everyone's attention.

I couldn't be prouder of my kids. Clearly, family is a part of why my career was so successful.

Call from the Hall

You never think of yourself in terms of being worthy of the Hall of Fame.

The idea simply does not enter your imagination. At least, not mine.

Hearing the news triggered quite an emotional week.

I actually received the word of my selection the day before I was to fly home to New Brunswick. My cell phone rang. Chuck Kaiton, president of the NHL Broadcasters Association, was on the line, giving me the good news and offering congratulations.

Subsequent calls arrived from Dick Irvin, someone I'd gotten to know well over the years and at the time the secretary-treasurer of the association, and Bill Hay, then the president of the Hockey Hall of Fame.

The next day I left for Moncton for the burial of my father, who had passed away that winter. As it happened, the Memorial Cup was being staged there at the time.

I'd been asked by the Hall not to leak the news before they could announce it later in the week but when my brother Noonan picked me up at the airport, there was no way I could keep the news from him, so we went out and had our own mini-celebration with some of my other pals, also sworn to secrecy.

When the announcement was made, suddenly I was the one being interviewed, instead of the other way around.

The next day we laid my father to rest in my hometown of Campbellton.

I remember standing over the grave following the prayer and telling him I was going to be honoured by the Hockey Hall of Fame. Quite a moment.

Afterward, I drove back to Moncton in order to attend some of the Memorial Cup games. Interestingly, the team that eventually won the tournament, the Quebec Remparts, was being coached at the time by Patrick Roy.

Turns out, Saint Patrick would be in the same Hall class as me, in the players category, but didn't know it at the time, as the broadcasting and writing honourees are always unveiled first.

During another round of celebrations, my wife, Nancy, phoned to inform me that my second granddaughter, Sydney, had been born. I'd planned to be back in Calgary for the birth but Sydney couldn't wait and arrived early.

My daughter, Tricia, and the baby were doing great.

More wonderful news.

My good fortune continued. After arriving back in Calgary, I notched a hole in one at the Jack Carter golf tournament at MacKenzie Meadows.

The Hall of Fame induction itself is something I'll never forget. There I was, in November of 2006, back in Toronto where I'd started my career calling Maple Leafs games to be recognized with that year's Foster Hewitt Memorial Award to be presented at a luncheon held at the Westin Harbour Castle Hotel.

Long-time hockey writer Scott Morrison of the *Sun* newspaper chain joined me on the media side as recipient of the Elmer Ferguson Award.

Also in attendance were Dick Duff and Patrick Roy, being inducted that night into the players category, and, happily for me, Flames owner Harley Hotchkiss, in the builders section.

The late Herb Brooks was being honoured posthumously. Herbie had been tragically killed three years earlier in a car accident, and was represented at his induction by his son and other members of the family.

I'd arranged for my colour commentator of 21 years on Flames broadcasts, Doug Barkley, to come and do the intro before I received my jacket from Bill Hay, the president of the HHOF.

Bill and Doug were good friends and I knew Bill from his tenure as president of the Flames, as well as Hockey Canada.

Rob Kerr from Sportsnet 960 was also in attendance, along with Steve Bujold from my hometown radio station CKNB in Campbellton, New Brunswick. Lanny McDonald, a Hall of Famer himself and a great pal, also took in the festivities.

Having co-workers and long-time friends on hand certainly helped me along.

Following the luncheon, a photo session to commemorate the event was held, including myself, Harley, Patrick Roy, and Dick Duff, who'd been an assistant coach with the Maple Leafs while I was broadcasting in Toronto and someone I'd gotten to know quite well.

After that official function, we adjourned to a room my brother and pals from down east had rented for a couple relaxing beers.

Soon after that, it was time to get ready and to head over to the Hall of Fame for induction ceremonies, held at that time in the Grand Hall. For this event, I was only able to secure six tickets, which were taken up by family. Thanks to Doug MacLean, Columbus GM at the time, and then St. Louis Blues president John Davidson, I was able to get all the others seats in an adjoining room.

Midway through the evening, I'd say, the magnitude of the honour really hit home for me when NHL commissioner Gary Bettman mentioned me from the podium and showed a brief film clip of me working on a broadcast.

Pretty overwhelming.

We were so wrapped up with what had just happened, none of us went over to look at my plaque, hung on the wall in the Hockey Hall of Fame underneath the Foster Hewitt Memorial Award citation.

The highest honour was awarded to me at the Hockey Hall of Fame on November 13, 2006, the Foster Hewitt Memorial Broadcasting award. The plaque hangs proudly in my home and another is in the Great Hall of the HHOF in Toronto.

I'd received a plaque for myself earlier at the luncheon, as is the custom, but to miss out that night by not seeing the main plaque up there with all the other worthy recipients was quite the oversight.

In fact, it was nearly two years before I was finally back to the Hall, during the Flames' visit to Toronto, to actually see my plaque on the wall. Better late than never, I suppose.

Another great moment for me came shortly after the HHOF evening. Prior to a game between the Flames and St. Louis Blues, Harley and myself were honoured at the Saddledome, dropping the ceremonial first puck before the game.

The only problem was missing the first minute and a half of the broadcast of the game, hustling up to the press box.

Luckily, Rob Kerr filled in admirably for me, and had quite an exciting 90 seconds in his first chance at calling an NHL game, with a Calgary goal and a fight. "Well, it's all yours now," he said when I arrived, stepping aside. "I've had my biggest thrill in the business."

Mine had happened a couple of days earlier in Toronto.

One Final Trick

Toward the end of my career, with games becoming much more low-scoring, I'd decided to yell "Yeah baby!" after every Flames player would score a hat trick.

The last one I called, though, turned out not to have my signature line attached.

This arrived late in the 2013–14 season, March 22, the Flames were in Edmonton, in my final time broadcasting a Battle of Alberta game, up north at Rexall Place.

Through its incarnations—Northlands Coliseum, Edmonton Coliseum, Skyreach Centre—it was probably the visiting building I'd broadcast more games out of than any other. So it was pretty emotional.

I have a lot of memories—both good and bad—over the years in that arena.

On this night, Calgary winger Curtis Glencross would score three times, the Flames inflicting an 8–1 beating on the Oilers. Immediately following Curtis' final goal, the team's seventh, I had a second or so to decide whether or not to yell out a "Yeah baby!"

I chose not to, given that it had turned into such a one-sided game. I didn't want to rub the scoreline in. Maybe 10 or 20 seconds later, though, I was kicking myself for holding back, being that it was a hat trick goal and the opponent was Edmonton.

I actually apologized afterward to Curtis.

As memorable as those three goals were, probably the one that stood out most from my final working visit to Edmonton was by centre Matt Stajan in the second period.

That game, you see, marked Matt's return to the lineup after the death of his and wife Katie's infant son, Emerson, shortly after childbirth.

Seeing Matt look to the heavens and pumping his fist after scoring on a penalty shot brought tears to everyone's eyes.

In a building in which I'd witnessed so much great hockey, so many memorable moments, a final one, as well as a farewell hat trick, to add.

Johnny's First, My Last

The first game Johnny Gaudreau played for the Flames turned out to be my last game in the broadcast booth.

That night at Rogers Arena, he'd score the first goal of what promised to be a dazzling NHL career.

It would also mark the final Flames goal of my broadcasting career.

Lovely bit of symmetry there.

April 13, 2014, was the final game of the regular season, the Flames and Vancouver Canucks both already eliminated from playoff contention.

Johnny had just completed his third year at Boston College and there'd been oodles of speculation on whether he'd agree to sign an NHL contract or opt to complete his senior year at BC, which would've freed him up to sign on with another organization.

He'd been the Flames' fourth-round draft choice in 2011. Another fourth-round selection from the year before had been centreman Bill Arnold, Gaudreau's teammate at Boston College, and his linemate their final season together on campus there.

Deals were struck for the two players days after the Eagles suffered a 5–4 loss to the Union College Dutchmen in the Frozen Four semifinal. Gaudreau had also just collected the Hobey Baker Award, emblematic of the NCAA's top player, in Philadelphia.

Johnny arrived as a high-scoring winger, Bill a two-way centreman. Just talking to Gaudreau that one day at the Westin Bayshore, you could sense an air of confidence.

In both young men, actually.

Interestingly, that night would turn out to be the only time Bill Arnold would ever play for Flames, spending a couple of seasons at the AHL level before being allowed to walk away, unsigned.

Johnny, as everyone knows, has blossomed into a bona fide NHL star, the 2017 Lady Byng Trophy winner and one of those rare talents capable of lifting fans out of their seats.

His first goal arrived in the second period that night in Vancouver, at the 15:22 mark, with the Canucks already leading 4–0. Difficult to generate a whole lot of enthusiasm given the game's lack of importance, but Johnny, as always, provided an injection of excitement and it sure seemed to signal a new star arriving in the NHL constellation.

I called a few thousand Flames goals during my career and the last one was courtesy of the team's present-day scoring star, Johnny Gaudreau. (Getty Images)

As I took the elevator up to the press box that night, I knew it marked my last game, even if I hadn't made any sort of announcement.

Few people knew of my plans at the beginning of the season. I didn't want any fuss. No distractions. I just wanted to do my job, go about my game preparation, do my broadcasts as I had for more than three decades.

I wasn't interested in any farewell tours or being asked a bunch of questions about retirement plans and all that type of thing.

I prepped for that game in my usual manner, did my customary morning skate interviews, had my afternoon workout at the Westin Bayshore Hotel gym, wrote game notes and finished the opening.

On the bus heading to the arena it really hit me that this was going to be the last time.

I'd invited a long-standing friend from my hometown of Campbellton, Brian Flann, who lived in Vancouver, to come to the game and watch adjacent to our broadcast location. Brian had gone through some very tough health issues for a couple years but had gotten back to pretty good shape, so it was nice for him and me to share that game together—even if he didn't know my plans yet, either.

I'd considered telling him though, because he was in the broadcast booth for one of the first games I called play-by-play for, with the Campbellton Tigers back in the 1970s. (Two weeks later, after I'd announced my retirement, Brian called and told me he knew there was something on my mind that night. He had an inclination something was up, even if he couldn't quite put his finger on it.)

I must admit, the personal emotional significance of the evening was eating at me. Still, I was determined to maintain a normal broadcast.

I signed off in my normal manner, reminding listeners that the Flames would be back on The Fan 960 for the 2014–15 season and wished them all a great summer.

On the flight home, I had a couple of quiet beers to privately celebrate my career and made the rounds, as I always did following the final game of any season, thanking the players, coaches, trainers, and management for their assistance in helping me throughout the course of the season. On the surface, anyway, a normal way to wrap up.

Inside, though, I knew it was going to be the last time.

Not so very long after that flight home from Vancouver, on April 13, to be exact, I officially retired after 33 years of broadcasting Flames hockey.

Johnny's first. My last.

Anyhow, that's the connection Johnny Gaudreau and I will always share.

The end of one era, as it turned out, and the dawn of another.

Thank You, Flames

The final game I broadcast was, by choice, without fanfare.

The send-off was anything but.

I must admit I had a difficult time controlling my emotions at the retirement media conference held at the Saddledome.

So many friends and colleagues on hand to help me say good-bye to a job I loved.

Afterward, my son, Jeff, and I went to the Calgary Golf and Country Club for a couple of hours with some friends in a room that Bill Creighton had set aside for us. We were able to unwind a bit and reminisce.

Later on, I did a few interviews with local TV and radio stations, as well as a couple out-of-town interviews by phone. The response was overwhelming.

Then I went to watch my granddaughter Haylee play soccer.

The next day, on the way to the airport, I had an on-air chat with long-time radio friends Don Stevens, Joanne Johnson, and the Coach on XL 103. Over the next three seasons in retirement, I'd talk Flames on their program three times a week.

I did a lot of summer golfing at the Cottonwood Golf and Country Club, which is owned by long-time Flames Ambassadors president Lyle Edwards.

In September, just before the start of the new Flames season, my first in memory not cramming, The Fan 960 staged a nice testimonial dinner at the Calgary Italian Club, set up by Kelly Kirch.

It was great to mingle with so many colleagues, friends, and associates.

A friend, Frank Sisson, offered his Phoenix home to Nancy and me after I'd mentioned how nice it'd be to get away for a couple of weeks to coincide with the first game, sure to pull at my heartstrings a bit, given the circumstances.

The original idea was to go to Phoenix and then to Toronto for the 2014 Hockey Hall of Fame induction ceremony and take in the entire weekend festivities—I'd missed some of that experience when I'd been enshrined eight years earlier due to game commitments in Vancouver. But those plans had to be altered when my two brothers and sisters announced they were arriving in Calgary to attend a night the organization had arranged for me on November 18, prior to a game against Anaheim.

The team set up another media conference the day of that game. In the morning, we happened to bump into Ducks coach Bruce Boudreau.

Back in his playing days as a junior, Bruce used to come to New Brunswick in the summer. I'd also had the pleasure of broadcasting his first game NHL game with the Leafs back in the 1970s.

After chatting for about 15 minutes with Bruce, reflecting on the summer ball-hockey games we'd play when he was back in New Brunswick, I was due in the Flames' dressing room.

Coach Bob Hartley had asked me to talk to the players.

Bob ended his comments by referring to me as the Flames' seventh man that night. I joked that, "I'd love to be the seventh player, but you shouldn't expect me to score any goals."

I then thanked them for all their assistance and wished them all the best.

Unsurprisingly, the evening was filled with nervousness and emotion. The Flames had sent a limousine over to pick up me and my family, plus another one for my out-of-town guests.

At the Dome, we were guests for dinner in the owners' lounge with Murray Edwards thanking me on my career and Flames alumni president Jamie Macoun presenting me with a jersey signed by most of the players from the 1989 Stanley Cup team.

Following the meal, my immediate family and I made our way to ice level and the remainder of the crew were ushered into the Flames' owners box to watch the ceremonies and then the game itself.

The night the Flames honoured me on November 18, 2014, they unveiled the Peter Maher Broadcast Booth, much to my surprise. Fittingly, seen high in the background unveiling the citation are my three colour commentators: (left to right) Doug Barkley, Mike Rogers, and Peter Loubardias. (© Calgary Flames)

We lined up at the Zamboni entrance at one end of the rink and I had my son take the notes for my speech and place them on the lectern that was out on the ice.

Just seconds before the players would take to the ice, a thought struck me and I told Jeff that maybe he should go back and put my phone on the notes, fearing that when the players skated by, the wind would blow the sheets away.

That turned out to be a wise move.

Going out onto the ice for that ceremony was a feeling I'd never before experienced, a truly once-in-a-lifetime moment, surrounded by my family and hearing the applause from the crowd.

Just a tremendous ceremony put on by the organization I'd covered for 33 years.

The video tribute included input from management, current and former players, as well as my two long-time colour commentators, Doug

Barkley and Mike Rogers. The capper was Mike, Doug, and my final year colour man, Peter Loubardias, unveiling a sign naming the radio broadcast booth in my honour.

That was really stunning. It left me speechless.

Finally, I did get to address the crowd, thanking everyone for their great support, and ended with as vibrant a "Yeah baby!" as I could muster. The biggest emotional wallop arrived, though, after we'd all exited the ice and my daughter came on the ice to sing our national anthem.

That moment topped 'em all.

After all of the activities on the ice, my family and I then joined the Peter's Posse gang, along with many Flames owners, in the owners' suite. That's when I finally had a chance to relax a bit and have a beer. Unfortunately, I didn't have too many beers, because near the end of the third period, with a victory by the home team in play, a member of the Flames entertainment staff asked if at the end of the game I'd give it one final "It's in the win column!" should the Flames prevail and then a "Yeah baby!"

The Flames came through with three in the third period, grabbing a 3–2 lead. But wouldn't you know it? The Ducks scored a goal late in the third to force overtime.

I was at the location they'd indicated; I also asked my three grand-girls, Haylee, Sydney, and Kate, to sit with me so that the cameras would focus on us and they could look up to see themselves on the JumboTron again.

That was something they'd giggled about during the course of the night.

Well, we sat. For quite a while as it turned out.

There was overtime plus a shootout and after the third Flame, Sean Monahan, scored, Corey Perry of the Ducks shot just wide and it was, finally, my cue to scream into the microphone.

So, at long last, a fitting ending to the game. Afterward, the Flames hosted another reception in the Chrysler Club, but not before Peter's Posse, as we were exiting the owners' suite, were told by the hostess there that they'd set a record for beer consumed during the game.

There was a lot of pride for my pals from down east in that bit of news.

A week or so later, I attended an owners' meeting and personally thanked them for all the support they'd given me during my career and the wonderful appreciation night they had for us.

I also thanked all the workers at the Flames for making the retirement evening a truly wonderful one.

Good Guy Award

Late in my career I was flattered when Roger Millions, the host on Sportsnet TV broadcasts and Scott Cruickshank, then hockey writer for the *Calgary Herald*, approached me about having an award named in my honour.

The idea was to have a media panel vote at the end of the year and select a Flames player deemed to be most co-operative that season with the writers and broadcasters. A donation would be made in the winning player's name to the Flames Foundation for Life.

They asked if they could call it the Peter Maher Good Guy Award.

I was a little bit stunned by that, but pleased and quickly agreed.

Interestingly, the first four times the award was given out it went to a player who was produced by Calgary minor hockey and had listened to my broadcasts as a kid growing up in the city. The first three times the winner was Joe Colborne. The third time Joe won the award and I made that presentation, I told him during the ceremony that if he keeps it up, his and mine would be the only names on the trophy.

As my career was unwinding, my Calgary media colleagues decided to honour the Flames player deemed most obliging at the end of each season. For some reason, they asked to call it the Peter Maher Award. (© Calgary Flames)

But after winning it in 2015–16, Joe moved on, signing as a free agent with Colorado.

The tradition continued the next season, with first-year Flames goalie Chad Johnson the selection. Johnson also played his minor hockey in Calgary and talked about listening to my play-by-play, noting the 2004 run to the Cup Final.

Even though I didn't know Joe or Chad until they became NHLers, it was certainly nice to hear them recalling listening to my past work when they were youngsters.

Being a Calgarian isn't a requisite for winning the award, but it was the case early on. In season five, 2017–18, it changed, with Toronto-born but long-time Flame Matt Stajan selected.

Broadcast Impact

I continue to be staggered by the impact my 33 years calling hockey games had on people.

When you're working, the job at hand is your focus, getting prepared for a show or a game.

During my career, receiving letters from fans, particularly from the sight-impaired who thanked me for being their eyes during Flames games, was always special, and frequently moved me to tears.

Only in retirement, though, did I begin to truly comprehend the scope of what I'd been doing for over three decades. E-mails, texts, and letters came pouring in, congratulating me.

The day after I called it quits, I was travelling to Las Vegas to indulge in a bit of R&R. At the airport, I saw my photo on the front page of both Calgary newspapers, which kind of threw me for a loop.

During that flight, a lot of fans recognized me and dropped by to say thanks. Even the flight attendant sent me over a free beer.

Late in the first season of my retirement, I hosted one of the Flames' Dressing Room Experience events. After chatting and mingling with fans, ex-Flame Perry Berezan and I, along with team sales executives Mike Franco, Craig Smith, and Luke Dauray, were scheduled to visit a few suites.

On the way to the upper level of the Dome, we had to pass through the iconic Platinum Club during the first intermission. When the patrons spotted me, they all stood and cheered. I was floored. Mike, Craig, Luke, and Perry, in contrast, were very amused.

After visiting the suite, we had to pass through the club again and this time fans started chanting my name.

There is no way to prepare yourself for something like that, and only then does it begin to hit home how much you meant to people's enjoyment of the game.

Another time, walking through the concourse with Theo Fleury, I found myself stopped a number of times for photos and/or a signature.

Theo's accustomed to such adulation. I am not.

The phenomenon truly is extraordinary. Every once in a while I'll be driving and stopped at a red light, and the person in the car the next to mine will recognize me, start honking their horn, waving, or rolling down the window for a word or two.

Voice recognition is one thing, but being recognized in that way really left me speechless. Often, I'll be asked, still, "Are you...Peter Maher?"

So many people have told me I was the voice of their youth, in the car or at home with mom and dad. Many regaled me with stories of

With the crowd standing and cheering, I departed the Saddledome ice with a final thank-you salute to the fans in my long-time home away from home. (© Calgary Flames)

being under the blankets in bed at night with the earphones on, pretending to be asleep but listening to the broadcast.

I'd receive requests from fans, often with friends or loved ones in the hospital, to record a voice message using my signature "Yeah baby!" or "You can put it in the win column!" lines. I'm more than happy to oblige.

Thinking about it now, back in the 1980s and early 1990s, before the advent of sports specialty channels such as TSN and Sportsnet, a full half of the games were available only on radio.

A lot of my following must've been developed during those radio-only days.

Whatever the reasons, through the years, in wins and losses, my audience and I connected.

And for that, for the ability to resonate with the thousands upon thousands who grew up listening to our broadcasts, I'll be forever grateful, and humbled.

It's amazing to look back on.

A lucky guy, Peter Maher.